anthropologists in the field

SAMENLEVINGEN BUITEN EUROPA/*Non-European Societies*

waarin opgenomen/including

ACTUELE ONDERWERPEN/*Occasional Papers*

onder redactie van/edited by

prof. dr. A. J. F. KÖBBEN (Amsterdam), prof. dr. R. A. J. VAN LIER (Wageningen), prof. dr. G. W. LOCHER (Leiden) en prof. dr. L. H. JANSSEN S. J. (Tilburg)

anthropologists in the field

edited by

DR. D. G. JONGMANS University of Amsterdam
DR. P. C. W. GUTKIND Mc. Gill University, Montreal

ASSEN 1967

VAN GORCUM & COMP. N.V. - DR. H. J. PRAKKE & H. M. G. PRAKKE

Printed in the Netherlands by Royal VanGorcum Ltd.

introduction

D. G. JONGMANS AND P. C. W. GUTKIND

For the benefit of future fieldworkers the Institute of Cultural Anthropology of the University of Amsterdam regularly organizes a series of lectures on fieldwork. Anthropologists recently returned from the field are invited as speakers. Rather than reporting on the results of their research, they are requested to give an account of how they set about it, of the difficulties they had to face, their dealings with authorities, interpreters and informants, of the pleasure and pains of participant observation. In short they are asked to show how research is done.

The success of these lectures has led to the compilation of 'Anthropologists in the Field'. A number of authors were invited to contribute to this volume. They were asked the same questions as the speakers in the lecture series. In addition we have included four articles already published:

J. A. Barnes, in *British Journal of Sociology* (1963) 14:118-134; A. N. J. den Hollander, in *Kölner Zeitschrift für Soziologie* (1965) 17:201-23 (original title: Soziale Beschreibung als Problem); P. E. Josselin de Jong, in *Bijdragen tot de Taal- Land- en Volkenkunde* (1956) 112:149-168 (original title: De visie der participanten op hun cultuur); and finally E. R. Leach, in *The Ceylon Journal of Historical and Social Studies* (1958) 1 (1):9-20. We are most grateful to the editors of the journals mentioned above for their permission to reprint these articles.

Existing literature offers little data on how anthropologists carried out their research. The last forty years hundreds of monographs have been published,

yet a careful study of them reveals that at least sixty percent of the authors make no mention whatever of the methodology employed; perhaps another twenty percent devote a few lines, or two or three paragraphs, to this important topic; while only the remaining twenty percent give us some clear idea about how they carried out their research: this is hardly a satisfactory situation.

In the world of natural sciences it is customary to give a description of the experimental set-up and the procedure followed as well as an estimate of the reliability of the results achieved, thus making it possible for other people to carry out a retest if they so desire. In cultural and social anthropology the possibility of testing results will largely have to remain a pious wish.

Anthropology is not an experimental science nor will it ever be one, however much its scholars look for quasi-experimental situations and use exact methods and techniques. The anthropologist, who wishes to test the reliability of the results of a village study, will never find another village identical to the first one. Moreover, he will never be able to eliminate the time factor. Not even a re-study of the original village is the perfect answer, for the reason that the first investigation, if it was intensive, did not leave the village undisturbed. Yet, if we are to strive in earnest for greater reliability, we shall have to make more room for re-studies as is rightly argued by Dr. Garbett in this book (ch. 7).

Since he usually operates by himself we are obliged to take the fieldworker at his word, but we are entitled to know what this word is worth: he should inform us about all factors relevant to an evaluation of his work. These include data concerning his own origin, ideology and attitudes. For the sake of the researcher as well as of his work, some people have pleaded for psycho-analysis, so that the fieldworker might become aware of his idiosyncrasies. We, in our turn, ought to be acquainted with these if we are to evaluate his work. Ultimately we should like to see his field-notes too, for between these and the final monograph, as den Hollander (ch. 1) points out, a process of stream-lining takes place. In short, the quality of the fieldwork will benefit if the fieldworker learns to regard himself, together with his work, as a problem. Nevertheless exactitude is not the alpha and omega of fieldwork. The question has been asked whether anthropology belongs to the humanities or to the sciences. Our answer is that it belongs to both. The social life of man is a panorama of organized complexity. To unravel this demands exactitude *and* artistry. Only if, in our writing, we can combine these opposite qualities is our place as scholars assured.

Chapter 1 gives an extensive exposition of the problems we are concerned with here. Chapters 2,3 and 4 discuss the pros and cons of participant observation and survey methods respectively. Chapters 5 to 10 deal with more specific subjects. In conclusion the book contains a detailed and annotated bibliography which, we trust, may be of service to the experienced as well as to the tyro in the field.

Chapters 1, 2, 3 and 9 were originally written in Dutch and have been translated by Mrs. M. J. van de Vathorst-Smit. Our thanks go to Prof. A. J. F. Köbben for assisting us by word and deed and to Miss C. Jonker for preparing the manuscript for the press.

contents

I

social description;
the problem of reliability and validity

A. N. J. DEN HOLLANDER

Introduction. In the social sciences we are concerned with social reality in many and various forms. The amount of knowledge the individual scientist may acquire in the course of a lifetime by direct observation is very small, in many cases even practically nil. We are all obliged to depend predominantly on the fund of observation recorded by others. The customary means of recording and communicating knowledge gained through observation is verbal description and this has of old taken place on a large scale. Many scientists no doubt share the experience of the present author; having read, professionally, innumerable sociological accounts of tribes, villages, towns, town-quarters and other local communities, one feels a certain uneasiness not unlike the vague feeling of discontent and doubt with which one is afflicted after having carried out such a task oneself.

One may 'know' a community through reading an account of it, but when visiting that community personally one will nevertheless feel out of touch and a little surprised. It is like a river on a map; the line 'is' the river, yet it is not, for in the process of abstraction the resemblance to life has got lost. Our perception of reality is made up mostly of particulars whereas description or symbolic representation are based on generals which do not make for easy recognition of the object. That is why a child is surprised on seeing a river it only knew, so far, from geography lessons; surprised, not because this is that river, but because it is so different from the way it looked on the map. The line on the map *is* the river but in another way it *isn't*.

One wonders how reliable the results of much socio-descriptive work really are; how valid and how 'true' in their representation of reality?

The question that interests me is to what extent it is possible to observe social reality and describe it sufficiently 'correctly' to make the knowledge gained scientifically valuable and communicable to others. If some other person were to repeat the job, would his results be the same? Is it really like this? How useful, for scientific purposes, is this descriptive work? It seems to me that the problem extends beyond the general social description of local communities. For our present purpose, however, we shall limit ourselves to this field.

It has long been customary, in the social sciences, to make a distinction between descriptive work and theoretical work. Ethnographers were supposed to supply the data for ethnologists; 'purely' sociographic work had to provide sociologists with the necessary factual knowledge concerning the object of their speculations. Although the significance of this distinction has never been generally disputed it seems that in the course of the last few decades it has come to be regarded as less essential. But even if the distinction has grown more vague it still exists and one can hardly object to it. As long, that is, as we keep in mind that the two fields of activity interpenetrate and that there is no reason why description should be accorded a lower status than theorizing; an unfounded but rather persistent valuation. And as long, too, as it is not implied that sociological description is exempt from problems, as if it were a technique that may be handled according to prescription and tradition by any more or less competent person.

Description is full of problems. Many of these have been recognized by various authors who incidentally mention them in their writings. Many other problems which these authors doubtlessly experienced in the course of their work, whether descriptive or theoretical, are not explicitly mentioned, perhaps because they were considered inevitable or insoluble. Little attention has been paid to this complex of problems as a whole.

The discrepancy between reality and representation is an old issue, but it was not until the turn of last century that it was considered in its application to the social sciences: it occupied Max Weber, Pareto, Sorel and others, although they were interested in different aspects of it. Ever since their time the theme has kept occurring in one form or another. In recent years American socio-logists especially have discussed it in relation to the theory of cognition. I do not propose to follow these authors – they vary greatly in their approach to the problem, which again is different from ours – nor do I intend to present a historical survey of all that has been written about the many aspects of the subject. I would rather discuss some general factors that give every socio-descriptive report its own stamp, basing my observations on my experiences both as a 'describer' and as a reader of the descriptive efforts of others.

On comparing alien to own, and vice versa. Our understanding of an alien society is often influenced by our tendency to relate this society to our own, by our wish to acquire further insight into our own through the other or to find support in the other for a presupposition about our own society. In the eigh-teenth century it was believed that the lost paradise was to be found among the primitive peoples and the misconception of the 'noble savage' coloured the description of the autochthonous societies of America and the Pacific. Later, at the time of evolutionist ethnology, we were hoping, through a study of primitive peoples to recapture our own past. In the same way Europeans think they can get a preview of their own future in observing daily life in the United States. This tendency has always blinded Europeans to the many archaic traits in American culture, its colonial lag. The same tendency plays a part in many of the false notions concerning Europe that exist in the United States. Our ideologies often play an important part in this. They affect not only our observation and description but also our theories.[1] At present we realize how

---

[1] Calverton (1931) especially points this out, although he undoubtedly exaggerates in stating that 'our social scientists are not interested in objective facts, but in theses that will justify existing attitudes and institutions' (p. 16). On p. 24 he speaks of 'cultural compulsives', which, according to him (p. 29), make objectivity impossible in the social sciences. See also Evans (1953): 57 'Each age tends to support its metaphysics with a fictional zoology . . . The eighteenth century, exalting order and reason, found Nature orderly and reasonable. The nineteenth century preferred to contemplate the 'law of the jungle' and the 'survival of the fittest'.

much the theories of Tylor, Morgan, Westermarck, Spencer, Sumner, Tönnies were subject to this, how closely they were tied up with the social and historical environment of their authors. It has been pointed out that the ethnographies of the Pueblo cultures reflect the differences between the ideologies of their various authors.[1]

This brings us to a related phenomenon, our tendency to project our own culture onto the alien one. This manifests itself, for instance, in a rather naïve error of perception. To the 'strange' people or the distant village the visiting anthropologist or sociologist is an outsider and viewing it from the outside he is more readily tempted to regard this foreign collectivity and its culture as a 'unity' and to treat it as 'a whole', than he ever would his own, for example his national, culture. This symptom of projection has its positive side, too, for it gives a person the courage to undertake a task which would otherwise seem (and in fact is) hopeless. It is an error which makes possible the illusion of the feasibility of 'an ethnography', 'a sociogram'.

In the description of the social structure of this illusory 'whole', a special preference for a division into three parts may frequently be noted. Division into two, four or five certainly occurs far less frequently. Is not this triple division a consequence of the duality to which our logic is so much attached and which may explain our preference for pairs of contrasting concepts? Simple observation teaches us that in the social sphere there is a 'high' and a 'low' and also that there is obviously rather a lot that is neither high nor low but in between. In this way three status groups within the 'whole', 'spontaneously' present themselves, in each of which if the 'whole' is at all numerous further perception will inevitably again distinguish a higher and a lower section. Thus we have three, or six, status-strata or 'classes', but the reader is left doubting whether the described reality compellingly prescribed this conclusion.[2]

For western man, triple division is a habit of thought. Apart from its traditional meaning the number three has an emotional value and thus it has always

[1] Bennett (1946).
[2] See Davis' review (Davis 1942) of the well-known study by Warner and Lunt on Yankee City (Warner and Lunt 1942) and also Hollingshead's comments (Hollingshead 1948). In addition, Gordon (1958): 88, note 12.

influenced scientific thinking without much objective reason.[1] There is a Dutch saying that 'all good things consist of three parts' – apparently this should also apply to the structure of an alien human aggregate.

Value judgements in social description – and they are hardly ever lacking – are clear proof of the writer's naïve projection of values belonging to his own culture or sub-culture. In these cases understanding is frequently veiled by judgement. Those European travellers who made disparaging comments about the low yield per acre of agricultural land in such new countries as Canada, Australia or Argentina failed to realize that the relative costs of land and labour respectively, differing as they did from those prevailing at home, led farmers in these new countries to use land 'wastefully' and labour sparingly; this being, indeed, the most rational method there. Extrapolation of their own values and customs is what makes our American visitors speak of the 'low position of the wife in Europe' and in the same way Europeans discover a modern matriarchy in the United States.

In social action, projection is more often present than absent. The present enthusiasm in western countries to teach the entire world to read and write is partly due to the fact that reading and writing have become such a matter of course for us. Illiteracy may be undesirable in (present day) western society but it is not necessarily a sociopathological phenomenon in every culture. By premature forced or 'planned' acculturation knowledge and skills are disseminated in societies where they have no function as yet, where no large-scale need for them exists nor is likely to develop in the near future. The socially destructive effect may be considerable.

Since social 'problems' are a matter of definition they may easily arise from ascribing to others the reactions which an educated middle-class person of western culture would show in their circumstances. It is lack of imagination that makes us think that the overpopulation of slums is inevitably an affliction to the inhabitants. They experience this quite differently. Constant company

[1] Révész (1957): 16: 'Die dreigliedrigen Bildungen sind aus der empirischen Forschung entstanden. Sie besitzen zwar keine logische Notwendigkeit, trotzdem haben sie eine grosze Ueberzeugungskraft', which he deems (: 35) 'beinahe rätselhaft' and he states (p. 36) that 'ihre Richtigkeit ohne Notwendigkeit intuitiv erlebt wird'. Cf. also Scharman (1959): 13 on the metaphysical and religious significance of the number 3.

and conversation give them a feeling of security. They dislike being alone and would find the comparative social isolation of more prosperous people hard to bear.

Many charitable actions of the socially powerful manifest an unthinking projection of their own values. The parks 'for riding and strolling' that were laid out in western cities during the 19th and 20th centuries did not at all correspond with the needs and wishes of the masses. They reflected the tastes, preferences and habits of the rich bourgeois whose ideals of what they wished to bring to the people were based on the parks of English country manors and on French palace gardens.

On factuality, objectivity and induction. In some ways our scientific manner of approach to an alien social reality smacks of eighteenth century thinking, being based on the tonic error that nothing less than the sum of all that is knowable determines what one ought to know. This encyclopedic misconception still pervades our educational system and it is perhaps by this road that it has crept into social description. Teachers like to impress on their students that any description should be as full as possible, that it should 'keep strictly to the facts', that one should proceed 'objectively' and draw one's conclusions 'strictly inductively'. None of this, though, is ever possible and those who propagate these requirements have never realized what exactly took place in their own mind while they were doing social-descriptive work.

Scientific 'facts' in their own right do not exist. No 'fact' is ever 'pure' and 'objective'. Significance and interpretation are never simply contained in the facts. One cannot simply gather or discover facts. What we call facts are really constructions of the mind, isolated from a complex and as yet confused reality, with the help of definitions and classifications we have made ourselves. We find 'facts' by a process of selection which inevitably entails evaluation, the criterion used being: is it relevant for what we are doing, will it be useful? We note and mention them because we already have an idea about the way they are linked up, – an idea only partly produced by these facts. It is a mental game of leapfrog with influences working both ways. On this basis we pay attention to one thing and not to another; it makes us observe in a particular way and perceive particular things and it determines the way our findings are provisionally put together. In the course of this we are forced by what we observe to modify the provisional assumption, which then opens our eyes to other 'facts' and so on.

The differences between descriptive and theoretical work are, therefore, less than is generally believed. They are not essential. Social description, too, if it is to have any significance, will be looking for the general behind the particular and the process by which this is achieved is the same as that by which hypotheses originate.[1] It seems to me that a failure to realize the exact nature of this process has produced much unnecessary discussion on the relation between sociography and sociology. In the same way the disdainful attitude of some theoreticians towards those who specialize in descriptive work is mostly due to insufficient (theoretical) insight on the part of the former.

All 'perception' is essentially a combination of taking and giving, of passive sensory behaviour and mental activity. The results are subjective because they are to a large extent our own creation. Much observation is mere visualizing of what one expects to find and much reflection is really a looking for confirmation of preconceived notions. For this reason it is not possible to draw a strict dividing line, as some would wish to do, between scientific and unscientific thinking. Scientific theories and scientific concepts also are arrived at by a priori reasoning. What is important is the way we use existing knowledge – how much, how well, how significantly – and whether we seek in the first place to confirm the apriority, or to test it objectively.

The insight thus acquired by reaching across the facts is usually founded on astonishingly few data. Initially these really stand midway between 'data' and 'illustrations'. Those who indignantly reject this suggestion, asserting that it is just this difference that matters, fail to recognize the manner in which sociological insight comes about.

We are still suffering from the effects of the erroneous notion that general

---

[1] Redfield expresses this rather well: 'The description and the explanation . . . are in part guided by the ideas the investigator brings to that community . . . These perceptions act upon what we find in the community, and are in turn influenced by what we find there. While we describe the community, we often try to systematize and to justify the revised preconceptions into what we may call a theory or, more modestly, a point of view'. (Redfield 1960: 147).

insight may be produced by strict induction. Although this is an exploded notion we still regularly come across all sorts of remnants of it. The customary manner of presentation of the results of sociological research is such a remnant; it keeps alive a wrong conception of the mental processes that lead to the conclusions offered by suggesting that these processes are of an inductive nature. It is not true, however, that mere accumulation of observations can produce generalizations as if through crystallization or sedimentation.[1]

The very basis of this conception is fictitious, for, as has already been stated: unbiassed, open-minded observation does not exist. Whatever we see or otherwise perceive is a function of something that we saw or that was otherwise planted in our minds before: in the first place our conceptual framework, together with all sorts of irrational preconceptions which may either close or open our eyes to particular aspects of reality. 'Induction', for us, is plausible guesswork. That is how we arrive at our hypotheses and our concepts, by inspiration, imagination, intuition, by a mental adventure. The adventure comes to an end only when we test our hypotheses by examining their deductive consequences: the argumentation should now be rigorous and strictly logical.

If social description is to be more than an unlimited registration of meaningless observations, the person recording these observations needs to possess, to a smaller or greater degree, a talent for intuitively divining connections, for producing general insight. This is an individual matter that cannot be tied down to one method to be followed by everyone. For this reason a person lacking such sensitivity and creativity will never produce anything of value in the way of description, not even by scrupulously following the directions of a great teacher. On the contrary, this only leads to caricatures of social description.

A highly rated quality is 'objectivity', but complete objectivity can be practised only by those who are either totally ignorant or totally indifferent. In social description prejudice and preference are attitudes that should be kept in hand but they need not be shunned and it is absurd either to pretend or to demand

---

[1] Popper rightly observes (Popper 1957: 134): 'I do not believe that we ever make inductive generalizations in the sense that we start with observations and try to derive our theories from them'.

their absence. A piece of social description that portrays social reality, one that is more than a bare catalogue, will teach us much about its author. His personality will colour his work; the culture and subculture in which he grew up will make themselves felt and so will the academic subculture in which he received his training. He will never succeed in completely freeing himself of the predominant attitudes, prejudices, assumptions and values of his own culture.[1] Because of this, the sociology and cultural anthropology of different countries have always borne a national stamp, both in their theoretical and in their descriptive writings.

Formerly this was perhaps more obvious but even nowadays such differences are still to be noted. There is no limit to the number of directions social description may take, but the same is not true of any given author. His description can never be a photographic reproduction. 'There is no one ultimate and utterly objective account of a human whole'.[2]

The personal factor in a narrower sense; local circumstances; communication. The research worker is not just an average representative of his culture; he has a unique personality of his own by which his description will be coloured just as it is affected by his general cultural conditioning. Every painting is to some extent a self-portrait of its maker, it will always contain a certain amount of self-projection. No extreme cases are needed to convince any reader of social descriptions that the authors among themselves show the greatest possible diversity.

Some are naïve and some are sceptics, some amateurs and some professionals. In their perception they are strongly influenced by the presuppositions, theoretical or otherwise, acquired during their training, maybe through the influence of an admired example. Many, if not practically all, field workers started their descriptive task with hardly any preparatory training. Even in the field some never succeeded in acquiring the necessary skill, and fear of

---

[1] These are the sort of questions Elenore Smith Bowen poses herself in her account, in the form of a novel, of her stay in an African village (Smith Bowen 1954), where she did not only learn a lot about headman Kako's people but also about herself.

[2] Redfield (1960): 136.

the task, incapacity, or laziness prevented them from producing any results. I know of several such cases of total failure. Others did produce something, some even did a surprising and admirable amount of work but really valuable results are only rarely achieved. Anthropological and sociological description is an uncommonly difficult job, full of snags and pitfalls, and yet it would be hard to name another example of such a difficult task being undertaken with, in general, so little preparation and training apart from the usual theoretical and linguistic instruction. There are textbooks for social description, though not many, and the really good ones are only of recent date. Note, moreover, that some scientifically important descriptive contributions in the field of the social sciences have been made by outsiders and amateurs. Personal talent and ability, evidently, are of the greatest importance here.

The effects of practice and experience in increasing professional skill are far less felt here than in other professions. Although there is an important creative element in social description it is wrong to suppose the social scientist to be inspired by the same sort of creative urge as the artist. Authors of valuable, talented descriptive reports often produce no more than one piece of work. If this is outstandingly good a subsequent academic appointment, with all the attendant obligations, may effectively prevent the person in question from doing any more descriptive work. Advancing age, too, lessens the inclination, for field work makes great demands on the scholar. It requires lots of time, it often means considerable privations, and if not blood, yet sweat and tears. Apparently a strong creative urge for this kind of work is rare and curiosity proves an inadequate substitute. There are so very many things one can get to know with less trouble.

Nor should we overestimate the spontaneous interest on the part of social scientists for the innumerable facets of human existence, the 'richness of life'. Professional sociologists often show an interest that is obligatory rather than spontaneous and irrepressible. On the whole, it seems to be activated, directed and nourished by particular assignments, by the desire to take an academic degree or by professional literature, rather than by an unsatiable curiosity about the undigested social reality that surrounds us. As a rule, they have neither an extensive nor an intimate knowledge of the everyday world around them, often not appreciably more than scientists in other fields, and less than a lot of people with everyday experience like general practitioners, rent-collectors, district nurses or social workers. Every person, of course, has some amount of social experience and the extent of such 'naïve, empirical knowledge' may be considered irrelevant; nevertheless one would expect sociologists, social psychologists or cultural anthropologists to have more of it. They sometimes display a staggering ignorance with respect to their own society. It is not unusual for a man who is familiar with the taboos of an extinct Australian tribe to have not the slightest notion of his charwoman's family life.

Whatever the reasons, descriptive activity usually decreases with advancing age, even for those who have proved themselves singularly capable at it. Improvement through maturing, practice and experience, therefore, takes place to a much lesser extent than in the case of artists.

The things a field worker observes, and the way he observes them, depend on his personality as much as on his object. If he is attached to a museum at home chances are that he will be particularly interested in material culture. Others show other preferences, frequently for formal aspects of the culture investigated – kinship rules, for example – since these formal aspects are easiest to observe, or at least to get information about. Some follow a printed guide for description or the instructions provided by the leader of an extensive research programme; others take an independent course. But everyone remains dependent on his own personality which means that his descriptive work will always be somewhat like impressionist painting. Romantics will have a particular eye for what is exceptional in a culture whereas realists will note rather what is ordinary and most usual. But even the most realistic person will give a slanted picture of the people he describes. He, too, will achieve not so much the truth as rather a transposition of his own personality.

Many an error can be avoided by keeping in mind that the persons observed are different not only in their perception but also in their means of expression, their categories of thought, their sensibilities. Much more than this consciousness we cannot, in all fairness, require of the observer. He can make allowances but he cannot be anyone but himself. Every social structure, for example, and particularly a stratified structure is nothing but a product of the observer's mind, of his point of view which is usually that of an extensively educated person belonging to the economically secure middle class of his own society. His experience of life and his social optics are not necessarily the same as those of most members of the community he observes. Social stratification, even in one's own society, is never an objective fact or a truth accepted by everyone. We know that the way one subdivides social space in one's own society differs according to one's social optics. Of the village or town observed by a particular author we usually have only one report, his; by which its social structure is then 'defined'.

Observation is affected to a high degree by the intention of reporting on one's findings and by the means the observer has at his disposal to achieve this end. Intuitively he ignores much that is there, and that he knows to be present but either doesn't consider describable or doesn't feel himself able to cope with as a reporter. To alter slightly Paul Valéry's well-known statement: it makes a world of difference whether you see something with or without a note book in your hand. This is another reason why the strange village 'will be described in a way in some significant degree determined by the choices made, perhaps quite unconsciously, by the student of the community'.[1]

Only rarely do we find the investigator reporting just how he set about his work. How long was he in the community and during which seasons? Was he alone or accompanied by his wife? Had he visited the community previously? Did he know anyone there before his arrival? How, and where, was he housed? What local help did he hire? Who collected the basic material? The local situation the observer has to cope with is always important. It is usually more or less structured by the stranger's presence. The mere fact of knowing they are being observed may produce a change in the people observed. Their reactions towards the visitor must both be distinguished from their community life and interpreted through it.

At first his being a stranger[2] gives the observer certain advantages. He knows nobody here, and he will be leaving again soon, so there is no great risk involved in confiding in him. In the beginning he is overwhelmed with confidences. All sorts of people warn him against all sorts of others. Here, for once, is an

---

[1] Redfield (1960): 136.

[2] In this capacity one continually experiences the truth of Simmel's well-known observations on the subject (Simmel 1908: 685 ff.).

opportunity to air one's grievances to someone who is apparently willing to listen and who is not capable of judging whether the information offered to him is correct or not. Soon all relations with him will come to an end. Everyone wants to forestall everyone else with his confidences. In the course of a few days an incredible amount of information may thus be poured into the visitor's ears. These confidences do not lead to any personal relations with the volunteer informants. They soon grow indifferent, when they find that the visitor lends his ear to others as well and that he is really no use to anyone nor will be so in future. Or else they soon understand that he is not going to accede to their requests, which are not always quite proper and something of which, they suspect, may stick in the stranger's memory. During this first stage the field worker gets to know a lot, but it is a sort of knowledge that does not help him much and that, moreover, is quite different from what every member of the community knows by a life time's experience plus a residue of traditional experience handed down by previous generations.

During his visit the investigator is sometimes respected, sometimes not. In some cases people simply refuse to believe that he is occupied with something quite as futile as he pretends: learning about the ordinary things that everyone knows. In the Appalachian mountains, in 1931, it proved quite impossible for me to make the inhabitants understand or accept my reasons for asking them so many questions. It seemed to them that I was hiding my real motives and the fact that I was doing this so successfully in this case added to my prestige. It might equally well have caused distrust and rejection. In a town in southern Georgia (1932) it was rumoured after a few days that I was a scout for a rayon concern and might help to get a rayon industry established in the town. My denial reinforced the rumour, everyone tried to convince me of the excellent qualities of the town and its population – the observer had turned into a fairy godmother and serious work was no longer possible. Departure was the only solution.

It is impossible, in a community of any extent and differentiation, to remain 'socially free-floating'. One is soon faced with the necessity of choosing. There is a minimum of social contacts one needs and the investigator is identified with his house and means of transport, with the class, family, or clique with whom he associates most. Questions that are frankly answered by working men cannot be put to middle class people. One rarely learns much about the wealthiest and most powerful people, at least not directly. It is impossible to approach them on their own social level. The same is true of the very poorest but in their case there are always other informants who know a lot about them. In the case of the wealthy and powerful there are not. Few sociologists have the privilege, like Amory, of coming from these circles and not everyone has the flair and talent to penetrate into them, like Lincoln Steffens. Even his information was concerned rather with the mechanism of power than with the daily life of those who exercise it. Such persons are very reticent and inclined to formalize and limit the length of every conversation. That is why we know very little about the subculture of the 'upper ten', 'society' or 'smart set'. The most isolated, xenophobic village is incomparably more accessible than the social summit. When, if at all, the phenomenon of power is treated in descriptive studies of western society-fragments the description is based on observation and deduction from a lower or middle level rather than inspection on the upper level.

The sociologist's position with regard to his object is clearly different from that of the ornithologist or the historian. The reactions evoked by his personality and position affect the reality he is trying to understand, which in itself is constantly changing. It is amazing that so many have found their way out of this labyrinth so well. They deserve our profound respect.

Though all these problems may be pointed out, what is the use if we cannot say how they are to be overcome? One remains an outsider, a 'white man', 'a gentleman', 'a non-farmer' or whatever else one is or is not. These attributes determine one's position. Field-workers are more often men than women; perhaps that is why so many of the groups described make such a masculine impression? They consisted for about fifty percent of women, but as a rule we read little about the female half of society, about their outlook, their role in transferring culture to their children, their peculiar preoccupations. The true reason is, probably, that the principal informants and interpreters are practically always men, even for female ethnographers, whose picture of the culture studied therefore not infrequently also has a masculine touch. The problem is not unknown to historiography, either. Much of the presentation of history is male oriented because the male scribe has evolved as the main custodian of tradition. The point met with less interest on the part of historians than one might expect.[1]

A much heard piece of advice to future investigators is to 'try and become one of them'. This is of course quite impossible and even, past a certain degree, undesirable. One cannot be 'one of them' and keep aloof, be an uncommitted and co-reacting observer at the same time. What is required is that 'blend of critical detachment and discerning sympathy'[2] which the Lynds so pre-eminently possessed. By definition every 'describer' stands to some extent outside the action in which he is involved. He does not enter fully into his role, he is actor and spectator at the same time. If he has a talent for description this talent becomes a barrier separating him from 'objective reality'. He will never be 'one of them', never completely join in their emotions or fully participate in their experiences. He will watch it all rather coolly, more like a dramatic critic than like an ordinary theatre-goer. The situation conditioning his task performance requires this. Being 'one of them' would mean acquiring many of the handicaps which make it impossible for a member to write a report on the life of the group as a whole. Many doors are closed and thus more is lost than is gained.

In social description it should be always mentioned how, through whom, and about whom, the information was acquired. Some ethnographic accounts and group studies were based on information furnished by one informant only. Apart from the evident general objections against this procedure, we should take into account that such an informant is inevitably a marginal figure in his own society, or at least a peripherous one with respect to his own culture. He is never 'typical' of his group. The same may be said of bearers and interpreters selected from the community to be described.[3] The preferences that move researchers in the field in their selection are sometimes hard to understand. I have known an excellently trained but inexperienced and opini-

[1] Ferguson is quite aware of it in his tracing of the development of modern male feeling and thought (Ferguson 1966).

[2] Stein (1960): 313.

[3] These interpreters, naturally, also possess certain personal traits which exert on the data a similar effect as the anthropologist's. A clear illustration is found in Berreman (1962): 10; 13 ff.

onated American sociologist to choose, in a land of Muslim and Hindu, the only Christian from among the large number of bearers and interpreters available – contrary to all well-meaning advice. The person selected, moreover, had a bad reputation. In his new capacity the man proved a great failure. Such mistakes are all the more painful since the time available is always limited. In all such decisions where an irrelevant preference on the investigator's part may assert itself, a modicum of common sense and the slightest bit of intuition are worth more than the best theoretical knowledge.

The range of the investigator's contacts with the collectivity described by him is often thought wider than it really is. Especially in those cases where there is a considerable cultural disparity between the investigator and his object most of the data will be obtained from a small number of informants interrogated for the purpose. Usually it is not so much a matter of 'catching' reality as of deliberately bringing it out. The former would no doubt be better, but it takes too much time besides requiring a constant alertness which is hard to keep up.

The interrogation of a small number of informants, a procedure followed by many an anthropologist, is based on the implicit supposition that in a primitive culture every person is acquainted with the entire cultural heritage of the group. This is a wrong assumption to begin with and equally mistaken is the idea that everyone who ought to know a thing does actually know it. This is not the least bit true. At the moment of interrogation people may prove to be totally ignorant of certain past events which undoubtedly closely concerned them at the time of occurrence. Maybe they know, really, but either it is too great an effort for them to remember, or they are afraid a positive answer may elicit further questions of which they are tired as it is, or for which they have not the time. Not always because they have something else to do – outside the Western culture area 'spare time' is so plentiful that the concept as such hardly holds water – but because they do not wish to do anything. The most frequent answer I received when working in East Bengal was 'ahtcha', which can mean: 'yes', 'no', 'I don't know', 'that is so', 'be it so', 'well, well', 'I suppose so', 'you're right' and usually: 'I dont' care one way or the other but you can have it any way you want if you'll leave me alone'! It is in the line of western thinking to reward people for their trouble and we frequently find investigators paying for information. The people studied may think according to different lines, so this procedure entails all sorts of risks.[1]

Misinterpretation, prejudice, distortion and other forms of inaccuracy both on the part of the observer and on that of his informants are of far greater importance than ignorance, unwillingness or deceit on the informant's part. The interrogator – often an interpreter whose accuracy is hard to check – must be very careful not to ask leading questions in his zeal to find a conjecture confirmed. Laziness, politeness, and subservience on the part of the persons questioned will readily bring forth the desired answer. One never knows whether a question 'gets through' correctly – that is, whether the answer given applies to the question the interviewer had in mind but had to ask via an interpreter, or by using pidgin or some other lingua franca. Even within one's own culture a wrong word or an obscure phrase may have catastrophic consequences in an interview. In addition to this we are insufficiently acquainted with the facial expressions and gestures of members of another culture. They too have a store of conventional extra-lingual means of expression, which, however, convey nothing to the western interviewer. As for unintentional co-expression – in this respect the contact situation is, in Lewin's words 'unstructured'[2] as far as the stranger is concerned.

In the case of sociological research within our western culture the communication problem is not entirely absent either. The interviewees' capacity for verbal expression is generally far smaller than the interviewer's, which means that their replies are usually far less subtly formulated than the questions are in the interviewer's mind. A large number of persons may be reached by using a questionnaire, but the drawbacks of this method are well-known. Unexpected difficulties are encountered when one tries to use a questionnaire for obtaining information from people who are not accustomed to reflect on the precise meaning of words and phrases. No question seems to be clear enough. Answers contradict one another. Often they are not answers to the

---

[1] Not in all cases: in some cultures it is thought only natural or fitting to be paid for supplying information or even to demand payment as a matter of course. My colleague A. J. F. Köbben who pointed this out to me, experienced this in the nought-for-nought culture of the Baulé (W. Africa) and also to some extent among the Djuka (Surinam).

[2] See Lewin's analysis of the adolescent and his environment (Lewin 1951: 135-154).

corresponding questions but only to what the person questioned thinks he is asked. With such answers anything can be proved, even if the questions are carefully formulated not to betray the interviewer's presuppositions. The questionnaire is an important, an indispensable, instrument of research but it must be handled with the greatest caution especially when investigating simple cultures and sub-cultures or any 'alien' community.

Formal aspects and homogeneity; on fixation and arranging, smoothing out and choice. A bit of experience will enable the observer to avoid a number of mistakes encountered in naïve reports. Motives that are no more than rationalizations ('do you want your sister to marry a negro?') he will recognize as such and refuse to accept as explanations. He will know that people like to talk about the qualities they lack, as if they wished to make themselves believe they possess them.[1] He will realize that certain things are not talked about as long as they exist in full force – 'tradition' being an example – and that something is wrong with them when they keep being mentioned. There are many such cases where some simple insight into human nature and knowledge of life may preserve one from making gross errors. There still remain plenty of pitfalls that are extremely hard to avoid.

No investigator ever finds out 'everything'. What he ultimately learns is a very small fraction of the immense knowable whole. On numerous subjects every child in the place is better informed than he is when his research is concluded. On the other hand a good 'community study' contains more information than any one member of that community possesses. It is possible to live in a community for a considerable length of time and remain ignorant of certain things which everyone there knows, but about which according to a local consensus 'it is better not to talk'. This is not so very serious, since it only causes incidental lacunae. Other illusions cover a wider range. Owing to a common preference for the formal, more easily observed, aspects of culture instead of the informal and for constant interrogation instead of detection, the

---

[1] In an Eastern country where the public officials certainly did not excel by their sense of duty, their replies to my expressions of thanks were a stereotyped 'It is my duty, Sir'.

investigator learns more about the norm, about how things should ideally be, than about how they really are. He finds out more about the moral code than about morality, more about precepts than about actual behaviour. This in turn leads him to ascribe to norms, attitudes, ancestors, demons and all sorts of beliefs a greater influence on behaviour than they have in reality. He is apt to overrate the coercive power of ceremony and ritual.

The observer is also liable to overrate the homogeneity of the culture observed, since he concentrates most on adults, men, and the members of a majority group, within a larger whole that is rarely socially homogeneous. The sub-cultures of the generations may show interesting differences. There may be a certain tension or conflict between them. The report usually shows as little of this as of other contemporary conflicts or of the numerous personal differences between the members of a community, their ambitions, antagonisms, friendships, cliques. A community of some size, with a hierarchical structure, usually possesses various value systems. Which of these is officially accepted is a question of power. But, although one system may finally acquire general acceptance, because it is impossible to live in protest and conflict all the time, this democratic basis of an undemocratic principle varies greatly for different societies. We learn too little about recessive norms, even if secret protest organizations and all sorts of other forms of expression such as folklore clearly show they exist. The investigator's mental constitution, a product of his social origins or education, will cause him as a rule even in a strange society and culture, to concentrate on dominant values. For the great diversity of what is tolerated, the innumerable nuances of what 'also' exists and of what is 'also' possible or permissible, for all this there is a blind spot in his observation. He cannot and does not wish to be an all-round observer and we must not expect his general report to contain an exposé of the sub-culture of the 'underdog'. It is a part of a community's 'impression management' to see to it that the investigator's contacts with low-status groups are limited. These are the people,[1] nevertheless, to whom we ought to listen in order to find out about the non-official culture and about forms of behaviour that deviate from the norm, especially, too, on the part of persons of standing.

[1] Cf. Barnett (1953): 339 ff.

One of the reasons for this is that the observer freezes his object while in reality it is a continuous whole of human interaction, a drama that cannot be stopped at any given point. The very intention of producing a description, the 'notebook in one's hand', freezes the object in motion and we cannot expect in this way to get an insight into social processes. Such an insight could only be acquired by watching a course of events that would show us things against a background of time. This is why most sociological reports are deficient regarding those aspects of culture that can only be got to know in motion. Many cultures and sub-cultures offer practically no opportunity for looking back in history. The absence of a time dimension gives the description a peculiar flatness, a lack of that colour and fullness which would be characteristic for a present of which we know the past and may guess the immediate future. For a study of social change, of course, description on one temporal plane is useless. Only a renewed enquiry after a lapse of time may offer useful data in this respect.

Everyone who has some experience in this field knows that in noting down data as they present themselves one is continually tempted to fit them into some tentative arrangement on the spot. For the most 'concrete' facts there is little objection to doing so, but one always has a tendency to go much further.

We do not know how to move in a chaotic reality, do not know how to handle it, and when we describe it we do so as if it were organized. Conditioned by a culture which worships reason like no other, and moulded in a sequence of educational institutions which inculcate the high values of logical thought, clarity and a sense of order, our mind habitually looks for order where chaos reigns, longing to discover a pattern and a structure, preferably a coherent one with an inner logic. Our passion for neatly smoothing out a disorderly social reality, again, fails to do justice to the complex variety of all social life. Already in our observation and once more in writing down we try to avoid dissonance. This determines the slant both of our observation and of our reporting. We avoid or reduce any information that creates dissonance and welcome anything consonant.[1]

[1] Festinger (1957): passim; p. 3: '... dissonance, the existing of non-fitting relations among cognitions, is a motivating force in its own right. By the term cognition ... I mean any knowledge, opinion, or belief about the environment, about oneself, or about one's behavior'. P. 137: 'If a person

This rather arbitrary way of imposing order, the satisfaction of our need to round off, straighten, and smooth out and the illusion of well-functioning systems are partly a result of the fact that even after concluding an investigation the anthropologist or sociologist still has a very imperfect knowledge of the society he has studied. Anyone who does not agree would do well to read the reports of foreign observers on his own society. For is not our appreciation of such writings due, in part, to the fact that the authors' observations are sometimes not altogether wide of the mark? And to their amusing conclusions and their rectilinear exposé, based on a minimum of knowledge? Such reports by amateurish authors are always grossly deficient, as we Dutch have had ample opportunity to note. Much has been written about our country by visitors from elsewhere, but there has been little professional investigation of Dutch life by foreign sociologists. What research did take place was usually concentrated in one facet or problem. As soon as a more general approach is attempted it becomes apparent how extremely difficult it is, even for professional sociologists, to understand a strange society. Such writings have a sobering effect on the reader: what reason has he to believe he would do better himself in similar circumstances?

Since a society may be viewed from many different angles, the personal hobbies of the observer, the dogmas of his teachers, the 'school' that trained him, everything that directs his vision, plays a part in his total cognition. He may, for instance, have a penchant for ecological aspects, for man's relations to his natural environment. A half-yearly change of residence may lead to the discovery of a 'summer' and 'winter' culture, as Mauss found with the Eskimo. But do the Eskimo themselves see this caesura in their culture? Do the Nuer themselves attach as much importance to their half-yearly migration as Evans-Pritchard, their ethnographer, does? I asked myself this question once when I yielded to the temptation of such a central point of view when investigating the life of the Hungarian tanya peasants in the Alföld. Not much imagination

is involuntarily exposed to information that will increase dissonance, then in addition to the usual procedure whereby he may reduce this dissonance, there are also set up quick defensive processes which prevent the new cognition from ever becoming firmly established', for (p. 260): 'the human organism tries to establish internal harmony, consistency, or congruity among his opinions, attitudes, knowledge, and values. There is a drive toward consonance among cognitions'.

was required on my part to realize that the tanya population themselves did not attach nearly as much importance to this fact as their foreign visitor did, who kept hammering on what was to them the most ordinary thing in the world. Of course the informants' view on their own culture and society is not the 'real' truth either, but we might at least accord them an equal voice with the foreign observer. It cannot be denied that their knowledge is infinitely greater and – to return to an image used at the beginning of this article – they are, after all, the river that is being mapped.

Social description is often not so much a study of actual behaviour as rather a systematic description of certain patterns of behaviour which are proclaimed 'typical' and/or 'general'. In thus imposing an order (of his own) on a disorderly body of human interaction the observer naturally notices many 'exceptions' and 'contradictions', which, being a conscientious person, he will note down as soon as they present themselves to him as such. These 'exceptions', however, have come into being through rules, configurations, or models which are not necessarily inherent in the observed reality but which were determined by the observer. The 'exceptions' do not fit in with his highly simplified picture or with his method of collecting data.[1] Many contradictions are nothing but normal modalities that integrally belong, as counterpoints[2] or otherwise, to the great, complicated, never totally cognizable whole, which allows all sorts of possibilities beside the officially prevailing[3], which is never as strict and implacable as it is made out in writing by an ordering mind. Nor is it in this form that the official order exists in the minds of the members of the observed society, even of those who maintain the status quo. Evidently such a system is just not logical in structure, but why should it be logical?

It is significant that one never finds these 'exceptions' or 'contradictions'

---

[1] An interesting example is found in Garbett (1960). A comparison with the results of a previous investigator, Bernard, moves Garbett to say (p. 27): 'This example also shows how preconceived methods of collecting fieldwork data can seriously affect the resultant description of a social system which an anthropologist presents, and how important it is not to dismiss the exceptional case which does not fit in with the general pattern for, as in this example, it may 'prove the rule'.

[2] Wertheim (1953).

[3] See for instance Berreman's felicitous use of the concepts 'back region' and 'front region' information (Berreman 1962: passim), in imitation of Goffman (1959).

marked as such in one's diary notes. They are hardly ever there in ink, appearing only in typescript. The informants, even the thoughtful ones, apparently see nothing incongruous or remarkable in them. Their 'contradictory' character arises only in the mind of the outsider. Nevertheless they are essential parts of the prevailing order, just as 'normal' and 'regular' as the 'general order' observed by the investigator, which as a matter of fact could not exist without these 'exceptions' and 'contradictions'. There is no problem really, or rather the problem is a sociological, not a social one. The problem we seem to observe is not present in the society but in our cognition. It arises from the observer's tendency to objectify the subjective, to project his own mental categories on the observed material.

Excessive attention for some matters is often accompanied by a neglect of other aspects of the object studied. That we should close our eyes to things we have learned to keep secret in our own culture is understandable enough, but scientifically it is disastrous. 19th Century ethnographers, for instance, paid little attention to the sexual life of primitive peoples. The effects of this prudishness, especially on the part of missionaries, were perceptible for a long time afterwards. A mistaken delicacy which apparently did not permit the mention of anything extraordinary, abominable, disgusting or 'unnatural', and all sorts of hypocrisy, have withheld important information from us in a great number of reports.

Between observation and reading: the problem of communication. Observation is followed by registration. Usually the investigator begins to write his report while still engaged in observation. In this writing many of the influences we have mentioned as affecting observation make themselves felt once more. The two phases cannot really be separated but there is a difference in the sense that influences which assert themselves in an unconscious or scarcely conscious manner at the observation level will reach a higher degree of consciousness at the writing stage. Putting into words the contents of the mind means being confronted with them. By using language we externalize thoughts that have been brought to a clear state of consciousness. Things one preferred to disregard at a previous stage now become conscious omissions.

While writing, one is already associating with one's readers. 'Indecent' or 'smutty' passages may offend an employer or publisher, although this seems to happen less often now than before the second World War. Any such passages that do occur in the original publication often disappear in translation. Translators are known to leave out offensive passages, even actually to falsify texts. Right to the present day publisher's office employees lend a helping hand, texts also being abridged by them for the sake of keeping down the price of the book. The asterisks of Hakluyt Society publications * * * unfit for translation * * * have obscured entire paragraphs. It is on these grounds that Friederici declares these publications to be worthless to cultural and religious history.[1] The inaccuracy and scant scientific value of old illustrations, as for instance those of Cook's voyages, are due to prudery. In contemporary studies important information may be withheld on ethical grounds, for instance when publication might harm informants or when they have been promised secrecy, or because of restrictions imposed by some official body.

These are simple forms of incompleteness and distortion. Other influences affecting reports are less easy to diagnose. The conceptual framework with which the author is accustomed to work, his presuppositions and preferences, assert themselves once more. They determine, to some degree, both what he selects for his writing down and the way he does it. In order to understand the society described, the reader must identify himself with the observer. This is the only way for him to experience the described piece of reality from the inside. It is extremely difficult, however, to write one's report in a way that enables the reader to do so. We should therefore be mild in our judgement of the numerous deficiencies that are so easily and frequently noted. All sorts of projection mechanisms that already played a part in observation do so again in the writing: the description becomes still more ordered, more logical, more systematic and more 'arrested' than the real thing was or could be. The observer did not see it thus. Nobody could ever see it thus. It is like someone's life history. We don't get to know it, as novelists used to offer it to us, from birth to death. If they were to give it systematically the other way around it would still not be satisfactory. In real life such stories are told neither forwards

[1] Friederici (1927): 392 ff.; 397.

nor backwards; we learn them both forwards and backwards. The same is true of the way we see social reality: it differs radically from the view given by the usual, though perhaps in this form inevitable, presentation of the result. No sensitive author can ever be satisfied with the result and everyone who has passed through this ordeal will know the frustrating feeling created by the inadequacy of man and means. Description again deprives the object of much of its dynamic character after observation has already sinned in this respect. This is partly due to the fact that the author is apt to use a system of concepts which is attuned, one feels, to a condition rather than to change: 'class', 'rank', 'institutions', 'structure', 'stratification', 'pattern of resources'. He knows that this helps to enforce an undesirable tendency but he can do little about it.

The awareness that one is addressing an audience may affect one's report in various ways. An author, if he has something to say, will want to convince his readers. The truth, however, rarely looks veracious. Arranged truth, which is no longer truth but a striving for effect, has a much greater semblance of veracity. That is why the builders of the Greek temples added a slight curve to lines that had to look horizontal and why their columns are not purely geometrical in shape. That is why an altogether credible, readily acceptable story is nearly always somewhat contrived. 'Les vérités fabriquées sont plus vraies que les vérités nues'. It is not usually possible in social descriptions to point out actual instances of yielding to this tendency, but they may sometimes be suspected. On occasions, in one's own work one feels the necessity to brace oneself against such concessions to one's readers. After all, our aim is not to turn out a flawless piece of work calculated to achieve a maximum of effect, but rather to report as truthfully as possible.

This consideration makes our problem all the greater. How are we to find the right words to communicate our findings? There are many fairly objective elements of culture, the general characteristics of which, their frequency and so on, may be determined and put down in writing with a high degree of reliability, but this is not true of other aspects of culture and social structure. Language is by no means an ideal medium for this purpose. Language did not develop primarily in aid of our cognitive powers. It is too concrete for a direct representation of social reality, too simple to do justice to every subtle distinction. There are many products of the mind for which we have no words and have to resort to metaphor. This is one reason why linguistic usage is such a very personal matter. This again hardly facilitates communication. We cannot expect all sociologists to use their language with the same degree of accuracy, flexibility and sensitivity to nuances. The one is more skilful and gifted than the other. It is, essentially, an artistic rather than a scientific skill and the personal factor plays an important part. The term papers of young students already show the talent of a few and the hopeless incapacity of others for finding the right words to evoke in the reader or listener the same images as were present in the author's mind. In this respect our situation differs radically from that of the natural sciences.

Every language is itself a product of culture and everyone knows how difficult it often is to find in one's own language the right expression for a concept that does not exist in one's own culture – a notorious stumbling block for translators. How are we to understand a strange culture through empirical definitions, derived from a culture – our own – that differs so much from the alien reality we try to grasp? The result will never be completely satisfactory. However sensitive and striking our description, it can never be sufficiently close and direct to produce truly identical shapes or sensations. The problem of communication, first between the investigator and his object and again between the author and his readers, would seem so serious that we may well be surprised at the amount of success that is nevertheless achieved.

Even the most subtle and inventive use of language offers no solution for the circumstance that a social 'fact' is shrivelled and stunted by being written down. Though thoughts may be more diffuse than words, their content is greater. The limited usefulness which words do possess, by virtue of their greater clarity, is only too often cancelled by an undisciplined use which has blurred their meaning to such an extent that we are obliged to resort to professional jargon in order to regain the original advantage of words over thoughts.

The structure of 'civilized' languages, too, entails certain dangers. By their tendency to reduce a heterogeneous mass of phenomena to categories they offer a far more schematic picture of reality than would occur to those whose minds have not undergone the influence of such languages. Western cultures are more verbally inclined than primitive cultures[1] and the same difference exists between the subculture of the western university graduate and that of the rural population he studies in his own country.

Age is another factor. Young people show a preference for the unusual words of contemporary professional jargon and take fewer personal liberties than those who have long been in the profession. The influence of previous experience with another object, perhaps in a different culture, is as important as the influence of one's education. The descriptive work produced by young scholars often displays the hobby -horses of their teachers, sometimes even to the extent of borrowing their pet expressions.

True art can undoubtedly describe social life more effectively than science will ever be able to, but the liberties which are the prerogative of art, added to its essentially different aim, preclude our looking in this direction for a solution of our problems. All the same it must be stated that social description is a creative activity in which the artistic element has a positive significance.

There has been no lack of attempts to banish the latter element, for science does not feel quite comfortable with it. It is an old ambition, following the example of the natural sciences, to quantify elements of social reality and thus make them accessible for mathematical manipulation. Great ingenuity has been displayed in subjecting to statistical treatment even such aspects of society as do not, by their nature, easily lend themselves to such operations. It must be conceded that this does open a way to greater objectivity, reduction of the personal note, increased accuracy, and even, perhaps, to conclusive argumentation. For carefully worked out functional relations between quantitative variables, mathematical treatment is the obvious procedure. Many questions that arise in this connection, however, remain unsolved for the time being. This approach will never be able to replace the *verstehende* method of verbal description and appraisal and, what is more, the statistician usually applies the latter method himself, far more than he would care to admit, before starting on his calculations.

---

[1] Which does not imply that primitive peoples make less use of speech or show no appreciation for eloquence – the opposite may be true! What I mean is that an accurate use of language, in speech or writing, as an essential part of many actions, of law, administration, etc., or as a means of recording culture, is less important with them.

He, too, does not work 'haphazardly'. His research is also based on a tentative theory of the context of human behaviour. The chaos of collectable material is not organized by observation, registration and processing alone. Hypotheses, conceptualization, a priori speculation are still necessary and it remains to be seen whether the part played by presupposition and projection will be smaller. These factors cannot be eliminated by 'confining oneself purely to the facts' since this is simply not possible. The statistical approach involves some new dangers as well, such as overrating the significance of 'averages' (maybe the one thing that does not exist) and reducing a whole category of phenomena to one denominator for the sake of quantification, with a total disregard of differences and nuances due to factors of time and place.

It is customary nowadays to prefer the mathematical approach of a complex of factors to the intuitive descriptive approach, partly because the former is thought to make it possible to 'measure' the force of separate factors. Those who propagate this view are apt to forget that all these factors are significant only within the total context and as a part of the whole. They only exist as such and an analysis of the whole produces sham creations, the 'weighing' of which by mathematical methods is still, necessarily, based on a verbal system. In spite of their undeniable and admirable inventiveness the numerous recent attempts at mathematical analysis of factor complexes have not fundamentally changed my views on this matter. It seems to me that little real progress has been made and I doubt whether any may be expected.

Conclusion. The reliability of anthropological and sociological description has received little attention as a problem in itself. For the various reasons named above their value should not be overrated. In a number of cases a social aggregate was studied and described more than once within a reasonably short period of time. In those cases where both investigations were carried out by the same person, or where the second was based on the first it is not surprising to find a great deal of similarity.[1] Where two investigators worked indepen-

---

[1] See Lynd and Lynd (1929) and id. (1937); Redfield and Rojas (1934) and Redfield (1950); Lewis (1960) and id. (1951); West (1945) and Gallaher (1960); Firth (1936) and id. (1959); Miner (1939) and id. (1950); Whyte (1943) and the postscript in the second edition (1955): 'On the evolution of Street Corner Society'.

dently, however, the results were often far from similar.[1] This is only to be expected considering the numerous operative factors, as we saw above. These make it doubtful whether the word 'reliable' may be used at all in this connection. For by what standards are we to judge reliability?

Deliberate deceit does not occur much in science, but inadmissible negligence does. In social description we depend entirely on the accuracy and sincerity of the author since, especially with exotic objects, there is little likelihood his work will ever be checked. A newspaper reporter has a more compelling external motive for being conscientious than any scientific reporter in the social field. Those journalists who were known as 'muckrakers' for their activity in social exposure in the United States between 1892 and 1911 were paragons of accuracy. They had to be, considering the judicial consequences of any lack in this respect. The academic man reporting on society in a scholarly treatise is not faced with civil suit or criminal charge.

Since a 'reliable' author may still produce a distorted picture, the question of 'validity' arises. How 'true' are his results? How representative, for instance, is the information offered? Did he use the right word in every case? If something occurs 'much', 'not much', 'often', 'repeatedly', 'frequently', 'rarely', 'usually' or 'quite a bit', what exactly does the word mean? What means have we of testing? How has the relative force of various factors been assessed and on what grounds? Who, in the collectivity described, would be able to judge the validity of the report? As we already said above, the precariously small foundation on which the generalizations of many social reports are based would be a source of general amazement if it were known. This has contemptuously been called 'anecdotalism' and much ethnographical and sociographical work is in fact barely disguised anecdotalism.

At the same time it is also true that a purely statistical analysis, processing and presentation of material is only seemingly objective, to say nothing of 'induction'. It has the added drawback of lacking all verve or colour, of draining the life from everything while the results, when presented, fail to evoke any picture of group life. The results of research in the social sphere are by

---

[1] Compare Dollard (1937) and Powdermaker (1939); Redfield (1930) and Lewis (1951), and id. (1960); Garbett (1960) with the study of the same community by Bernardi in 1948 (Bernardi 1950).

no means always meaningful and many results of mathematical operations are convincingly 'true' but devoid of all meaning. Even if they do have some significance the danger, or probability, remains that as a result of these methods thought will wither and intuition will be discouraged. We cannot but agree with Nisbet that: 'Anything that shrinks the field of experience and imagination, that in any way diminishes the sources of inspiration, that routinizes the workings of the intelligent mind, is to be regarded with suspicion'.[1] Similarly we will have to endorse the view of Stouffer and Lazarsfeld: 'Some of us are extremely interested in helping put sociological research more in the direction of verification. But that cause will not be served by an insistence on an exclusive technique which too often may yield trivial results where valid, and pretentious nonsense where invalid'[2]. My admiration for many recent attempts to achieve cool objectivity in social description by means of mathematical formulas is only too often tempered by the consideration: 'le mieux est l'ennemi du bien'. Although this good may not be so very good, though there are many justifiable objections to verbal description, characterization, speculation, generalization and interpretation, we cannot do without it however little cogency there may be in the validity of its results.

We are forced to conclude that neither one extreme nor the other will do, that we shall have to accept a compromise while constantly keeping in mind the dangers of both methods. The verbalists should always, in every case, provide a clear and complete statement of their approach, and of the working situation, explaining how the data were obtained, from and through whom, how they were arranged and how conclusions were drawn.

In recent years there has been a considerable improvement. Well-trained anthropologists are profoundly aware of many of the difficulties mentioned and systematically avoid them in their precise and detailed studies. In the sphere of sociological description the question of scientific value applies mainly to community studies or 'sociographies'. Aspect studies and other less comprehensive investigations are less prone to the shortcomings mentioned. The reasons are obvious and follow from our discussion.

---

[1] Nisbet (1962).
[2] Stouffer and Lazarsfeld (1937): 201, quoted by MacIver (1954): 131.

A few very general difficulties cannot be eliminated and make themselves felt all the time. This may be why, in spite of all the progress made in ethnography, old ethnographies are still so readable and by no means hopelessly out of date. There are a multitude of descriptive sociological studies of local aggregates and they all have a stamp of their own, an incidental character. They are less concerned with each other than is customary in the field of science and they evince a discontinuity in conceptualization and general approach. The generalizations of the one are not consistently compared with those of others. It is not with impunity, evidently, that they are situated in the borderland between art and science.

This position is, however, by no means unfruitful. These studies have taught and keep reminding us that all social perception is subjective and one-sided.[1] Unwittingly they have called attention to the close connection between institutional organization, the daily life of the people and the social structure of the aggregate. They give us an opportunity to examine the effects in 'the provinces' of decisions made in the national centre of government and administration. More perhaps than any other descriptive work they have drawn the attention of sociology to social hierarchy and status criteria and to the differences between reality and social stereotype. They offer a possibility of viewing a general problem (e.g. 'unemployment') or phenomenon (e.g. 'social mobility') within a total social context.[2] From an educational point of view they are useful for young students in freeing them of the tendency to overrate economical and political aspects of society – a residue of pre-university education – and in pointing out the dangers both of excessive generalization and of being too specific. Finally, these studies have contributed more than any other research to our knowledge of daily life, of the 'genre de vie' in the United States, Mexico, Sweden, France, the Netherlands, Austria or in whichever country they were carried out. They are an excellent introduction for those who wish to get acquainted with a strange people and we would reluctantly do without them in any 'area-study'.

---

[1] As Redfield puts it, reports by different investigators on the same community provide us with 'a somewhat stereoscopic view' (Redfield 1960: 316).
[2] As is convincingly done by Stein (1960).

Since the twenties of this century a large number of sociographic studies have been published in the Netherlands. The majority of these were carried out by persons trained in an academic environment where there was little awareness as yet of the complex of problems treated in the present article. Most of these sociographies display in abundance the various shortcomings we have mentioned. The sociographic work of the Amsterdam school, carried out with the greatest industry and devotion both in this country and elsewhere, has not on the whole had a fecundating effect on sociology in the Netherlands. In my opinion it has even been a drag on its development. In any case this activity led more or less to a dead end which is no accident since it was based on fundamentally wrong suppositions. Of course this extensive body of work displays all the nuances in quality that are to be expected in view of the great differences in ability between the various authors. For some of them – disappointingly few, we must admit – this sociographic activity had a deeper meaning. They came to sociology through being confronted with social reality. They reacted to this and were forced to learn how to put their experiences into words, to assemble and organize them somehow into a readable whole. This need for coherence, among other things, made them feel the need for more theoretical insight.

Though, scientifically, there may be many objections to the wholistic social description of local communities and though perhaps it will never be capable of being carried out in a purely scientific fashion, we would yet reluctantly do without it. It remains one of the more attractive activities in the field of Social Science or, let us say, in the para-scientific field. Its attraction is, in fact, partly due to the fact that excellence here cannot be achieved exclusively through proficiency and experience of the craftsman but is still closely dependent on that very personal factor, the semi-artistic one, which is subject to so much censure. And even apart from these considerations we may agree with Chesterton that 'a thing that is worth doing at all, is worth doing badly'. However profitable it may be to reflect on the weaknesses of social description it would be unfair and even harmful to make perfectionist demands where perfection cannot be attained.

references

H. G. BARNETT (1953) Innovation, the basis of cultural change, New York etc.

J. BENNETT (1946) The interpretation of Pueblo culture: a question of values, *SWJA* 2: 361-374.

B. BERNARDI (1950) The social structure of the Kraal among the Zezuru in Musami, S. Rhodesia, Communication from the School of African Studies XXIII, Cape Town.

G. D. BERREMAN (1962) Behind many masks: ethnography and impression management in a Himalayan village, *Society for Applied Anthropology Monograph* # 4, Ithaca, N.Y.

V. F. CALVERTON (1931) Modern anthropology and the theory of cultural compulsives, in: V. F. Calverton ed., The making of man, New York.

K. DAVIS (1942) Review of W. L. Warner and P. S. Lunt (1942), The status system of a modern community, *AJS* 48 (# 4): 511-513.

J. DOLLARD (1937) Caste and class in a Southern town, New York.

B. EVANS (1953) The natural history of nonsense, London. (1st ed. 1947).

C. FERGUSON (1966) The male attitude, New York.

L. FESTINGER (1957) A theory of cognitive dissonance, Evanstone, Ill.

R. W. FIRTH (1936) We, the Tikopia, London.

R. W. FIRTH (1959) Social change in Tikopia. Re-study of a Polynesian community after a generation, London.

G. FRIEDERICI (1927) De preutschheid in de ethnographische literatuur, *Mens en Maatschappij* 3 (# 5): 392-404.

A. GALLAHER (1961) Plainville fifteen years later, New York etc.

G. K. GARBETT (1960) Growth and change in a Shona ward, Occasional Paper # 1, Department of African Studies, University College of Rhodesia and Nyasaland, Salisbury.

E. GOFFMAN (1959) The presentation of self in everyday life, Garden City, N.Y.

M. M. GORDON (1958) Social class in American Sociology, Durham, N.C. etc.

A. B. HOLLINGSHEAD (1948) Community research: development and present condition, *ASR* 13 (# 2): 136-156.

K. LEWIN (1951) Field Theory in social sciences. Selected theoretical papers, New York.

O. LEWIS (1951) Life in a Mexican village: Tepoztlán restudied, Urbana, Ill.

O. LEWIS (1960) Tepoztlán, village in Mexico, New York.

R. S. and H. M. LYND (1929) Middletown, New York.

R. S. and H. M. LYND (1937) Middletown in transition, New York.

R. M. MACIVER (1954) Social causation and change, in: G. Gurvitch and W. E. Moore (1945) Twentieth century sociology, New York.

H. MINER (1939) St. Denis, a French Canadian parrish, Chicago, Ill.

H. MINER (1950) A new epoch in rural Quebec, *AJS* (# 1): 1-10.

R. A. NISBET (1962) Sociology as an art form, *Pacific Sociological Review* 5 (# 2): 67-74 reprinted in: M. Stein and A Vidich (1963) Sociology on trial, Englewood Cliffs, N.J.

K. POPPER (1957) The poverty of historicism, London.

H. POWDERMAKER (1939) After freedom. A cultural study in the Deep South, New York.

R. REDFIELD (1930) Tepoztlán: a Mexican village, Chicago.

R. REDFIELD (1950) A village that choose progress: Chan Kom revisited, Chicago (2nd ed. 1962).

R. REDFIELD (1960) The little community, Chicago.

R. REDFIELD and A. V. ROJAS (1934) Chan Kom: a Maya village, Washington.

G. RÉVÉSZ (1957) Die Trias. Analyse der dualen und trialen Systeme, München.

TH. SCHARMAN (1959) Tertius miserabilis, Berlin.

G. SIMMEL (1908) Soziologie, Untersuchungen über die Formen der Vergesellschaftung, Leipzig.

E. SMITH-BOWEN (1954) Return to laughter, London.

M. R. STEIN (1960) The eclipse of community. An interpretation of American studies, Princeton.

S. A. STOUFFER and P. F. LAZARSFELD (1937) The family in the depression.

W. L. WARNER and P. S. LUNT (1942) The status system of a modern community, New Haven.

W. F. WERTHEIM (1953) Het contrapunt in de samenleving, in: Weerklank op het werk van Jan Romein: Liber amicorum, Amsterdam.

J. WEST (1945) Plainville, U.S.A., New York.

W. F. WHYTE (1943) Street Corner society, Chicago (2nd ed. 1955).

2   *participation and quantification;*
field work among the djuka (bush negroes of surinam)

A. J. F. KÖBBEN

'Gone are the happy days of ethnographic osmosis, when the fieldworker could sit down
and allow the fluid material from the primitive life around him
to percolate his intellectual and emotional tissues'. R. Firth (1954): 2

Introduction. The Bush Negroes of Surinam for the greater part live in the interior of this vast country, along the great rivers which form their traffic routes. Their precise number is not known, but it probably amounts to twenty-five or thirty thousand. The Bush Negroes are divided into a number of tribes, the largest of which are the Djuka and the Saramaccan. They live together in villages, averaging some hundreds of inhabitants, the core of which is formed by one or more matrilineages. They practise shifting cultivation in addition to which they have of old earned money through rendering transport services on the rivers and by selling timber. Nowadays many young Bush Negroes leave their villages to work as migrant labourers in the capital (Paramaribo) or elsewhere.

We know more about the history of the Bush Negroes than about that of most other non-literate peoples. From the last quarter of the seventeenth century onwards, large numbers of negro slaves were brought to Surinam from West Africa to work in the sugar plantations. Their life was extremely hard and in spite of the risks involved, many of them ran away to hide in the immense forests of the interior. These runaway slaves raided the plantations to procure tools and implements and thus were a menace to the colony. Time and again the administration organized expeditions in an attempt to wipe them out, which, however, proved unsuccessful. Ultimately, therefore, a treaty was sought, involving the acceptance of the *status quo* if the Bush Negroes would cease their raids on the plantations and hand over new escapees. This matter was finally settled just over two centuries ago, a treaty with the Djuka being concluded in 1760 and one with the Saramaccan in 1762. From that time onwards the Bush Negroes could develop their society practically without interference, although their relations with the whites continued to be strained. In doing so, they made full use of their African heritage, which does not mean, however, that they produced a faithful copy of their original society in West Africa. The great achievement of these people, in fact, is that they have succeeded, under most difficult circumstances, in developing a culture of their own.

Even today the Bush Negroes are to a large degree a nation within a nation. They harbour a considerable measure of distrust with regard to the outside world, an understandable attitude when we take into account their past history. The fieldwork reported in this chapter was carried out from August 1961 to July 1962 among the Djuka of the village called Langa Uku, on the Cottica river. During the same period Mr. (Now Dr.) and Mrs. H. U. E. Thoden van Velzen worked in the village of the Djuka's Paramount Chief on the Tapanahony river (from July 1961 to November 1962). Additional research among Djuka migrant labourers in the capital was carried out during a period of some months by Mr. H. Lamur. By this threefold approach we hoped to arrive at a better insight into the range of this culture. The fieldwork upon which this paper is based was financed by the Netherlands Organization for Scientific Research in Surinam and the Dutch Antilles (WOSUNA).[1]

Participation. I spent my year of fieldwork mostly in one small village, where I occupied a hut among the other huts.[2] Thus I was constantly in a position to watch the daily life of the village; its ordinary activities and ordinary gossip;

[1] For the history of the Bush Negroes see Stedtman (1796); Wolbers (1861), ch. 3; Van Lier (1949) ch. 1, 2, 3 and 6; De Groot (1963). An older source on Djuka society is Van Lier (1940). On the related Saramaccan and Boni see Herskovits (1934) and Hurault (1961) resp. For the results of the research-project here mentioned the reader is referred to Lamur (1965), Thoden van Velzen (1966) Van Wetering (forthcoming) and Köbben (1967b and forthcoming).

[2] I repeatedly interrupted my stay, however, for short visits to the capital, where my family lived.

small quarrels and big quarrels, and resulting palavers; the various crises in the lives of the villagers; sickness and death and their interpretation.

Diary, 11th to 16th March. 11th March. This morning Brother Mansooi started building his new hut. Yesterday he asked only one man to come and help him though he needs 5 or 6 for the job. But no worry: every man who passes gives a hand, for a few hours or for half the day. Papa Amoksi (the village eldest) sits and watches, offering a bit of advice here and there. No-one pays any attention to him, though. 11 o'clock. Uncle Pé comes by, stops and watches for a moment and wants to go off again. Papa Amoksi rebukes him for leaving. The man apologizes: he has hurt his hand. Even so he hasn't the courage to leave and hangs around for at least another hour. Father Sanka (the village headman) also arrives to lend a hand. When he catches sight of Brother Anaki he starts scolding him: the latter has made his wife pregnant again, while their first baby is still to small it can't even walk, 'he is robbing the child of its mother's breast'. Anaki grins sheepishly. The other young men are highly amused and ask me how 'we' do such things. 5.30 p.m. Ba Mansooi fetches a bottle of *tafia* and everyone present is rewarded with a good swig of the liquor. He whispers some derisive remarks about old Father Saité, who always arrives to 'help' at the moment drinks are being handed around. 12th March. This morning I bandaged Mother Faandi's foot. People are inclined to frown on me for doing this, after all she has had this dreadful tropical sore for years and there's sure to be a reason for it! They regard it as a sign of her being a witch. The old woman gave me two eggs. Brother Fanaili said: 'You can eat them as far as I'm concerned as long as you don't give me any'. The conversation turned to other people 'with an evil heart' and their doings. Uncle Jukun, who had had a few drinks, warned me against one such person: 'don't sleep at his place and don't accept food from him, *he is a witch*'. But there he went too far; you can insinuate as much as you like, but you are not to call anyone a witch in so many words. The others stopped him talking and said: 'sopi taki' (it is the liquor speaking). 13th and 14th March. Went to Pinatjaimi to attend Mother Saki's funeral. 15th March. As we are sitting in front of the hut talking, Sister Kolafu suddenly appears. In a voice trembling with rage she accuses her co-wife of every conceivable misdeed and announces her intention of fighting it out with her . . . Some hours later things really come to a head: screaming insults, the two women are tearing at each other's hair. People immediately come running to separate them . . . All this in spite of the fact that Sa Kolafu has been ill for quite a while now; tomorrow she is going to the doctor's policlinic in Tamarin, and afterwards to Agitiondro, the seat of the Great Deity, in order to ask him what has caused her illness and to find a cure.
In the evening the mother of Sa Meiba – that is the name of the co-wife concerned – comes and rails at the husband. When she has gone the latter complains of his hard fate: he is supporting two wives, but don't think they're grateful, oh no! Women are unreasonable, they won't learn to live together in peace. Uncle Jukun urges him to take Kolafu back to her own 'belly village' (matrilineal village) as soon as possible; it's no good to have two co-wives living in the same village, that's asking for trouble. 16th March. Last night about 10 o'clock a dog started to bark in the silence of the night, then another one started, and another. People came running and suddenly there was a terrible row of men and women. Cause: a man from another village was caught by the hut of Sa Pobieng

(her husband is in town, has been for a couple of months already). Ba Anaki tried to catch hold of him but he managed to escape. In the early hours of the morning the affair is discussed at length. Sa Pobieng insists that she is innocent and that she was just about to call for help. But the whole matter is thought rather suspicious and people agree to put her through an ordeal (*akondia*) in due time.

In sociological jargon this way of doing fieldwork is called 'participant observation'. May we use this term here? If actual 'participation' requires the fieldworker to be a Bush Negro among Bush Negroes, it is certainly not applicable. I share with other anthropologists, of course, the experience of being told by 'my' villagers that I was just like one of them; but I am not so naive as to consider this anything more than flattery or a form of compliment. It would not be right, for that matter – even if it were possible – to be completely absorbed into the group that one is studying.[1]

But we might also use the term to mean that the fieldworker participates in social life *in his rôle of fieldworker*.[2] And in that sense it may be applied here, as in the case of most anthropologists. If we wish to do our work properly, we should not work like an entomologist observing an ant-hill, but we must instead collect our material in interaction with the group. It is on the nature of this interaction that our information depends, the contents no less than the quality and quantity of it.

When I first arrived in the village of Langa Uku in my little boat, I was accompanied by a young man from this village, whom I had got to know in town, but I had no other introduction at all. At the landing-stage I met a man who was after only a short conversation, greatly interested in the work I had come for. He straightaway housed me in a hut of his that was being built. Two days later he allowed me to rent it for a year. It was only by coincidence that he happened to be in the village the day I arrived. As he said himself later: 'God kept me home that day in order that I might receive you'. Right from the start he regarded me as his protégé and confidant. This was certainly fortunate, for he was a key figure in his society. In addition he was exceptionally intelligent and quickly grasped what things would interest me. All the

---

[1] Cf. in the same vein Paul (1953): 438.

[2] Cf. Babchuck (1962): 225-228, who following a suggestion made by Raymond L. Gold, distinguishes between the 'participant observer' and the 'participant-as-observer'.

time of my stay he was involved in a power-conflict. He was a candidate for the position of village headman of Agitiondro, the most important village on the river. He explained to me all the factors that played a part in this conflict. My connections with him, however, had one drawback. His opponents never wholly accepted me. What made things worse was that these opponents were the priests of the Great Deity in Agitiondro and constituted the most important power-group in this society where power-groups are, otherwise, so conspicuously lacking. Fortunately my co-fieldworkers were in a favourable position to observe such a power-group in action elsewhere, so from the point of view of division of labour it would not even have been advisable for me to do the same. Otherwise I would have had to sever my connections with him, however painful it would have been to do so. Now I was able to watch the subtle ways in which these priests kept pestering both him and me. Even on the occasion of my farewell visit to Agitiondro an instance of this occurred. The oracle of the Great Deity imposed a stiff fine on my man (which he made sure to recover from me) because he had not notified the Deity beforehand of my intended visit, so that the latter had not been able to give me a worthy reception! Although the man in question was convinced that this decree of the oracle was 'the work of men', he dared not refuse to pay, for fear of vengeance on the part of the deity: 'the Great Deity can't help but punish if his priests want him to'.

In cases where a society is highly stratified, the same problem presents itself to a far greater degree. In an Indian village it is practically impossible to do research among the untouchables once one has been in contact with the dominant caste ... while it is equally impossible to avoid such contacts (Baks et al. 1965: 171-172). The nature of the information obtained by the fieldworker varies significantly according to the caste his interpreter belongs to (Berreman 1962: 10).

If what I said above about interaction is true, it follows that the attitude of the group, with respect to the research to be carried out, is important. Take my case: was it possible to explain my purpose in coming to the village? When I did so in simple terms, many people understood. A help was the fact that the population of Surinam consists of many widely different groups, which makes people conscious of cultural differences. Examples of this were proffered quite spontaneously: 'a Javanese can squat on his heels for hours, even if there's a box right next to him he won't pull it under his buttocks. We wouldn't be able to keep it up'. For a long time they continued to suspect there were other, hidden, motives for my presence, the most common assumption being that I was a missionary of some church rivalling with the catholic mission, simply because such persons are known in the region. That is why, on my arrival there, I stated with great emphasis that I was in no way connected with any church whatsoever. This assertion, however, missed its mark. It was thought bizarre and obviously a lie. I was white, so I belonged to the church of white men. They can't conceive how anyone can be irreligious or not belong to a church. Fortunately this did not prevent them from showing me the expressions of their religion. They would make libations on my behalf if I undertook anything as dangerous as, for example, going into town by plane. Similarly they thought it quite natural that I should make libations to their deities, since they don't regard their own religion and Christianity as incompatible.

At first I tried to make myself popular by giving children small presents of sweets and pictures. But that had a negative effect. Presents should be given to the elders who, in turn, may pass something on to lower ranking persons, thus gaining prestige. I also gave small presents of food to a poor imbecile woman, Sa Pusa, simply out of pity for the neglected creature. People could only wonder at this and it gave rise to a standard joke which was always followed by screams of laughter: 'Uncle Andilé is making up to Sa Pusa'.

People never showed the least surprise at the fact that I had come from the other end of the world to study, of all places, their own poor village. They considered themselves the navel of the world and praised my wisdom in choosing their village and not one of those worthless other Cottica villages. Until recently I believed that such an egocentric attitude was characteristic for mankind everywhere, but Berreman (p. 9) tells us of 'his' village in the Himalayan mountains that the inhabitants never got over their surprise at the fact that he should have chosen them, of all people, as an object of study.

The better informants get to know quickly what interests the researcher and keep this in mind in their contacts with him.

Diary, 7th Jan. Pa Daose is whispering conspiratorially with a few fellow villagers. When I curiously inquire what it is all about he says: 'it's nothing . . . but do you know that such and such had a fight yesterday?' At my instantaneous reaction: 'Did they? Where, and what about? Tell me about it!' all those present burst out laughing. Daose says to them: 'You see, it's just as I predicted, *fighting*, that's what he's interested in'.

At first people gave me much spontaneous information about technical matters (such as laying snares, plaiting mats, etc.) to which I always paid courteous attention, even taking notes for duty's sake. All the same they must have sensed a lack of response on my part, for they gradually stopped coming to me with such data.

The personality and interests of the research-worker are thus a significant factor in determining the contents of his report. Pure description does not exist.[1] Young anthropologists are sometimes urged to write down 'everything' they see.[2] Anyone who were to follow this advice literally would need a book to report on one day in one small village. It may be objected that 'everything' in this case means everything *that is significant*, and that anything insignificant should of course be omitted. But then what is 'significant'? It is impossible to offer an objective criterion for this. It depends on the pre-occupations of the researcher and on the theories to which he is addicted. Take an example: a two-year-old is whimpering in front of a hut; the mother comes out and slaps the child; the child stops crying. Should the fieldworker make a note of this trivial incident? If he is interested in, say, political structure he will most likely omit it. The odds are he won't even notice it at all. For a man who is interested in Culture and Personality, however, this incident is very important indeed, since his theory claims that the formation of personality depends greatly on how the mother treats the young child, in this case on whether she fondles it or slaps it when it cries.

There are other selective mechanisms, too, that play a part in fieldwork. I personally find it difficult to extricate important information from persons who are antipathetic to me. In doing social research one should, of course, keep one's personal antipathies concealed, and I acquitted myself of this task to the

[1] The consequences of this situation with respect to cross-cultural comparisons are discussed in Köbben (1967 a): 11. See also the chapter of den Hollander in this book.

[2] Cf. the advice given by Lévi-Strauss (1963: 280): 'On the observational level the main, one could almost say the only rule is that all the facts should be carefully observed and described without allowing any theoretical preconception to decide whether some are more important than others'.

best of my ability. In several cases the persons in question were not aware of my negative feelings towards them, yet they never became valuable informants. This is obviously a shortcoming on my part, for presumably this sort of selection of informants will result in a warped picture of society.

Informants should preferably be intelligent, but intelligence is not enough. Being an informant is a profession that needs to be learned. The informant has to sense what the researcher is looking for. He must learn to be accurate in matters which in his experience do not call for accuracy; he mustn't start inventing when he doesn't know the answer to a question. I was glad, therefore, to have a basic group of regular informants. The highest degree of proficiency was reached by the only informant I had taken into paid service. Sometimes when I asked him a question he would be plunged in thought for a while, finally to reply: 'I'd rather not answer this question at all, for I don't know exactly'. Part of his job was to help me with the language. I was soon able to converse easily in Djuka, but I still missed a lot when people were chattering among themselves. I would note key-words and try to reconstruct the conversation afterwards with my informant. Djuka is a so-called Creolized language with a very simple grammar and as such it is much easier to learn than, for example, West-African languages.

Together with this informant I carried out a house to house survey, more about which will be found in the section below. Before we started, I tried to explain my purpose to him. At first I didn't succeed, but after a while he evidently understood and spontaneously proceeded to introduce my questions as follows: 'he (the ethnographer) wants to know very exactly all sorts of things about you, so that when he is present at a *kutu* (palaver) that concerns you he'll be able to follow what it's all about'. I couldn't have wished for a better explanation.

After having worked for me almost a year, this man met the informant who was employed by my co-fieldworkers. The two men exchanged experiences and together pondered on the nature of their work. They were completely agreed about the object of anthropological fieldwork: *soso konku taki*, 'simply collecting gossip' – not at all a bad definition of the bizarre activities of the ethnographer.

The nature of the interaction that takes place is determined to a great extent by the fieldworker's *status* among the group he is studying. In Western society, as has often been pointed out, his status is generally not high. This means that interviewers are denied much valuable information.[1] The Djuka are not accustomed to research-workers, and therefore don't know how to 'place' them. My being white and rich – however primitive my life among them, I was irrevocably rich – undeniably gave me extra prestige and, consequently, the attention of the group. Status, however, is a double-edged sword. If the researcher is held in great awe, people will try to play up to him, and nothing can be more harmful for research than this. I did find some symptoms of it among the Djuka, but only faint ones, while on the other hand I was flatly refused certain information in some instances. Real subservience, as is found in highly stratified societies[2] is foreign to the Djuka.

One's being white, however, does not only lend status, it also evokes distrust, especially in the beginning. In the long run, though, this initial distrust, instead of being a disadvantage, rather proved the opposite in my case. That was when they noticed how very differently I acted from the way other white men act, or at least from the way they imagine white men to act.

On the other hand my prestige suffered from the fact that I tried to speak their language and tried to conform to their customs. This brought about a pupil – teacher relationship and in my position as pupil I inevitably made a stupid and clumsy impression, and often felt horribly clumsy and stupid myself. Anthropological fieldwork is an exercise in modesty! Needless to say the advantages of adjustment much surpassed the disadvantages of my loss of prestige.

Diary. 17th Oct. Went with a group that set out to cut trees. I also attempted to wield the axe but acted so clumsily that Da Sanka told me to stop it. He was afraid I would cut my leg or have a tree fall on me. I was allowed to watch from a distance, with the women and children. 18th Oct. This afternoon at the mortuary feast for Ba Milanda I played the game called *agi* with five others. I won only from one of them, a woman, whose astonishment at the fact was not very flattering to me. 12th Jan. I owed Da Amoksi five guilders. When I saw him sitting under the village tree with a number of others I wanted to pay him. Although I know that for these people it is bad form to pay anyone in public – it should be done in the privacy of the hut – I did not realize this at the moment. Everyone

---

[1] Cf. Junker (1960): 95-99; 106-110. Blau (1964): 27-31.
[2] For examples see Miner (1960): 164-167; de Schlippe (1956): IX-X.

was alarmed. I was gently reprimanded and apologized profusely. 20th Feb. I'm given a small part to play in a trial (really only for fun). I try to acquit myself of this to the best of my ability but only succeed in provoking hilarity. Pa Daose comes to my aid and prompts me. 22nd Jan. At the funeral of Sa Bobi I am asked to make a libation. I am a bit nervous, for there are many people present, also from other villages. I do it carefully and as beautifully as possible and evidently I am successful this time: there is a murmur of approval. 12th March. In future I won't have to sit idle when everyone is helping to build a hut. Ba Mansooi has taught me how to make a roof-covering. He checks my work carefully (he doesn't check the work of the others). 15th April. Went with a hunting party today. When we had been walking through the forest for hours I asked my companions how they would find their way back. Great amazement: 'wouldn't you manage by yourself?' – When they were stalking the game they asked me to stay behind. I'd make too much noise, I suppose, which would scare the game and spoil everything. 28th April. This afternoon my informant told me a long story about *kunu* (the avenging deity). I thought I understood him and told him so. But when I tried to repeat the story in my own words, as it is my habit to do, it turned out I had missed the point completely. He was clearly irritated at my failure and so was I in turn. 2nd June. Ma Jeje is a classificatory *tia* (aunt) of Ba Apaitiki's, but he didn't know what the exact relationship was. With the aid of my genealogy I was able to explain it to him in detail. He exclaimed in astonishment: 'You know something about the village that I don't know'. His compliment gave me an intense feeling of satisfaction.

An ethnographer is a prying busybody and as such he is a potential danger; a nuisance, moreover, with his never-ending questions. If people tolerate his presence in the village, they do so on account of compensations which may be either of a material or of an immaterial nature.

Diary, 18th Oct. 10.30 p.m. Sa Dow came to see me at this late hour, and whispered: 'Uncle, life is hard for an old woman who has two co-wives. Have you got a piece of tobacco for me, I won't be able to sleep otherwise. And give me a piece of paper to wrap it in, or someone will see it and I'll have to give them some'. 18th Dec. Today we went to Ricanaumofo for the mortuary feast. Twelve adults came with me in my boat, and all their luggage as well (chickens, cassava bread, bottles of oil, cans of rice, pagnes and what not). The boat was almost ready to sink with the load and still more people wanted to join me. My informant angrily shouted that we were full up. I was pretty glad! Now he was the one to be unpleasant, not I. The captain (village headman) said that it was quite an honour for me, since, as he was also on my boat, I was allowed to fly the captain's flag. 14th Jan. The rain keeps on pouring down, people stay in the village all day and the anthropologist receives a lot of visitors. In his hut there is coffee, tobacco, and always something to eat. I get exhausted trying to follow the lively conversations, but I can't very well turn half of them out of my hut. 18th Jan. The village headman comes in with two strangers. After the customary greetings he almost orders me to put on the 'turning thing' (tape recorder). I have to stifle my vexation at being interrupted during an interesting conversation. This means hours of playing tape after tape of uninteresting music . . . but I just can't deprive the good man of this triumph in front of his guests. 12ᵗʰ Feb. Ba Banè's mother from Malokokonde came to ask me to treat her son for his wound which has got badly infected. I've decided to agree, and to go there regularly for some weeks for that purpose. This is an unlooked-for opportunity to consolidate my connections with the people there. 14ᵗʰ Feb. Sa Alieti, big, fat and as strong as a horse, asked me to buy a pair of drawers for her in town; with those on she'll be able to fight much better than when she's only wearing her pagne! 28ᵗʰ May. Tonight Ba Mansooi and Ba Afende are to play *apinti* (drums) for me and my guest. The scoundrels called me aside and said they're very sorry, but the ancestors demand that there'll be *tafia* (liquor) for a total of 25 guilders. I gave them 10 guilders for four bottles of *tafia* which will undoubtedly be speedily emptied by the onlookers. 15ᵗʰ April (in Paramaribo). I spent some hours in writing out an application for a concession on behalf of Da Frouwa and in pleading his cause with the authorities. I hope it'll be successful, for he is expecting the world of my intervention and he'll be sure to blame me if the affair doesn't come off. 3ʳᵈ June. Da Basi: 'When you go back to Holland I suppose you'll go straight to see Queen Wilhelmina; tell her we are poor and ask her whether she can't do something about it'.

Village life is rather monotonous and the anthropologist's presence creates a welcome diversion. People never grew tired of asking me about my country, my 'village', my house, my family. They also liked me telling them stories about West Africa (where I had previously done fieldwork) and an album of photographs from that region was an object of general interest. This enabled me to provoke reactions which were of importance to me.

Diary, 16 Feb. The conversation turns to Pa Femu, the prophet who caused great commotion in the Cottica region fifteen years ago. I suspect that his movement was mainly directed against *wisi* (witchcraft and sorcery), but people don't say so in so many words. I don't want to ask any direct, and therefore suggestive, questions about it. 5ᵗʰ March. I showed some photos of meetings of the *Deima* movement in Ivory Coast, telling people how the prophetess 'saw' witches and dealt with them severely. There is a prompt reaction: 'Just like Pa Femu, he also 'saw' witches. He used to tie them up and make them sit for hours in the burning sun. Everyone threw away his *wisi*'. – Remember that it is a few weeks since we talked about Pa Femu.

It was my impression that the Djuka quickly got used to my presence and did not let it affect their behaviour much. The so-called thermometer effect was negligible in this case, or even non-existent. When I had been there only two weeks a quarrel arose which ended in a fierce fight taking place right in front of and even partly inside my hut. I don't believe the parties involved would have behaved otherwise if I had not been there.
Apparently the situation can be different elsewhere, at least Berreman (1962)

in his field report cited above says that the people in his village were constantly bent on making a good impression on him ('impression management'). Of this he gives some striking instances. I did my best to interfere in the life of the group as little as possible, and thus to persevere in my rôle of participant *observer*. In some cases this took some effort on my part.

Diary, 29th Dec. in Ricanaumofo. I am asked to have a look at a patient, a girl about twelve years old. She is in coma. I say I can't do anything myself but that I'm willing to take her to the hospital immediately (only a few hours by boat from this place). The family thank me courteously and say they want to think it over for a little while. I realize they don't want me to take her: they probably expect the child to die and would rather keep her home for that reason. I am reflecting whether I'll assert my authority (if any) and take the child away, if necessary against their will. For a multitude of reasons I finally reject this plan. 2nd Jan. The child in Ricanaumofo has died. I feel a bit guilty. With reason?

Since an ethnographer studies people and not insects, his fieldwork also causes emotions in himself. Personally, I lived under great psychological stress and felt little of the proverbial peacefulness of 'country life'. Few books touch on this subject,[1] but I know that the same is true of quite a number of other field-workers. Perhaps it is even a *sine qua non* for field work.

For many weeks my informants would not tell me the name of the woman who, in times of slavery, was the first to run away into the forest, according to the legend. I passionately hunted for that name and it was not until I had it noted down that I realized it was a fairly irrelevant piece of information! What I couldn't bear was that, in spite of all my efforts, these people did not trust me sufficiently to divulge this secret to me. As a fieldworker one gets to know one's own faults pretty well. I myself am too impatient and grow restless when there is nothing to note down for some hours. I never got round to quietly reading a book (though I did sometimes feel an almost physical need to do so), vaguely fearing I might miss something essential if I did. Something I found hard to bear was the lack of privacy. Someone might come and offer me a glass of *tafia* as I was still in bed at half past five in the morning. My breakfast was always shared with others. This continued all day long and in the evenings the number of visitors would reach a top varying from five

[1] But see the excellent novel of Elenore Smith Bowen, 'Return to Laughter'; also Paul (1953): 440-441.

to as many as twenty. My permanent informant felt himself obliged, as a matter of course, to put his hammock up in my hut and keep me company at night. If ever he was unable to come he would send some 'younger brothers'. A person who is obliged to sleep by himself in a hut is to be pitied and anyone who wishes to do so is either angry or sorrowful or has an evil heart (is a witch). As a result I had practically no opportunity to do anything *but* my research. Again, however, a certain degree of single- or even narrow-mindedness may be a necessary prerequisite for fieldwork.

Is it more difficult to carry out research in this Bush Negro society than in western society? It may seem more difficult and certainly is in some respects. Much depends, however, on the subject studied. Take for instance the relationship between husband and wife. In our society this is almost entirely a private matter, but with the Djuka it is less so, for which reason it is easier to get more information.

The affair Ba Asindo-Sa Kalima. Asindo and Kalima are my next-door neighbours, a friendly and cheerful couple. 15th March. My informant is accosted by someone who tells him in confidence that a man took up with Sa Kalima at the mortuary feast in Pikin Santi. My informant hotly tells me 'you see now why it's as well to have two or three wives; you can't trust any of them!' 17th March. Asindo is informed. He subjects his wife to a severe interrogation but she denies. 'But she wept all night and that's a suspicious sign'. The village headman is also told of the affair, since he should know about things like this. A conference is held and it is decided that Kalima will have to subject herself to the ordeal. 28th March. Kalima successfully stands the test. There should be no more gossip about her now (there still is, though). 7th April. Tableau! In Kalima's bag Asindo finds two notes which he asks me to read to him. I'm sorry for Kalima, but they're very incriminating. Asindo is profoundly indignant and loudly declares what he thinks of that 'shitty ordeal'. During the dancing that same evening he tries himself what he so condemns in his rival: to take up with someone else's wife.

During the days that follow the affair is the talk of the village and leads to all sorts of fights and quarrels. Asindo is awaiting the return of his father who is to plead his case for him. But to everyone who will listen he shouts 'I'm divorced already'. He has put Kalima's possessions out of the hut; Kalima herself is living at a camp some distance from the village with her mother and her child. But in confidence Asindo tells me 'If I get a divorce it'll be to my loss'. 18th April. Asindo's father has come back and urges him to make it up with Kalima: 'my wives have also deceived me but I never sent them away on that account!' 28th April. Trial: Kalima's lover is sentenced to a fine of two bottles of *tafia*. 30th April. Sa Kalima sends to tell Asindo that she can't eat or sleep for grief; he's going to make it up. 11th May. The family is re-united. Together with some other relatives they have a ritual ablution to cancel the effect of the angry words that have been spoken. Plenty of reason for that!

Quantification. Participant observation is what distinguishes the anthropologist from most sociologists. Sociologists *may*, of course, apply this technique as well, but unfortunately they seldom do. The difference in approach might be defined as follows: a sociologist will ask what happens if a cow is stolen, an anthropologist will wait till a cow is actually stolen and observe what happens then. This is the strength of anthropology, and at the same time its weakness. The disadvantage of this method lies in the fact that no numerical data become available in this way, only uncontrollable impressions.

An instructive example is the legendary story of those two anthropologists who studied one and the same African society; one said that divorce was 'relatively important' there, the other that divorce was 'relatively *un*important' ... the former was an Englishman, the latter an American. If an anthropologist wishes to indicate the degree in which phenomena occur – divorce, cross-cousin marriage, suicide or what not – it simply does not suffice to use such terms as 'much' or 'little'. He must give exact percentages. If he fails to do so his data will be largely useless since they cannot be applied, for instance, in cross-cultural comparison. Participant observation alone, therefore, is not enough. It must be supplemented by a more quantificational approach.[1] By now this notion is generally accepted by anthropologists. Most fieldworkers nowadays apply some form of survey and are thus able to present statistical rules in their reports in addition to jural rules.

The problems attached to the collecting of reliable numerical data in the type of countries where anthropologists usually work should not be under-estimated. Even in the case of simple personalia mistakes may occur through misunderstanding, through distrust on the part of the persons questioned, or through negligence on the part of the interviewer. This is all the more true in the case of attitude questions. We are indebted to the Africanist Marwick (1956: 149-159) for his report of a failure in this sphere. Tired of the continual remarks that it always took such a long time for him to produce results he organized a public opinion poll (with standardized questions) in some villages which he did not otherwise know. Besides Marwick himself (as a white man) there were two other interviewers (negroes). The most significant difference produced

---

[1] This point is more fully discussed in Colson (1954): 43-48; Köbben (1967 a): 9-10.

by this experiment proved to be between his own results and those of this two interviewers! But the latter also booked significantly different results between themselves. Apparently the interviewees allowed their answers to depend rather on the persons of the interviewers than on their own opinions.

The best results will usually be obtained when the anthropologist collects his numerical data himself in a community which he knows well through participant observation, or else if others do so under his guidance. In such cases he has the necessary *rapport* with the population and is better able to evaluate the answers obtained and to interpret them correctly. Such a survey means a lot of boring routine work (although while digging one repeatedly hits on unexpected treasures) but, as Elizabeth Colson (1954:45) says: 'perhaps the new depths of insight into human organization to which it should lead will at least partially compensate the fieldworker for the loss of his old freedom'.

In the course of my fieldwork among the Djuka I collected 20 data concerning 176 persons (all adults of the village of Langa Uku). This survey, carried out beside my other activities, took me a full year to complete.

What was it that made this work proceed so laboriously? Take for example the simple matter of counting the population (no-one knew approximately how many people were living in the village). People at first objected: 'Where are you going to take those figures? Perhaps you'll take them to other villages! They'll be jealous when they find out how many children we have here'. It was only after I had been there some months and after I had made the necessary libations (like everywhere else the living here help their ancestors drink) that I was permitted to take my census. But this was by no means the end of my problems. Mothers, for instance, who had had many children die at an early age, would rather not talk about this. They refused to give the correct numbers, not so much out of grief at the fact itself, but rather because it is a suspicious matter: it might be explained as proof of the fact that they practice witchcraft. On this very important demographic point, therefore, I was unable to collect reliable figures. Had I known this society less closely, I would probably not have been aware of this source of error and might have believed the figures I obtained to be correct, and have published them as such with a clear conscience.

Another problem is presented by the fact that these people have little sense of exactness.

Diary, 6th Jan. Today I interviewed Ma Baba. She knew I was coming and had of course heard from others what questions I'd been asking. She knew, moreover, that at the end of the interview she would receive a small present (a piece of tobacco or a can of fish). The old lady was willingness itself, yet the interview proceeded laboriously. I asked her how many times she had been divorced and she started telling me a long story: lots of times, she said; she'd had plenty of husbands, etc., etc. I asked her once more *how* many times and all I got in reply was a similar story. It took a long time before I finally got it out of her: how many times; the names of all these husbands, their matrilineal groups and how many children she'd had with each of them. She thought it so absurd of me to want to know all this exactly, that I ended up considering it rather absurd myself.

Finally there are problems of a more technical nature to be overcome. If one wants to find out the number of inhabitants, one naturally starts by counting the number of huts (no easy matter in itself) proceeding next to determine the number of persons that live in each hut. Djuka men, however, are very mobile. A man who has two wives – this is true of 30% of the married men – will have two families living in different villages. In addition he often also has a hut in his mother's village and finally he may have another hut in a camp in the forest. Such a person cannot be counted as a full member of the village community. I solved this problem by giving each person a rating in points. The maximum number was 10 points for a man who lived permanently in the village, the minimum 3 for one who spent about one third of his time there. Between these two, ratings of 5 and of 7 points were possible. Needless to say in this way an arbitrary factor crept in.

These people are quite aware how difficult it is to count them. During my stay in the village the government made an abortive attempt at a census. A group of men amused themselves one evening by telling each other about the various ways in which they had misled the censustakers. 'They can count everyone, the Creoles, the Hindustani, the Javanese, but not us ... you (addressing me) are getting a long way'.

In addition to counting numbers I tried to determine *ages* as far as possible. This information is indispensable for the correct interpretation of other figures, for instance those concerned with polygyny, divorce and number of children. In determining ages I based myself on two key persons, the village headman (about 50 years of age) and my permanent informant (about 25). I found out the age of the former by asking him how big he was when the first bauxite boat went to Moengo. This event made a great impression on these people (far greater than the first or second world war!) and the bauxite company was able to tell me how long ago it took place (forty years earlier). With regard to my informant's age I had one thing to go by, namely the fact that he went to mission school for a few years as a child. I next asked everyone whether he or she were older or younger than these two men. Although the Djuka have no idea of their absolute ages, they fortunately know relative ages quite well.

I further collected data on polygyny; divorce; number of children; adoption; membership of matrilineal group and place in the genealogical system; agricultural plots; who is the medium of a deity, and of which one; connections with the mission (school, baptism). Some comments about three of these points.

Adoption. Adoption in various forms takes place frequently among our Djuka. When asked for reasons, they give only meaningless answers: 'I give her my child because she will look after it well; because she is a kinswoman of mine; because I am fond of her . . .' The importance of statistical research is evident in this case, since it shows us that adoption does have a function in that it spreads children over the various households more evenly than nature does. This in itself is not a surprising discovery to make, but the people themselves proved to be not in the least conscious of it, and even denied the fact when directly questioned about it. I may note in this connection that in many other cases they are well aware of their own institutions and capable, as far as the more intelligent among them are concerned, of discussing them sensibly.

Place in the genealogical system. The inhabitants of Langa Uku say: 'all of us together are one family'. And so they are, if affines are regarded as belonging to the family, since they may all be fitted into one genealogical system. For the purpose of collecting genealogical data I again based myself on the village headman as a key figure, asking each person what his or her relationship was to him. Only for the tyros in this science need I add that the fieldworker must not be misled by classificatory terms. If a man tells me he is the headman's 'bala' (brother), I have to ask him next whether Ma Baba, the headman's mother, is also this 'bala''s mother, or even specifically whether she is the woman who gave birth to him. If not, I have to ask further questions until I know the precise relationship.[1]

Mediumship. In my village 20% of the adult population were mediums of some deity, on the Tapanahony river 37%. Even before my co-fieldworkers and I had collected these data it was already our impression that the Tapanahony people experienced their religion more intensely than the people of my region, but this was no more than an impression. We took the percentage of mediums as an operational definition of 'intensity of religious experience'. The difference indicated above we regard as a confirmation of our hypothesis. I mention this to show that phenomena which would appear not to lend themselves to a quantitative approach may sometimes be approached in this way after all.

Have I reason to be satisfied with the results of my survey? Clearly not, I could have asked for more data, actually I am sorry I didn't. There are lacunae left where I inadvertently failed to ask a certain question and undoubtedly there are errors. But worse is the fact that my data concern only 176 persons, all of whom, moreover, are from one village. The factor of chance has therefore not been eliminated. It is true that I may compare my results with those of my co-fieldworkers concerning two villages on the Tapanahony and to a large extent also with those of Hurault (1961) concerning the closely related Boni people. Even so I cannot be sure that my figures are representative of Djuka society as a whole. This is a shortcoming of many anthropological studies for which it is not easy to find a solution, unless a large number of fieldworkers together were to concentrate upon one people. It is a curious fact that anthropologists on the whole do not seem unduly worried about this. It is true that the societies which they study are usually more uniform than Western society, but one still wishes they might borrow some of the preoccupation with significance tests that is characteristic of sociologists. In her paper already cited above, Elisabeth Colson (1954: 50-52; 58) gave some attention to this problem. Characteristically she takes rather a light view of it:

[1] For more details see Notes and Queries (1951): 54-56. Schusky (1965): 53-70.

"Whether or not my material for the areas studied is in any way representative of the Tonga people as a whole, I do not know. This is a problem which may be of some concern to the administration and to the technical assistants who are trying to deal with the Tonga as though they were a single unit. I do not think that it is a problem which needs to concern the anthropologist who is trying to make a study of the interrelation of social factors in a single social system. After all, each area studied does represent a unit in which the people are in close social relations with each other. The factors which exist within that set of relations can be dealt with as though one were dealing with an isolated society."

These words were written twelve years ago, and since that time the anthropologist's interest in applied research has steadily grown. He is now in the same position as the administrator in that it is as important for him as for the latter to know to what extent data from one village may be extrapolated. There is another objection that may be raised against Colson's view. She avoids the requirement of representativeness by treating the two or three local groups which she studied as a cultural isolate, whereas in fact these are merely some rather arbitrarily selected villages from among hundreds of such villages which together form the Tonga tribe. Thus we are deprived of an important dimension of social reality, namely those social relations which transcend the local community. In the case of the Tonga, who have an extremely simple political structure and therefore few supralocal relations, this is not too grave a shortcoming. When societies with a more complex structure are studied, however, this method is inadequate.

When I was working among the Djuka I collected data outside my village only on one point, namely the total number of the population of the eleven villages which, together with Langa Uku, form a cluster. I proceeded in the following way. I knew the ratio huts: persons in Langa Uku. I assumed this ratio to be the same in the other villages and counted the huts there, thus arriving at an estimate of the number of persons.

Even this simple undertaking took a lot of time and work, for in each village I had to explain at length in a *kutu* (palaver) what I had come to do, why I wanted to do it and that there was no harm in this. I considered the possibility of counting the huts in secret but I did not want to do so on account of my informant . . . until a solution was offered.

Diary. 19th Jan. Today went to Pikin Santi to count the huts. The *kutu* took a long time and the gods proved to be very thirsty indeed. As we were going back Fanaili (my informant) said: 'It is really a waste of time . . . couldn't we count the huts clandestinely from now on?' 15ᵗʰ April. To Agitiondro for the great mortuary feast. Took advantage of the occasion to count the huts, which wasn't easy since they are planted pell-mell with no sort of order while moreover we were continually interrupted by other visitors to the feast who greeted us. To have some means of checking our results Fanaili and I each counted separately. He came to a total of 219 huts, I had 215. I resignedly wrote down the average, 217, in my notebook, but Fanaili was not so easily satisfied: 'no, we must do it well if we do it at all, let's start again'.

references

N. BABCHUK (1962) The role of the researcher as participant observer and participant-as-observer in the field situation, *HO* 21 (# 7): 225-228.

C. BAKS ET AL. (1965) De betrouwbaarheid van informatie in een kastesamenleving in Gujerat, India, *Sociologische Gids* 12 (# 3): 167-174.

P. M. BLAU (1964) The research process in the study of 'Dynamics of bureaucracy', in: Ph. E. Hammond ed., Sociologists at work, New York and London.

G. D. BERREMAN (1962) Behind many masks; ethnography and impression management in a Himalayan village, Ithaca, N.Y.

E. COLSON (1954) The intensive study of small sample communities, in: R. F. Spencer ed., Method and perspective in anthropology, Minneapolis.

R. FIRTH (1954) Social organisation and social change, *J.R.A.I.* 84 (# 1): 1-20.

S. W. DE GROOT (1963) Van isolatie naar integratie; de Surinaamse Marrons en hun afstammelingen, 's-Gravenhage.

M. J. and M. S. HERSKOVITS (1934) Rebel Destiny; among the bushnegroes of Surinam, New York.

J. HURAULT (1961) Les noirs réfugiés Boni de la Guyane Française, Dakar.

A. J. F. KÖBBEN (1967a) Why exceptions? the logic of cross-cultural comparisons, *CA* 8 (# 1): 3-34.

A. J. F. KÖBBEN (1967b) Unity and disunity; Djuka society as a kinship system, *Bydragen Taal-, Land- en Volkenkunde* 123 (# 1): 10-52.

A. J. F. KÖBBEN (forthcoming) Law on the village level; the Cottica Djuka of Surinam.

B. H. JUNKER (1960) Fieldwork; an introduction to the social sciences, Chicago.

H. LAMUR (1965) De levensomstandigheden van de in Paramaribo werkende Aukaner arbeiders, *Nieuwe Westindische Gids* 44 (# 1-2): 119-133.

C. LÉVI-STRAUSS (1963) Structural anthropology, New York, London.

R. A. J. VAN LIER (1949) Samenleving in een grensgebied, 's-Gravenhage.

W. F. VAN LIER (1940) Aanteekeningen over het geestelijk leven en de samenleving der Djoeka's (Aucaner Bosnegers), *Bijdragen Taal-, Land- en Volkenkunde* 99 (# 3): 129-295.

M. G. MARWICK (1956) An experiment in public-opinion polling among preliterate people, *Africa* 26 (♯ 2): 149-158.

H. MINER (1960) Culture under pressure: a Hausa case, *HO* 19 (♯ 3): 164-167.

NOTES AND QUERIES ON ANTHROPOLOGY (1951), London, 6th ed.

B. D. PAUL (1953) Interview techniques and field relationships, in: A. L. Kroeber ed., Anthropology today, Chicago.

P. DE SCHLIPPE (1956) Shifting cultivation in Africa; the Zande system of agriculture, London.

E. L. SCHUSKY (1965) Manual for kinship analysis, New York etc.

E. SMITH-BOWEN (1954) Return to laughter, London.

J. G. STEDTMAN (1796) Narrative of a five years expedition against the revolted negroes of Surinam (etc.).

H. U. E. THODEN VAN VELZEN (1966) Politieke beheersing in een bosnegermaatschappij, Leiden, Afrika Studiecentrum.

W. VAN WETERING (forthcoming) Djuka witchcraft beliefs; a sociological approach.

J. WOLBERS (1861) Geschiedenis van Suriname, Amsterdam.

3   *social surveys in non-western areas*

J. D. SPECKMANN

Introduction. Since the end of World War II, modern research methods which were originally used exclusively in Europe and North America have increasingly been applied in non-western areas. I refer here particularly to the individual questionnaire in so-called sample surveys. 'In the last 15 to 20 years', says Elmo C. Wilson, 'large-scale sampling has become fairly commonplace in the major urban centers of the world, and each year finds pollsters pushing on into remote backlands, where until recently only itinerant peddlers or the most intrepid politicians ventured' (Wilson 1958:230).

This development of social research in non-western areas has given rise to some criticism in anthropological circles. In the critics' opinion the questionnaire, particularly, is not a suitable instrument of research outside the European-American culture area. Though the standardized interview may be adequate for the western world, in non-western countries where communities are more traditional and more homogeneous, interviewing of individuals by means of a questionnaire would seem to be of little use. In such circumstances some social scientists continue to have greater faith in the trusty, familiar techniques of anthropological research: participant observation and open-ended interviews.

This uneasiness about the application of new research techniques was put into words by Leach in his article An anthropologist's reflections on a social survey (Leach 1958, also included in this volume). In the Netherlands, too, critical reactions are to be heard. Three years ago the anthropologist Köbben, though certainly no opponent of sample surveys in non-western areas, made critical remarks about certain inquiries which had used questionnaires. In connection with an investigation by Eister (1962), who was interested in the religious attitudes of villagers in Pakistan, Köbben says: 'A cultural anthropologist would have spent some time living in a village for this purpose. Eister, however, sent interviewers armed with questionnaires. The latter contained attitude questions of the stereotyped sort: 'If someone does not carry out his religious duties should he be: severely punished, punished after an attempt to reform him, not punished but persuaded that his behaviour was wrong . . . etc.' 'To be quite truthful', Köbben remarks, 'I have very little faith in the results of this inquiry. I am afraid that in many cases the interviewees answered according to what they thought the interviewer thought they thought, or: what they thought the village headman would wish them to think' (Köbben 1964: 38-51; 45).

Every research technique, of course, should be handled judiciously. This is equally true of the traditional anthropological approach. It is often hard to evaluate the reliability of its results since many anthropological monographs lack a detailed and critical account of the research-methods followed.

Moreover, formal training of anthropologists often pays little attention to methods and techniques of research. John Beattie, for example, says: 'On just how when one got to the field one went about one's task, on the practical techniques which would be useful in collecting the kinds of information I wanted, I was perhaps less adequately informed. It was unusual in English anthropology courses at that time (it still is) to give very detailed formal instruction on methods of field research. Sometimes, indeed, one rather got the impression that field work was simply a matter of getting into the field and being there; once there one would absorb information by a kind of osmosis, helped, no doubt, by that invaluable vade-mecum, *Notes and Queries on Anthropology*'. (Beattie 1965: 5).

In spite of the discussion that is going on between a number of sociologists and anthropologists, and among the anthropologists themselves, concerning the methods and techniques of social research, the number of sample surveys of non-western areas is increasing every year. This development is due to a change in the nature of the problem and in the object of research. The small, isolated, more or less homogeneous tribal group which was the original interest of anthropologists, is becoming rare in the non-western world. The current problems of the new nations are concerned with large social groupings: nations, towns, trade unions, cooperatives, bureaucratic bodies, political parties. Social research is confronted with more complex non-western societies and with problems that concern social groupings transcending those of tribe or village. This means that the familiar techniques of participant observation can no longer be considered sufficient. The larger social units of more heterogeneous composition force us to use large-scale sample surveys. Partly with a view to their various development projects, the new nations themselves are particularly interested in information concerning the social and economic situation of the country as a whole. This has led, for one thing, to a sharp increase in demographic surveys. Furthermore, the growing demand for information by commercial and industrial institutions has greatly stimulated research of market analysis. Also the public opinion survey has grown fast in developing new countries. According to Wuelker, there are presently various competent research institutes active in these fields in Asia (Wuelker 1963).

All this, however, does not answer the question to what extent criticism of the results of survey-research in non-western countries is justified. Mitchell does not speak very favorably about the reliability and validity of sample surveys in developing countries. 'For example, validation checks conducted in the course of fertility studies sometimes reveal major discrepancies in simple factual information; a validation check performed in the course of a study of capital formation in a rural area of a developing country showed a 15 per cent discrepancy in basic economic figures'. (Mitchell 1965: 665). According to Mitchell, this situation is chiefly the result of a lack of proficiency and competence on the part of the investigators. Much criticism of surveys refers to investigations characterized by this shortcoming.

Mitchell also discusses the objections of certain anthropologists with regard to public opinion surveys in non-western countries. Two problems may be distinguished here: does public opinion exist at all in non-western societies? and if so can these opinions be recorded by using standardized questionnaires? These questions could be briefly answered as follows: It is true that mostly standardized questionnaires are inappropriate research tools in small, homogeneous, and well-integrated tribal societies – but, as we have stated already, there are not many of these societies left. As to the question if individual or public opinion exists at all, we may quote Wilson and Armstrong, who wrote that 'there is no justification for ruling out opinion studies simply because opinions do not result from a person's interaction in voluntary associations as they usually do in the West. Opinions which reflect the customs and traditions of autonomous, *gemeinschaft*-type, communal groups, . . , are of equal significance to any other type of opinion. However, it is important to distinguish between patterns of opinion which characterize groups at varying stages of modernization'. (Wilson and Armstrong 1963:50). Sample surveys moreover are not exclusively concerned with opinions, attitudes and values as some people appear to think. A large number of surveys aim at collecting mainly factual information.

As far as the use of questionnaires is concerned, critics tend to object most of all to the precoded questions. Their argument is that in this way the interviewee is prompted to give answers which in normal circumstances he would never have formulated. Mitchell, however, rightly remarks that: '. . . this is precisely what a well-designed interview schedule is supposed to do, and it presumably has many advantages over traditional research procedures. Rather than collect masses of partially relevant and irrelevant materials, the survey researcher attempts by prior inquiry to isolate major dimensions he wishes to study. And, rather than pore over his notes in attempt to substantiate (more typically, to illustrate) his major hypotheses, and rather than be in a position where no information is available to test alternative hypotheses, the survey researcher, in the ideal situation, collects data permitting him to perform both of these tasks'. (Mitchell 1965:675).

Many investigations show, moreover, that with respect to the standardized interview there is no longer much difference in attitude between respondents in non-western towns and those in Europe or North America.

Critics have tended to overstress the drawbacks and limitations of the questionnaire-approach in non-western areas. In actual practice, however, we find that this technique often produces quite positive results.

For my study of family and kinship structure among the East Indian population of Surinam (Speck-mann 1965) I used questionnaires both in rural areas and in town. I found that certain questions, which would certainly have presented grave difficulties to the interviewer in a European environment, elicited an open and direct reaction in Surinam.

When I wished to determine the divorce frequency among the East Indians, and especially the motives for dissolving a marriage, the majority of interviewees answered without reticence. Some respondents remarked, for instance, that they had beaten their wives, after which the marriage had been dissolved. It would be difficult, I believe, to elicit such a reaction during an interview with a married man in Europe!

It is true that the use of questionnaires in non-western areas confronts the researcher with specific problems, but this does not mean, that the technique is useless. Much depends on the way the investigation is planned, on the introduction, on the construction of the questionnaire and on the selection, training and supervision of the interviewers.

It seems to me that in the discussion on methods and techniques of social research the traditional anthropological approach is often wrongly seen in opposition to the sociological inquiry, whereas, in fact, there may be a com-plementary relationship. A prerequisite for sound survey research is an exploratory preliminary inquiry, for which participant observation and open-ended interviews are usually most appropriate. The poor quality of many a survey is due to the researcher's failure to fulfil this condition. Questionnaires are drawn up at some European or American university or research institute. After some pretesting, resulting in a few changes in formulation, the questionnaires are handed over to the interviewers. In some cases of survey research there is such a strong focus on statistical and organizational problems that there is no place for reflection on the formulation of the problem and the method of approach by means of a preliminary inquiry.

Finally much discussion about techniques of research in non-western areas fails to take into account that the manner of collecting information is primarily determined by the nature of the problem and by the object of research.

Two years ago I was asked to carry out an investigation in the Niger Republic in Africa. In all the villages of the country with more than 300 inhabitants I was to investigate the existing water shortage, with a view to future allocation of new wells. It was plain that for such large-scale inventories the classical anthropological methods and techniques could not be used. If the instructions had been different, if, for instance, I had been asked to find out in what way the villagers made use of the new mechanical devices for drawing water introduced by the government, it would have been possible to obtain a clear picture by means of participant observation and open-ended interviews in a few villages.

The time schedule for the investigation in the Niger Republic included a preliminary inquiry for which the members of my team, six students from Leiden University, were to spend at least some weeks in a few villages in order to familiarize themselves with the social structure of the village community and to afford them an opportunity to reflect on the nature of the problem to be studied as well as on the construction of the questionnaire.

Much time was lost, however, in discussing the business side of the investigation and, since the time schedule was threatened, I had in fact a much shorter time for the pilot study. Difficulties of this sort occur frequently in survey research.

On the basis of my experiences in Surinam and Africa I will now analyse some problems connected with sample survey in non-western areas in greater detail.

The introduction of the inquiry. For the planning and organization of a survey the researcher is often obliged to depend on the cooperation of various official institutions. In order to select his samples, for instance, he needs detailed data from the statistical bureaus. Good maps and sometimes even aerial photographs are indispensable. Moreover, the researcher usually tries to recruit his interviewers from the research departments of the administration. In those cases where the investigation is carried out at the government's own request the assistance of various official instances is more or less ensured. Even so, it is wise to make explicit arrangements to this effect beforehand. The situation is different when the researcher undertakes the research on his own initiative. In that case, if he needs the cooperation of the authorities, he is obliged to introduce his investigation at length.

One of the problems with which he may be confronted at this stage is connected with the very specific notions about the nature of social science found sometimes in non-western countries. Lloyd and Susanne H. Rudolph, for instance, tell us: 'In the field of social science, knowledge for knowledge's sake or knowledge for the sake of greater realism, understanding, and effectiveness gains scant support or appreciation in India today'. (Rudolph and Rudolph 1958: 240). This attitude is by no means peculiar to India alone. In such cases it is very difficult to convince the authorities concerned of the desirability of the research. Because of this attitude one is obliged to present the planned inquiry in a simplified form with a particular stress on its practical aspects. It goes without saying that the researcher in this situation needs to have some talent for diplomacy.

It is important to start the introduction at the highest possible governmental level. Many countries have a highly centralized administration, and readiness to cooperate on the part of officials of middle rank offers no guarantee at all, since they have neither sufficient independence nor sufficient information to give any real help.

During a training survey with students in Spain we made the mistake of placing our hopes on the governor of the province where we were working. It turned out, however, that this functionary had a mainly representative task and that only the heads of the departments in Madrid were authorized to supply the required information and cooperation. The period of introduction had to be repeated in Madrid, our time schedule suffering considerably as a result.

Sound preparation 'at the top' facilitates the work of introduction at lower levels of the administrative organization, where a mere letter of introduction will then often be sufficient.

If the investigation is concerned with sensitive matters, the authorities may be opposed to social research. Sometimes this opposition is understandable and justifiable. In many developing countries, research in the political field is a precarious matter in view of the structure of existing political systems. In such a situation the researcher is faced with a difficult decision. If he decides to go through with the investigation he takes certain risks.

At the time of my investigation into family and kinship structure among the East Indians of Surinam I was also interested in the relations and mutual stereotypes between the different ethnic groups of that country. I realized that, in a society where the integration of the various population groups may be reckoned a central problem, I could expect little sympathy from the authorities for such an inquiry, which moreover might entail hazardous social and political implications. Not until the actual investigation was well under way and my experiences had convinced me that it would be possible to carry out the subsidiary inquiry quite noiselessly did I decide to proceed with it as a part of the survey.

Constructing the questionnaire. The difficulties that arise in the construction of the questionnaire for non-western research are not essentially different from those met in western surveys. It is true, however, that these difficulties are magnified by the special circumstances of the developing countries. The rules and precautions that have to be observed in western countries apply even more strongly.

It remains imperative for the western investigator, to familiarize himself with the local situation by an exploratory field study before starting the construction of the questionnaire. By doing so, the investigator becomes aware of local circumstances and can assess both the validity of his research problem, and the manner in which it is formulated in the first draft of the questionnaire. The pilot-study will also produce important indications about the definition of the population and about the ultimate sampling unit. This is not an easy task, particulary not in unfamiliar areas.

For my investigation in Surinam the 'household group', the sampling unit, was one of the concepts that needed to be closely defined. In addition it was necessary to indicate which members of the household group had to be interviewed. Owing to the fact that I spent five months before the actual survey on intensive preliminary inquiries, while actually living in an East Indian community, I was able to recognize the various types of household groups in this section of the population and thus learned to define the concept with some precision.

Another advantage of making a pilot-study is that if offers the possibility to sound out reactions to the projected questions. This is indispensable particularly in the case of questionnaires asking for opinions, attitudes, or motivations.

Since the particular wording and phrasing of questions is often a sensitive matter, it is both useful and important to try them out first on such people like local administrators, medical personnel, agricultural advisors, colleagues in the field, or others who are thoroughly acquainted with linguistic idiosyncracies and cultural biases.

One example of possible complications is the so-called 'courtesy-bias'. Particularly in Southeast Asia respondents will tend to answer questions in a manner which they believe to be pleasing to the interviewer rather than expressing their own views.

Emily L. Jones points out that the disturbing effect of the 'courtesy bias' may be counteracted by projection-type questions and by wording the questions in such a way that critical, negative, or impolite reactions become acceptable (Jones 1963:72).

Linguistic difficulties can pose serious problems in drawing up questionnaires for social surveys in non-western areas. When the investigator has composed and arranged the questions, the questionnaire has to be translated. It is commonly agreed that the 'back-translation' technique gives the most positive results. This technique demands that the text is first translated into the local language, and then retranslated into the original language by a different person. Any discrepancies between the two versions should then be carefully analysed. Instead of the 'back-translation' technique, Phillips recommends that two translators independently translate the questionnaire into the native language, compare their results, and discuss those questions that have come out differently in their translations. If no agreement is reached the investigator should enter the discussion and make his own decisions It may well happen that certain questions must be discarded because they do not lend themselves to adequate translation (Phillips 1959). The situation becomes even more complex when different languages exist side by side in one area. Some of those may not even exist in written form. In such cases the translation is usually left to the native interviewer, though this is a rather risky procedure since even after careful instruction the interviewer might not always use the correct equivalents for certain concepts.

In Niger we were confronted with no less than six languages. Translation of the questionnaire into all of these proved to be impossible, so this task fell to the interviewers. Since the questionnaire was mainly concerned with factual information, such as the number of wells in the village, the number of inhabitants, etc., few difficulties arose from this procedure. When the questions refer to more subtle matters such as opinions, attitudes or motivations this sort of solution needs to be avoided as much as possible.

The Sample. In non-western countries making a reliable sample is no simple matter. Often the investigator has only insufficient secondary sources of data on the population at his disposal, and thus lacks parameter information. He will then have to resort to a simpler sampling procedure, with a greater margin of error. Moreover it is difficult to compare the sample with other sources, relating to such variables as age, sex and marital status. Even the existing government registers are most often incomplete. In non-western areas, available listings of eligible voters are often used for this purpose. But our experience has shown that these listings are neither accurate nor up-to-date, and often give wrong names and wrong addresses.

Moreover the units used for registration purposes do not always correspond to the ultimate sampling units employed in the survey. The investigator will then be obliged to draw up a map of the territory under study and to mark all 'sampling units' on it.

In Surinam good maps were available for the various areas, showing among other things, all the house-sites in the area. One house, however, might shelter different household-groups. By discussing each map in detail with the local administrative officer I was able to determine where and to what extent this was so.

Such extensive preparations for determining the sample area obviously take time. In the absence of reliable statistical data, the investigator may decide to use a 'random-walk' or a 'quota-sampling' procedure, which allow the interviewer, within certain limits, to select his own respondents. This of course has the disadvantage of entrusting the composition of the sample partly to the interviewer.

There are practical limitations as well: the absence of roads may make some places or even whole areas almost inaccessible for interviewers. These locations then will be left out of the sample. Also the fieldworker may be unhappy to discover that certain villages marked on the map are simply not there.

For the investigation in Niger all villages in the sedentary zone with 300 or more inhabitants were to be visited. (over 2,000 villages altogether). We tried first to determine, from the copious maps we had at our disposal, which villages fell into this category. It had been suggested that the number of dots with which a village was marked on the map might give an approximate indication of its number of inhabitants. This method, however, when tested, proved to produce unreliable results. In order to localize these villages, therefore, we applied to the local administration for information on each area. Although their data were not always in agreement with the actual situation the results of this approach proved to be quite satisfactory.

Another difficulty was presented by the fact that at certain periods of time many villages actually consisted of two units, the central village and the so-called 'village de culture', the settlement on the agricultural land. In some cases the whole population had left the central village to settle permanently in the 'village de culture'. The location of the latter, however, was not marked on the map. The nomadic groups, too, presented many problems to the interviewers.

In certain groups it may be difficult for the interviewer to receive full cooperation of individuals or members of a household group whose answers, on the basis of the sample, should be included in the survey. The headman of a traditional village community may think it rather curious, to put it mildly, when instead of he himself a female inhabitant of the village is selected and asked about her political views. An explanation concerning the use of a 'list of random numbers' will be of little use here. In practice the solution is usually found in a quasi interview with the village headman, after which permission is asked to interview the selected respondent as well.

This list of complications connected with the making of samples in non-western areas might lead to the conclusion that the organization of social surveys there is a hazardous venture. Granted that in some investigations the quality of the sample may be called dubious (Mitchell 1965) it should be realized, that conditions in these areas are continually improving. In connection with his experiences in public opinion survey in Africa, Hoffman writes: 'The constant progress of demographic and cartographical knowledge will make the application of the public opinion poll technique both easier and more reliable. It should also be emphasized that surveys of this kind, though far from flawless, would not have been possible even a few years ago'. (Hoffmann 1963:64). In those cases where defective statistical sources and other limitations make it doubtful whether a reliable sample covering the whole country may be obtained, it is advisable to set up the inquiry on a smaller scale.

Recruiting, selection and training of interviewers; the interview situation. In the newly developing countries, competent interviewers are scarce and the recruitment of interviewers in those areas poses many problems. Certain government departments may have interview teams of their own. It is advisable to attempt to enlist these in the first place, more so because they are not always constantly employed. For my work in Surinam, for instance, I profited greatly from the assistance of two experienced East Indian interviewers who came from an agricultural planning bureau and who proved most satisfactory in the field.

All the same, this group, too, should be subjected to a thorough selection procedure, since their experiences are usually limited to different types of surveys.

Other possible sources of assistance may be found in the existing social research, social work and educational institutions. University students especially are often employed in surveys, although they are not always suitable for interview work. Armstrong and Wilson, for instance, tell of their experiences with Indian students: '(their) typical approach to problems tends to be moral and ego involved rather than neutral and impersonal', while in addition their university education has given them a disproportionate amount of self-conceit which adversely affects the 'rapport' that needs to be established in the interview situation (Wilson and Armstrong 1963:56). Students may be used providing they are given a thorough interview training and are closely supervised in the field.

The group of interviewers that had been promised to us by the government of Niger proved to be not available when we arrived.

Our inquiries in various institutions of social research and social work were also unsuccessful. On all sides we were told that it was impossible in this country to find persons who had sufficient schooling to qualify as interviewers. Finally an advertisement was placed in the leading newspaper of the town. To my surprise as many as sixty applicants presented themselves the next morning. Three days of selection, however, left us with only four really suitable candidates while three more were accepted with some reservations. Although I would have liked a larger team I had to be satisfied with the seven available interviewers.

In Surinam the inquiry in the town of Paramaribo was carried out with the help of final year secondary school students and students from the Law School. On the whole my experiences with this group were favorable.

The criteria employed in selecting interviewers depend to some extent on the nature of the survey. Nevertheless there are a number of conditions that apply in all cases. The first requirement is that the interviewer should belong to the same ethnic group as the respondent.

If I had employed Creole interviewers for my inquiry in Surinam, the reactions of the East Indian respondents would undoubtedly have been different from those expressed to the East Indian interviewers.

I remember one evening when called on an East Indian family, the head of which had been visited by one of my interviewers a few days earlier. My host profusely praised the Dutch, whose presence he considered necessary for the good of the country. A few days later, while checking the information obtained in the inquiry I came across this family's questionnaire. Towards the East Indian interviewer, I found, the head of the family had shown himself extremely critical of the Dutch in Surinam.

The interviewer should not have any moralistic bias but should be capable of developing a professional attitude towards his task, a task even more difficult than in western countries since he will often have to train the respondent in his role of interviewee.

The interviewer should also be capable of behaving naturally towards respondents belonging to a different social class. In most cases he will also need to be bilingual, since he will need to have sufficient command of the language spoken by the survey staff and must be able to speak at least one native language fluently. In addition, he must be prepared, if the survey extends to rural areas, to accept less comfortable conditions in outlying districts.

On the subject of the procedure to be followed in this selection some general remarks can be made. One thing is certain: selection should be thorough and a reasonable amount of time should be reserved for it in the schedule.

For the applicants in Niger the following selection procedure was devised. The candidate was first subjected to a written test which required him to write a short essay on the town or village from which he came, while in addition he had to solve a few simple arithmetical problems.

This enabled us to judge the level of formal education and the extent of his command of the French language. The written test was followed by an interview with two members of our staff, providing some information about the candidate's experience in this type of work, as well as about his personality and intelligence. During this interview the purpose and the plan of the survey was explained to the candidate, after which he was shown a few questions from the questionnaire and invited to give an account of the content and significance of these questions.

The conclusions of the two staff-members in each case were compared and in the majority of cases they showed a great deal of similarity. The results of the written test and the impressions obtained in the personal interview were finally expressed in one evaluation mark. This initial selection, with sixty candidates, took four days to complete.

Interesting information on interview training is given by Kurt W. Back and J. Mayone Stycos, who carefully recorded the reactions of their trainee interviewers for the 'Jamaica human fertility investigation'. (Back and Stycos 1959). This training lasted a fortnight and consisted, among others, of lectures on the background of the investigation and the theory of the interview, readings, interview practice within the group with the help of audio-visual aids and trial interviews in the field. The trainees were most appreciative of the lectures on the background of the investigation and the training in the field. In addition it was found that verbal explanations were more teaching aids than written texts.

Apart from explaining the background and purpose of the investigation it is important to give the interviewers some idea of the way the material is to be used. This will make it easier for them to understand and accept observations and critical remarks in connection with their completed questionnaires. Finally, efforts should be made to foster the morale of the group during the period of training. Two important factors in this respect are the stimulation of self-confidence and favorable conditions of employment.

Proper supervision of the interview team is necessary in western countries but for research in non-western areas it is an even more compelling requirement. If a large number of interviewers are employed it is advisable to split the team into small groups of no more than five men, and to place one supervisor in charge of each group in the field. Sociometric tests may be helpful to arrive at compatible compositions of these teams. As supervisors it is advisable at first to appoint members of the staff. At a later stage this task may in part be handed over to very competent interviewers.

The first checking of questionnaires should take place as soon as possible so that systematic mistakes can immediately be discussed with the interviewer.

My personal experience has shown that it may be most profitable to bring the groups together periodically for discussions especially if the teams are working long distances apart. During the early stages of the survey such group discussions should be held more frequently than later on, beginning perhaps with every four or six days. These meetings offer the opportunity to discuss the difficulties experienced in the field. Based on these discussions, new instructions may have to be formulated. Mutual contact, moreover, strengthens the morale of the group. It is comforting for the interviewer to discover that his problems in the field are shared by his colleagues.

It is necessary that the staff continually checks interviewer's attitudes during the interview. In spite of thorough training some interviewers fail to conceal feelings of superiority during interviews with less educated respondents. Wilson adds to this: 'feelings of national pride also occasionally lead interviewers to make up responses in an effort to mask what they regard as unseemly evidence of mass ignorance or apathy among their fellow citizens'. (Wilson 1958:232).

Finally I will analyse two other aspects of the interview situation in the field. The first one deals with the introduction of the investigation. Before starting with interviews in a village it is a rule of thumb to contact the village headman first, and explain the object and design of the survey to him. The interviewer may meet with suspicion, especially if he is taken for a representative of the central authorities or, even worse, for a tax official. The standard introduction should effectively refute such notions.

In Surinam my interviewers introduced themselves by saying they were doing this work for 'the Dutchman'. This was a sufficient description for I always spent a few months in the area before starting on the actual survey, so that everyone knew me by then.
Incidentally, I also made grateful use of an explanation which the East Indians themselves had thought up, namely that the queen of the Netherlands had sent me especially to find out how the East Indian group in this part of the kingdom were getting on. I had never thought of introducing my work this way myself.
Amusing in this connection was the reaction of an East Indian grocer who told me that he would be willing to give any information I asked for if I, on the other hand, would promise never to write a book like the one Katherine Mayo had written about India, for she had put the country in a very unfavorable light (Mayo 1927).

Experience has shown that anonymity is not generally appreciated by the respondents. Stressing this factor too much will usually have the opposite effect: it may make the informant suspicious. An atmosphere of suspicion may also arise because rumours about the investigation sometimes reach the area even before the arrival of the interview team. Such a situation may endanger the success of the survey because it commonly leads to negative attitudes. Kurt W. Back and J. Mayone Stycos suggest two possible solutions. One is to counteract the rumours by explaining the aims and purposes of the investigation in detail to local leaders beforehand. Another is to try and forestall the phenomenon by carrying out the interviews in such an area more quickly than originally planned (Back and Stycos 1959). In my opinion it may also be helpful to talk openly about any such rumours during the introductory stage of the interview and show their fallacy.

Another situation which we should be aware of in surveys of non-western areas is the influence of third parties when the interviewee is not alone during the interview. Curiosity of other villagers may lead them to follow the interviewer. Mitchell points out that this situation may have its positive side, in as far as the presence of others may induce the interviewee to be honest in giving factual information (Mitchell 1965: 679).

Usually, however, it is better for the interviewer to be alone with the respondent. There are various techniques to achieve this. Our interviewers reached good results by explaining the investigation to the bystanders and reading them a few questions from the questionnaire. Once their curiosity was satisfied they were requested to leave the respondent alone so that he might answer the questions without their intervention.

Organization of the survey. The researcher undertaking a large-scale social survey is faced with many organizational problems. To discuss these in detail would carry us too far and only a few will be mentioned here. In any large-scale survey the investigator will need to recruit collaborators to assist in directing the survey. Staff members may be colleagues or various other specialists.

In our investigation of water-needs in Niger Republic, which was to serve as a basis for priority ratings in the allocation of new wells, the staff included apart from the sociologist, a hydrologist, a civil engineer and a social economist specialized in agricultural problems.

No matter what the actual composition of the staff may be, detailed definitions of the tasks and responsibilities of each member should be made. The distribution of authority should also be made quite clear to each participant. This will not only affect the staff's efficiency, but will also contribute to a positive team-spirit. This will of course also be influenced by the specific personalities of team-members. On this subject Margaret Barron Luszki says: 'The frustration in team research from material, financial, scientific and emotional problems is usually higher than in individual research. The members must be able to tolerate this and be flexible in their adjustment to unexpected circumstances and unaccustomed work methods. Personal and professional security, emotional maturity, openmindedness and humility are other important characteristics'. (Luszki 1957:22).

Important aspects of organization in every large-scale survey include arrangements for transport, communication and supplies. Although unexperienced workers may think that these are trivial questions, experience has shown that problems of this sort need to be solved during the planning stage. Neglect may well hamper the progress of the investigation and even endanger the whole project.

In respect to transportation, when the survey covers large areas, the transportation facilities should be sufficient and meet the highest demands of suitability for the peculiarities of the local terrain. More than one survey has been badly delayed through cars that proved unsuitable for the terrain that had to be traversed.

Communication and supply are of specific importance when the interviewers are scattered over a wide territory. The official means of communication such as postal and telephone services are often unreliable and technically far from perfection.

In the Niger survey six teams were in the field, scattered over an area of more than 600 miles. Each team consisted of a European superintendent – a sociology student from the Netherlands – 1 or 2 native interviewers and a driver. During the first few weeks communication with the teams was maintained partly via the national broadcasting service. At fixed times the staff was given ten minutes to broadcast messages to the teams who had been provided with portable radios. This procedure proved to be unsatisfactory, however, since the team members were often unable to tune in at the appointed time. Another drawback was the fact that this communication worked only

one way. We therefore soon changed over to written and oral communication by utilizing the supply parties who provided the teams with food and gasoline.
The great distance at which the teams were operating made it necessary for the combined meetings to be held not every week as had been planned, but once every three weeks. In the intervals, however, I did visit each team at least once in the field.

In large-scale surveys administration and supply of the interview teams play an important part. It will usually be necessary to employ one or several persons who concentrate all their efforts on this part of the operation. The Niger survey owed its success, in part, to the efforts of the administrator and his assistants who also took care of the interviewers' supplies.

From the various aspects of large-scale sample survey in developing countries it may be concluded that research in these areas does not differ fundamentally from similar research in western countries. It is a fact, however, that in non-western countries the investigator is faced with greater difficulties and, far more than his colleagues working in well-developed western areas, he will have to rely on his own initiative and resourcefulness to find solutions. Social research in non-western areas makes high demands not only on the professional skill but also on the personality of the researcher.

references

K. W. BACK and J. M. STYCOS (1959) The survey under unusual conditions. The Jamaica human fertility investigation, *Human Organization Monograph* # 1.
J. BEATTIE (1965) Understanding an African Kingdom: Bunyoro, New York etc.
A. W. EISTER (1962) Perspective on the functions of religion in a developing society: Islam in Pakistan, Paper submitted to the 5th World Congress of Sociology, Washington.
M. HOFFMANN (1963) Research on opinions and attitudes in West Africa, *International Social Science Journal* 15 (# 1): 59-69.

E. L. JONES (1963) The courtesy bias in South-East Asian surveys, *International Social Science Journal* 15 (# 1): 70-76.

A. J. F. KÖBBEN (1964) Van primitieven tot medeburgers, Assen.

E. R. LEACH (1958) An anthropologist's reflections on a social survey, *The Ceylon Journal of Historical and Social Studies* 1 (# 1): 9-20; also in this volume: 75-88.

M. B. LUSZKI (1957) Team research in social science; major consequences of a growing trend, *HO* 16 (# 1): 21-24.

K. MAYO (1927) Mother India, London.

R. E. MITCHELL (1965) Survey materials collected in the developing countries: sampling, measurement, and interviewing obstacles to intra- and inter-national comparisons, *International Social Science Journal* 17 (# 4): 665-685.

H. P. PHILLIPS (1959) Problems of translation and meaning in field work, *HO* 18 (# 4): 184-192.

L. RUDOLPH and S. H. RUDOLPH (1958) Surveys in India: field experience in Madras State, *Public Opinion Quarterly* 22 (# 3): 235-244.

J. D. SPECKMANN (1965) Marriage and kinship among the Indians in Surinam, Assen.

E. C. WILSON (1958) Problems of survey research in modernizing areas, *Public Opinion Quarterly* 22 (# 3): 230-234.

E. C. WILSON and L. ARMSTRONG (1963) Interviewers and interviewing in India, *International Social Science Journal* 15 (# 1): 48-58.

G. WUELKER (1963) Questionnaires in Asia, *International Social science Journal* 15 (# 1): 35-47.

4   *an anthropologist's reflections on a social survey*

E. R. LEACH

The publication of two documents giving results of the Ceylon University Socio-Economic Survey of Pāta Dumbara (Sarkar and Tambiah 1957; Tambiah 1957) clearly represents a landmark in Ceylon social studies. Whatever criticisms may be levied against particular details of this pioneering work its importance cannot be questioned. It has two particular virtues which I should like to stress. Firstly, the field of study (58 Pāta Dumbara villages) is precisely delimited and the method of study exactly described. Secondly, the facts are presented in such a way that they can be subjected to reasoned criticism. These are simple but by no means common merits; all too often sociological writers, both in Ceylon and elsewhere, indulge in sweeping and specious generalisations without offering any detailed evidence in support of their conclusions.

The bulk of my present paper is taken up with criticisms of certain features of one of the Pāta Dumbara publications. I should like to emphasise from the start that this criticism does not imply that I feel any personal antipathy to the document in question (Sarkar and Tambiah 1957); indeed the contrary is the case. I myself am at present preparing for publication an account of a small village in the North Central Province which I studied by anthropological methods in 1954. Although my orientation and interests were quite different from those of the University of Ceylon Socio-Economic Survey team, a good deal of my data is strictly comparable, and I am struck by the wide extent to which I find myself in general agreement with Drs. Sarkar and Tambiah. But I cannot regard this as a demonstration that the methods of the two types of investigation are equally satisfactory. On the contrary I believe that Drs. Sarkar and Tambiah have really arrived at their conclusions by intuitive methods, and that it is only because they are both by instinct first class *anthropologists* that their conclusions are fundamentally correct. The numerical apparatus in which these conclusions are embedded seems to me to be very largely a complicated piece of self deception.

The issue is a general one and is not confined to the particular case of the Pāta Dumbara survey. The book under discussion, *The Disintegrating Village*, strikes me as being a particularly 'true to type' specimen of a certain kind of sociological report. In criticising this book, I am not criticising the authors, who have accomplished an exceptionally able piece of analysis, but the principles of method on which the book is based. The purpose of my criticism is to display, by a process of negation, the crucial points at which contemporary sociological and anthropological investigations differ, and hence to imply that social anthropology has a special contribution to make to Ceylon social studies such as is not at present provided by conventional sociology.

But first I must limit my categories. Sociology, in its widest sense, is an all-embracing sort of discipline. At the level of abstract theory, anthropology and sociology are virtually one and the same (Macrae 1957), and in terms of subject matter there is often no obvious distinction between sociology and history (*e.g.* Pieris 1956). But there is a more limited kind of sociology which is explicitly concerned with empirical research into contemporary social situations, and this is not only comparable but antithetical to social anthropology. For the remainder of this paper, when I write of 'sociology' it is to 'field sociology' of this limited type to which I refer.

In this area of field research, the differences between sociology and social anthropology do not lie in theory but in method. As a consequence of the fact that the principal research tool of the field sociologist is a command of statistics, it has become a necessary feature of sociological investigation that the 'results' should be expressed in numbers. It follows that the units of sociological investigation must always be entities which can be expressed in numbers.

The extent to which this criterion limits the subtlety of sociological investigation is not always appreciated; yet, if we observe what research sociologists actually do, we find that their operations are severely restricted. Sociologists count things; they count people and houses and fields and acres and answers to questionnaires and so on and so forth, and of course they are very clever with their statistical arithmetic. But is that enough?

I would be the last to suggest that statistical investigations are necessarily mistaken in aim or application, but they are certainly limited in scope. It is my thesis that there is a wide range of sociological phenomena which are intrinsically inaccessible to statistical investigation of any kind. It is in this area of non-statistical social fact that the social anthropologist is professionally expert. The difference in method between research sociology and social anthropology stems from this distinction. The sociologist and the social anthropologist start with different premises about the nature of their subject matter. The sociologist with his statistical orientation presupposes that the field of observation consists of 'units of population', 'individuals'; in contrast, the social anthropologist, with his non-statistical prejudices, thinks of his data as being made up of 'systems of relationship'.

Let me take a simple case, a household consisting of a man and his wife and their two children, son and daughter. The sociologist may categorise such a family in a variety of ways. He may treat it as a single unit – 'one family' –, or as four units – 'four individuals', or as two adults and two children, or as two males and two females, or as one producer and three consumers, and so on — but always the sociological analysis will reduce to a set of numbers.

But the anthropologist will never treat such a family as either a single unit or as a multiple of units, he must always see it as part of a complex. The family, as a whole, consists of an internal network of relationships and is, in turn, linked to other elements in the outer social world by a further network of external relationships. For the anthropologist, the head of the family is not a single entity; he is not an individual man who can be described by a series of numerical characteristics and thereafter 'processed' in a Hollerith machine. Instead he is a complex of roles – a husband in relation to his wife, a father in relation to his children, a property owner in relation to his house, and employee in relation to some external employer and so on.

Differences in field research technique then logically follow. The sociologist assumes that the truths he is seeking to investigate are statistical truths and, in the normal way, he endeavours to arrive at these truths by sampling procedures. Consequently the size of the 'population' which can be investigated may be large in relation to the number of investigators; and the length of the enquiry may be correspondingly short. In the Pāta Dumbara survey which covered 58 villages, 116 square miles and 17,561 households the main research team consisted of 2 professional experts and 29 students; apart from preliminary planning and various pilot surveys, the major part of the research was completed in 10 days (Sarkar and Tambiah 1957: vii, x, xiii, xvi).

In sharp contrast, an anthropologist will ordinarily confine his attention to a single very small geographical area and endeavour to investigate the total network of interpersonal relationships which exists within that small area. The truths which he thus discovers are particular truths and, if he is wise, he will be extremely cautious about attempting to generalise from these particulars. Again to quote an example; in 1954 I made a study of a single very small village in the North Central Province. The total population of the village, including children, was 146; the number of households – using the same definition as that used in the Pāta Dumbara survey – was 39. I carried out my investigations alone with the aid of an untrained clerical assistant and I lived in the village for about five months, a period which, in the view of most professional anthropologists was far too short.

It is easy to see that the more obvious criticisms which anthropologists can make against sociologists are the simple converse of those which sociologists are likely to make against anthropologists. On the one hand, the sociologist with his sampling techniques and his questionnaire investigations appears to be presupposing uniformities which perhaps do not really exist. In a sense, he is forced to assume that, already, before ever he starts his questionnaire enquiries, he knows, by intuition, just what are the significant variables concerning which it is worth while making enquiries. On the other hand, the microscopic investigations of the anthropologist may well be of such a particular nature as to have no general validity at all.

Both arguments carry weight and there is a commonsense implication that, if they hope to achieve conclusions which have a general as opposed to a particular validity, the sociologist and the anthropologist ought to act as a team. With that view I am very largely in agreement. In this paper, however, I am not so much concerned with the interdependence of anthropology and sociology as with their contradictions. To that end I shall now make specific criticisms, from an anthropological point of view, of certain features of the analysis given in *The Disintegrating Village* (Sarkar and Tambiah 1957).

But let me repeat again, my criticisms are directed against defects inherent of the particular application of those methods, which is mostly skilful and at times highly ingenious.

At p. xvi we are told that throughout the volume the 'sampling unit' is the 'household'. A 'household' is defined as 'persons who cook their rice from the same pot'. It is stressed that this is not identical with the elementary family, but the authors might have added that it is also not necessarily identical to the group of persons living under one roof or in a single compound. With this 'household' as unit, the authors then proceed immediately to an elaborate statistical analysis of the distribution of land ownership between households. Some of the figures offer fine fuel for political rhetoric; thus Table 2 (p. 2) contains the striking statistic that, out of 506 households examined, 335 owned no paddy land at all.

Now what are the realities of this matter? Let us try to convert the figures back into facts. For a start, being anthropologically inclined, I have to take into account certain features of Sinhalese custom. I note for example that: – (1) Sinhalese village girls tend to get married very young, but that every married woman, however young, has a separate cooking pot. Thus every married couple constitutes a separate statistical household, whether living in a separate house or not. (2) Property may be transmitted to an individual's descendants either by inheritance at death or at any other time by gift *inter vivos*. In practice, except in the case of dowry to the daughters of the relatively wealthy, most property is handed on only when the original owner has become elderly. Thus, if a man of means is living in a single compound with three married sons, the sociological analysis might record this fact with the statistic that 'three out of four households are landless'.

Now it is true that, owing to the random selection of households, we should not ordinarily expect that the separate households of parents and their children would appear in the same sample. But that is not the point. It is merely that my anthropological appreciation of the total situation has led me to suspect that a proportion of the 335 landless households were landless simply because the householders were young, recently-married adults who were heirs to still living parents. I have arrived at this conclusion by making the typically anthropological assumption that a social field does not consist of units of population but of persons in relation to one another. Let us then proceed.

In my researches in the North Central Province a feature that greatly surprised me was that the term *anda* – sharecropping – might include the relation between fathers and sons. In this area, if a married son worked a share of his father's land, the villagers often considered that he held it on a sharecropping basis. Furthermore I found that in a very large proportion of all cases of sharecropping, the owner and the sharecropper were close relatives, the sharecropper being often a potential heir to the owner. Obviously the sharecropping relationship in such cases is sociologically of quite a different kind from that in which owner and sharecropper are otherwise unrelated.

Chapter 2 of *The Disintegrating Village* is concerned with the analysis of share-cropping in Pāta Dumbara. It is a long and complex analysis and I do not question the accuracy of the figures. I note however that there is, throughout, an implied assumption that the owners and the sharecroppers are entirely different people. For example, it is stated that 'under the present system of paddy cultivation by sharecroppers the landowners have no incentive to introduce any permanent improvements to the land because they do not get the full benefit of such improvement'. The authors nowhere consider the possibility that in a substantial proportion of cases owner and sharecropper may be closely related. My own enquiries, admittedly in another part of Ceylon, suggested that sharecropping was largely an age phenomenon. All young men are sharecroppers, most elderly men are owners. By and large, the sharecroppers are the heirs of the owners.

I am not insisting that this must also be the case in Pata Dumbara, but the figures presented seem to be quite consistent with this possibility, and if this were the case then nearly all the inferences which the authors of *The Dis-*

integrating Village draw from their figures would be erroneous. Again it is the factor of relationship which breaks down the statistical logic.

A rather different point of criticism is evoked by Chapter V where the authors make some complicated, though ingenious, deductions from the fact that, in their statistics, agricultural holdings fall into two clearly defined groups – a high yield group and a low yield group. The authors do not tell us how they measured either the acreages or the outputs in question, so specific criticism of the figures is impossible. I am however struck by the fact that my small scale data from a North Central Province village show a precisely similar dichotomy.

What impresses me here is that when the sociologists encounter an unexpected discrepancy of this sort they accept the validity of their questionnaire data and simply analyse the figures so as to discover their statistical significance. In contrast, the anthropologist suspects the validity of the original data as such and looks for a source of error. The sociologist postulates a statistical relation between the 'high yield' and the 'low yield' plots; the anthropologist postulates a sociological relation.

In the North Central Province case the source of the category split turned out to be quite clear; it traced back to an original difference between English and Sinhalese methods of reckoning field areas. This is an entirely different type of explanation to that which Sarkar and Tambiah have deduced with the aid of their mathematical computers. In the North Central Province what has happened is this. Cultivated lands fall into two main categories; 'traditional' (*purāna*) village lands which have existed from ancient times, and 'acre lands' (*sinakkara*) which have been developed in the last 60 years or so, after purchase from the Crown. The village in question was surveyed by cadastral survey in 1900 and the whole of the *purāna* field found to be slightly over 42 acres, but the 100 odd individual plots within the 42 acre field were not, and have never been, surveyed. In the annual paddy census, which has been drawn up in virtually the same form ever since about 1870, land areas are reckoned initially in terms of seed sown (*pāla* and *lāha*) and then converted into acres by a rule of thumb which seems to have been unchanged since 1900. Presumably because of some initial misunderstanding between the villagers and the surveyor the conversion factor is 'away off'. The acreage of each individual *purāna* plot is meticulously detailed, but the total adds up to 63 acres instead of 42! A number of other villages in the area show similar discrepancies and I suspect that errors of this type type are general.

In contrast, all the *sinakkara* plots were individually surveyed at the time when they were first acquired from the Crown so that acreages for this latter class of holding are correct.

Now the consequence of overestimating by 50% the acreage of each *purāna* plot is to make it appear that the yield from *purāna* land is exceptionally low; moreover since the *sinakkara* land is generally held by the wealthier members of the community, a further correlation appears to exist between large holdings and large yields. The parallel with the Pāta Dumbara evidence is exact.

In the North Central Province case there are further complications due to the fact that *purāna* land and *sinakkara* land has a differential utility in relation to the *Maha* and *Yala* harvests and I am far from suggesting that all land is used with equal efficiency. But the facts I have stated are bound to make me suspicious of Table 36 at p. 40 of Sarkar and Tambiah's book. Can we be certain, in view of the very small size of many of the holdings that all the acreage figures are of equal reliability? And, for that matter, dare we trust the output figures at all? From bitter experience I know how unreliable figures of this sort tend to be.

But let me stress again the nature of my scepticism. The anthropologist does not doubt the power of the statistical apparatus which is the sociologist's major tool; what he tends to query is the quality of the original data which is fed into the statistical apparatus. The anthropologist has nothing but admiration for the things that the sociologist-statistician is prepared to do with figures; the doubts are concerned with how far the initial figures genuinely relate to social facts. Operating as he does at a very 'microscopic' level of social analysis, the anthropologist is constantly made aware of the difficulty of fitting items of human behaviour and experience into numerical categories. It is not that the numbers are necessarily false but that they draw the enquirer's attention away from what is of crucial significance.

Let me come to my final examples. In Chapter VII of *The Disintegrating Village* Dr. Tambiah discusses the contentious topic of the 'fragmentation of land through inheritance'. This section of the book is of a special interest to me since inheritance is a process which is of central importance for anthropological analysis.

There are two different features of Dr. Tambiah's account which I shall criticise; both centre round the argument that an excess of mathematics can mask much more than it reveals. Here is my first point.

At pp. 58-60 Dr. Tambiah cites figures to show that 'the inheritance of land is heavily weighted in favour of males', 'the son's average shares of paddy land being 2-8 times as much as the shares of the (first) sister's'. (p. 60).

Now my objection is not to the first part of this assertion; but only to the second. I do not seriously doubt that in Pāta Dumbara, as elsewhere in Kandyan Ceylon, there is a bias of inheritance in favour of males, but I maintain that the effect of reducing this bias to a precise numerical figure is entirely misleading. It gives a false air of scientific precision to what is, at best, a highly variable 'general tendency', and deters both author and reader from enquiring further into the cultural processes involved.

To reach his numerically precise conclusion, Dr. Tambiah has had to subject his original questionnaire data to what he describes as 'refined calculation'. He claims that these calculations show that the facts are in accord with what might have been expected from a consideration of the inheritance laws.

This is the crux. Dr. Tambiah makes the normal statistical sociologist's assumption that his questionnaire data can be treated as independent evidence. Individual questionnaires may be in error but, since the material has been collected on a 'random' basis, the errors will cancel out. If then mathematical analysis of the questionnaires produces results which are in accordance with 'legal expectation', this shows that practice and legal theory agree.

But can we really say anything of the sort? Might it not be that all the questionnaires have, from the first, been drawn up to accord more closely with legal principles than with empirical facts?

Anyone who has ever had first-hand anthropological field experience will know that *inheritance* is the very last topic on which one can expect an informant to offer candid and straightforward information. Moreover, in the Sinhalese situation, statements about inheritance of land are subject to two special types of bias, both of which are mentioned by Dr. Tambiah (p. 54). On the one hand there is the vigorously asserted cultural prejudice that *dīga* (virilocal) residence is respectable and *binna* (uxorilocal) residence ignominious. This automatically makes it 'respectable' for a man to claim that he works land inherited from his father while denying or minimising similar claims on the part of his wife or his sister. The other bias, which operates in the opposite direction, derives from the common adult assertion that 'we treat all our sons and daughters exactly alike'. Again and again in my own preliminary question-naire-style enquiries I found the same man maintaining the intrinsically contra-dictory propositions that, while he himself had inherited far more than any of his married sisters, he proposed to divide up his own property equally among all his sons and daughters.

The true facts in my North Central Province case were that there was a ge-nuine, though moderate, bias of inheritance in favour of male heirs but that this bias came to be heightened by a tendency on the part of male heirs to 'buy out' the shares of their *dīga*-married sisters.

As an aspect of this I found, just as did Dr. Tambiah (pp. 60-62), 'that the ratio of land received by daughters when compared with sons was slightly smaller for daughters of poor parents than for daughters of rich parents'. This bias I found was not due to any variation in application of the rules of inheritance; it was simply that when a *dīga*-married daughter (or for that matter a *binna*-married son) inherited a very small share of a very small plot in a village remote from that in which she (or he) was living, she (or he) often neglected to assert a claim and consequently the land remained in effective control of some heir who had remained at home.

I doubt whether 'tendencies' such as these can ever usefully be converted into numerical statistics, but certainly precise quantification of the kind of pre-liminary information which can be obtained by means of a simple questionnaire and interview technique seems to me to have no meaning at all. To my mind it is inconceivable that the Ceylon University research team, working under the conditions stated, could have obtained data which might merit the kind of mathematical analysis which Dr. Tambiah has applied. In effect, the decimal points and the percentages serve only as a smoke screen to mask from the author the important ambiguities inherent in his information.

This perhaps reads like a personal attack on Dr. Tambiah but that is not at all what is intended. I find Dr. Tambiah's discussion of Kandyan inheritance truly illuminating, indeed I repeat my patronizing comment that his sociological insights mark him out as a first class anthropologist![1] Yet I claim that the mathematical form of his presentation is a serious defect, because it implies a degree of precision in the initial observations which is unwarranted. At one stage (p. 62) Dr. Tambiah himself recognises that his questionnaire information represents only a first approximation to the social facts. That being so, the application of the whole gamut of Chi-Squared Tests, Regression Coefficients and so on which fill out the pages of his book is any less approximate by being processed through a mathematical formula.

Here again we are back at the basic difference of attitude adopted by sociologists and anthropologists towards their raw material. The statistical sociologist takes it for granted that the truth which he is seeking is contained in his questionnaire answers and that mathematical technique is capable of revealing that truth; in contrast the anthropologist is suspicious of questionnaire data as such. I maintain that it is in the very nature of questionnaire investigation that the 'results' tend to err in the direction of ideal stereotypes. Hence any attempt to investigate, by questionnaire research, the degree of fit between an ideal stereotype and actual practice is a waste of time. Dr. Tambiah's 2-8 'ratio of discrepancy in inheritance' seems to me to be just that. It is to the meticulous quantification that I object, not the broader statements concerned with sociological fact.

My second and final criticism of the analysis given in Chapter VII is more expressly concerned with the question of fragmentation. Because he is operating with a random sample of informants, Dr. Tambiah is able to assume that all the 'respondents' are of the 'present generation' – with the suggestion of course that they are coevals all of whom have acquired their land under precisely similar external circumstances.

In a comparable anthropological enquiry the 'respondents' would be localised in one place but spread over three or four generations in time, the older members of the 'sample' being the parents and grandparents, or even great grand-

[1] In 1958, when this was written, Dr. Tambiah was in fact a lecturer in *Sociology* at the University of Ceylon, in 1966 he is a lecturer in *Social Anthropology* in the University of Cambridge and a close friend and colleague of the author.

parents of the youngest group. It would then immediately strike the eye that the property status of any particular individual with respect to the rest of the sample depends primarily upon his position in the age cycle. A young man starts with nothing; a young adult may possess some acquired property and some inherited property but he is probably still accumulating; in contrast, an older adult has probably passed the peak and has begun to dissipate his property; a very old man may once again be landless.

As soon as we consider the facts in this light the concept of fragmentation begins to lose shape. Clearly certain statistics remain relevant. If the total area of cultivable land is limited and the population increases, and there are no alternative avenues of employment, then the availability of land per unit of population must decrease, and this is an important economic fact. But this has no logical connection with 'fragmentation through inheritance'. Dr. Tambiah (p. 79) asserts explicitly that one of the *causes* of fragmentation in the Kandyan area has been 'the existence of laws and customs of succession which compel the division of land among heirs on a fair division basis'. But this is not the case, and if Dr. Tambiah had not been distracted by his figures he could never have supposed that it was; for the effect of Kandyan inheritance rules is quite clear. It is not merely that in each generation there tends to be a division of property between sons and daughters; there is also and simultaneously, a recombination of holdings in the children of husbands and wives. If the population is stable, then the rate of division is no greater than the rate of recombination, and the average size of holdings will remain constant throughout, even though some estates will decrease in size and some increase. This is not simply a theoretical proposition; it is demonstrable. An anthropologist by concentrating his attentions on the population of a single small area over a limited period, and making full use of the excellent documentary records available to Ceylon research workers can show very precisely what really happens as a consequence of Kandyan inheritance rules. It is a complicated sequence of events that emerges from such enquiries, and the result is not easily described in words, let alone numbers; but what is quite clear is that it is *not* a self-destructive system. Taken by itself the inheritance system tends to perpetuate a stable structure of 'moderate inequality'; it inhibits extreme accumulation and also extreme poverty.

I set out to claim a place for social anthropology in contemporary Ceylon social studies, yet, so far, I seem to have done little beyond criticise one of the most enterprising pieces of sociological research so far carried out in Ceylon. Let me repeat, I am arguing by negation. My purpose is not to denounce all statistical types of sociological enquiry but rather to explain just why the social anthropologist claims to be able to reveal facts which escape the observation of the statistician.

Precisely because he uses statistics, the sociologist must operate with a random sample of population. This means that *by definition* the units of population must be assumed to be unrelated to one another. It follows that no characteristics of the population which emerge from the enquiry can possibly be attributed to the interrelationships existing between different units.

In contrast, the anthropologist explicitly concentrates on data which are *not* random. He purposely chooses a small field within which all the observable phenomena are closely interrelated and interdependent.

As observations, the anthropological and sociological enquiries are alike 'synchronous' – all the observed events take place at the same, or nearly the same, time. But whereas the sociologist must treat his population as a homogeneous field – all units alike are regarded as 'members of the *present* generation' – the anthropologist must take account of generational relationship. He can thus take account of social process – for the fathers of today were the sons of yesterday; today's child is the adult of tomorrow.

And it is this fact that is fundamental. As is demonstrated so clearly in *The Disintegrating Village*, the field sociologist is concerned always with synchronous allocations. To him the word 'inheritance' means no more than the division of a body of assets among a number of individuals. Property, in passing from generation to generation, is 'fragmented'. In contrast, the anthropologist looks at the same facts the other way round. It is the body of assets – the 'estate' – of a society which forms the constant continuing entity; it is the individuals who 'flow through' society from childhood to old age and death. 'Inheritance' – that is the changing body of rights in the continuing estate – is the crucial fact which marks off the stages in the continuing process of transition by which individuals move through the system from status to status.

Perhaps that is the place to stop. My sociological colleagues, will recognise with some amusement that, having started off to set a distinction between sociology and social anthropology, I have ended by proclaiming Max Weber as my patron saint. And so it should be. At the theoretical level, sociology and social anthropology are one and the same; it is only in the application of theory to research that our differences and antagonisms begin.

references

D. G. MACRAE (1957) Social theory: retrospect and prospect, *The British Journal of Sociology* 8 : 97-105.
R. PIERIS (1956) Sinhalese social organization, Colombo.
N. K. SARKAR and S. J. TAMBIAH (1957) The disintegrating village, Colombo.
S. J. TAMBIAH (1958) The structure of kinship and its relationship to land possession and residence in Pata Dumbara, Central Ceylon, JRAI 88 (# 1): 21-44.

5 *the participants' view of their culture*[1]

P. E. DE JOSSELIN DE JONG

It is the native point of view which really matters to us.
Coral Gardens and their Magic I : 139

One of the unmistakeable trends in present-day anthropology is the renewed interest in structural studies. Although one could spend considerable time trying to draw up a generally acceptable definition of 'structure' (and probably never quite succeed), I think it will be sufficient for our present purposes to observe that a corollary of most structural studies is that the anthropologist tries to express a phenomenon or group of phenomena in the culture he is studying in such a simplified manner that it can be rendered in the form of a model or diagram; he then tries to find out whether other phenomena in the same culture may be expressed in terms of the same model.

This trying out the applicability of a model is a tricky business, as a considerable amount of subjective judgement is involved. A description can be judged by its truth, but a model (an anthropological model, that is) is to be judged by its usefulness, its helpfulness – and what one anthropologist considers helpful, another may call misplaced ingenuity.

One way of keeping the structural simplification anchored to the bedrock of observed reality, is to subject one's model to the reactions of the people whose culture one is studying. This will be the theme of the present paper: it will describe the way an anthropologist, during his field work in Negri Sembilan,

---

[1] The above is an abbreviated version of an article originally published in Dutch (De Josselin de Jong 1956). Several theoretical questions discussed in the Dutch version have been omitted here, as they are irrelevant in the context of this volume. For the same reason I do not discuss in the present version the more far-reaching argument put forward by Bohannan (1957), with which I fundamentally agree.

a State on the west coast of the Malay Peninsula, tried to put the model he had been constructing to the test by confronting it with the opinions and the points of view of the people among whom he was working. In general, I should say a study of the participants' view of their own culture such as we are now going to undertake fits into the framework of anthropological research in the following manner.

The anthropologist describes a culture, or a part of it, on the basis of his field work. Such a description is always a simplification: one narrows down the total range of observable phenomena, varying per person or per group, to a smaller range, which one holds to be representative. One describes a culture construct, to borrow a term from Ralph Linton (Linton 1949:30).

Now one can try to find out whether the participants see their culture in the same way, i.e. whether they form the same culture construct, as the anthropologist does. It is precisely because these two culture constructs do not necessarily agree, that one is always obliged to state in one's description what is based on information and what on observation. In some cases the participants' information proves to be coloured by an ideal, which the informants present as a reality – and they may or may not be aware that reality does not correspond with this ideal. The anthropologist can describe such an ideal, and the participants' reactions to striking deviations from it. Furthermore, by a structural analysis the anthropologist tries to understand the factual data he has gathered by fitting them into a model of the structure which he holds to be fundamental to the culture in question. He can then consider in how far the participants also recognize basic structural principles in their own culture. We shall now discuss these three subjects successively. First a few data on Negri Sembilan, as an introduction to our main subject.

Negri Sembilan may be considered a Minangkabau colony in the Malay Peninsula. The Head of State is a member of a dynasty said to be the continuation of the now defunct royal house of Minangkabau. The territory is divided into a number of provinces, of which Rembau, Sungei Ujong, Jelebu and Johol are the largest and most important. The head of a province bears a title which we shall translate as Lord of the Province. This dignity is hereditary in certain matriclans, but is held by members of the two or more lineages of the 'ruling' clan in turn.

In Negri Sembilan as a whole twelve matriclans are recognized. The clan has a chief, and this dignity, too, is taken in turn by members of all the branches or lineages of the clan. The head of a lineage we shall simply call the lineage chief.

This system does not include the position of village headman. The village headman does not owe his position to the customary genealogical system, but to the political system of the State of Negri Sembilan: he is elected by the villagers, then confirmed in his post and paid by the State – so he is a State official, as is the officer immediately superior to him, the parish headman. I shall use the term 'parish' for an administrative unit comprising several villages. The use of a religious term for a purely secular entity may be surprising, but the origin of the village cluster was, in fact, the Muslim parish. A number of parishes together make up a district, headed by a District Officer. He is a member of the Malayan Civil Service. The boundaries of a district sometimes, but by no means always, coincide with those of a province. Village and parish headmen may be considered as links between the genealogical chiefs on the one hand, and on the other hand the D. O. whose position is quite foreign to the traditional set-up.

The provinces are often divided into halves, with such pairs of names as 'Coast' and 'Interior'. In these cases, the dignity of Lord of the Province is often conferred on a member of each half alternately.

As we said, the clans are matrilineal; residence is matrilocal; the lineages are exogamous, the clans not necessarily so.

Lineages, and through them, clans have their own communal property, principally land, which is meticulously set aside from a man's or woman's individually acquired property when landholdings and moveables are re-allocated after death or divorce. Differences of opinion on matters of inheritance are dealt with in the same way as other matters concerning the family and succession to traditional dignities, i.e. they are decided through the application of traditional rules and proverbs by the customary hierarchy: lineage chief, clan chief, and provincial Lord, and sometimes, in political matters, the Head of the State. In striking contrast to the matrilineal commoners is the patrilineal organization of the ruling dynasty.

To conclude this brief survey, I would summarize the essential social structure

of Minangkabau (and therefore, at one remove, also of Negri Sembilan) as
follows: Minangkabau social organization is based on dualism and asymmetrical connubium; there is evidence for the recognition of two descent principles,
viz. in the relationship between the predominantly patrilineal royal house and
the predominantly matrilineal commoners.

My observations date from the period just before Malaya's independence, and
were principally made in Rembau province and Jempol province, in two villages
called Chembung and Padang Lebar respectively.

There is a quite considerable difference between these two provinces. Rembau
has long been settled and has been largely brought under cultivation. It offers
the prospect of a broad, gently undulating padi plain, bisected by a main north
– south road. There is intensive local traffic on the roads, which keeps up
until well after dark. This was possible (at the time of my stay) in spite of the
'Emergency' measures necessitated by communist terrorist activities, as
Rembau was a White Area, i.e. free of terrorists. Even after only a few days
one is struck by the signs of a certain prosperity of quite a long standing.
Jempol on the other hand is more isolated, 'up-country' or *ulu*. Padang Lebar
is the principal village in a row of twelve, all in a line up a narrow valley,
enclosed by jungle. As a lifeline to the outer world there runs one road, at that
time barred by a tall wire mesh gate, which was opened twice a week for a
convoy of two buses and some private cars and lorries, escorted by police
in armoured cars. The area at the back of the valley had only been 'opened',
as Malays put it, as recently as three generations ago. Jempol, one of the lesser
provinces, lies between Johol and Jelebu.

When one compares Rembau, wide open to foreign influences, with Jempol,
isolated and far more self-contained, one might well expect to see the latter
province acting as a bulwark of conservatism, as opposed to Rembau as an
outpost of modernism. But on the contrary, the inhabitants of Rembau pride
themselves on their 'orthodox' upholding of *adat*, traditional customs, and the
other provinces acknowledge this specifically Rembau sense of tradition:
Rembau tetap berpegang kepada adat (Rembau stands firm by custom) is a phrase
one hears time and again, outside the province as well as within. Later on in

the course of this paper we shall try to find an explanation for this paradoxical state of affairs.

How the participants see elements in their own culture It goes without saying that a full description of 'how the participant sees his own culture' would be as extensive as a complete ethnographic description, and would in part coincide with it, so we shall first select one single example which I think is interesting as it illustrates how participants may have a totally wrong impression of elements in their own culture, and other examples of the way participants may discuss culture elements among themselves. First an example of participants' 'mistake'.

It refers to *nikah ta'lik*. This is a procedure by which immediately after the Muslim marriage ceremony has been performed, the spouses contractually agree that the wife is entitled to divorce if the husband deserts, maltreats, or neglects her, or makes himself guilty of any other misdemeanour the spouses may wish to specify in the contract. In Indonesia this procedure has been strongly propagated by feminist organizations, as it offers the wife some protection against possible harsh or neglectful treatment. In Negri Sembilan, where due to various factors the women's position is strong, one might suppose that *nikah ta'lik* almost loses its raison d'être. And in fact, when I asked after it, I was told in Rembau as well as in Jempol that it was seldom practised, although it was no *great* rarity. Actually, however, the register of marriages kept by the *kadi* of Rembau showed that of the 275 marriages he had inscribed in 1946, no less than 210 were *ta'lik* marriages.

Now this, and other similar cases of participants having formed a completely incorrect idea of the actual situation in their society can be explained by lack of interest. As the *nikah ta'lik* procedure does not introduce any startling innovation in Negri Sembilan life, it has not brought about any considerable change in the position of women or the tenor of family life. Now it has been introduced (I do not know how) it is accepted passively, as not much more than a formality, and one hardly realizes when it is and when it is not practiced.

Our conclusion: the participants' incorrect views on points of fact connected with a particular cultural element *may* be an indication that that element is considered unimportant, that it has little 'value'. (Linton 1949: 72).

This situation that one irreflectively accepts one's own culture is of course very usual (even where it does not manifest itself by incorrect opinions), and is often only altered by an observer coming from elsewhere and asking questions. It may also be altered when a contrast-situation arises: participants are made sharply aware of their own culture, and start discussing it, when that culture somehow or other comes into contrast with another.

In Negri Sembilan three such contrast-situations kept on arising. The first is the contrast between Negri Sembilan, and its matrilineal institutions, as opposed to the surrounding Malay States, with a cognatic kinship system, and all the differences that this implies. The second is between Negri Sembilan, the colony, and Minangkabau, the mother country. It would take us too far to discuss these two at present, but something can be said about the third, the contrast between the matrilineal custom, or *adat*, and Islamic Law. This contrast, which in Minangkabau has led to a controversy of long standing and evergreen actuality is also of the greatest importance for Negri Sembilan. The contrast manifests itself in a number of issues: *adat* protects family and clan property and favours women, Islamic Law holds individual ownership of property to be normal and favours men. *Adat* demands exogamous matrilineal kingroups, but Law does not recognize genealogical units of that type. In last instance these and other such contrasts proceed from an opposition between two systems each of which in principle claims dominance over the entire life of the community, in spite of conciliatory proverbs which claim that the two systems support and supplement each other, e.g. *adat bersendi shara', shara' bersendi adat* (Law supports Custom, Custom supports Law). The protagonists of the *adat* are in the first place the clan chiefs. Islamic Law naturally has the clergy as its paladins. However, the common man too is most interested in the conflict. It touches him principally in its reference to inheritance. Debates on the merits of the two systems are still the order of the day. This is no abstract, 'academic' interest. Material selfinterest colours the villager's views, but often a moral conflict is involved as well. A person considers himself to be a good Muslim, but is also (particularly when he hails from Rembau) attached to *adat*.

In 1951 all these factors: a lively awareness of the contrast between the two systems, hope of material profit, private conflicts between people in positions of authority, and moral dilemmas, came to a head and led to a whole series of private and public meetings, actions and counter-actions involving political parties and government authorities, and to a veritable torrent of pamphlets, broadsheets, and publications in the Malay press. A truce during the month of the Fast took the edge off the debate which, however, continues to the present day, be it in a less emotional atmosphere. These events took place in Rembau, and had few repercussions beyond that province.

Earlier we said that at first sight it seems paradoxical that a province like Rembau, open to outside influences and 'progressive' should be more attached to traditional culture than the isolated province of Jempol. We now see that not only *adat* is strongest in Rembau, but that the anti-*adat* agitation by the protagonists of Islam also met with most response in that same province. It seems to me there is a direct relation between these two facts, which might be formulated, perhaps a little too rigidly, as follows: the faithful adherence to *adat* is based on continual thinking and discussion about it. This attitude is stimulated by a clear awareness of the peculiarities of the *adat*, of its own individuality as opposed to cognatic systems and to Islamic Law. The conscious upholding of tradition as well as the fanatical attacks on it are both aspects of a general 'interest': in Rembau there is simply greater interest in the prevalent social organization than, for instance, in Jempol. This again results in several features one can observe in Rembau: greater attachment to, but also clearer realization of the imperfections and a more brusque rejection of the *adat;* greater influence of the traditional office-holders, a more important rôle of the provincial Lord's office as centre for the formation of public opnion, etc. And finally: can the greater interest in its turn be ascribed to the higher level of development and prosperity, the more intensive traffic within the province and the more frequent contacts with areas beyond it – that is to say, to a more marked contrast-situation? I shall leave this last question open, and not hazard a conclusion.

Of the three contrast-situations mentioned above, the last (the *adat* versus Law contrast) arouses the strongest emotions on the part of the participants. It is a real conflict, namely a conflict between two systems struggling for dominance. We shall now turn to conflicts within a single system.

What the participants consider to be ideal. It is particularly in conflict-situations that the ideal comes to stand out clearly: one faction stands fast by an ideal, the other faction abandons it or pits a different ideal against it. This may be illustrated by a conflict of current importance for Negri Sembilan.

In Rembau the Shahbandar is one of the traditional office-holders who assist the provincial Lord. He is always a member of the Biduanda clan, but each lineage within that clan in turn has the right to designate one of its members as Shahbandar. In 1946 a vacancy occurred. In conformity with tradition, the chiefs of the several lineages assembled to decide which lineage's turn had now come. The conclusion they reached was that neither lineage Kota nor lineage Gadong had so far supplied an incumbent for this office. Which of them was now to be selected? Now it is the rule that the Shahbandar is at the same time the heir-apparent to the dignity of provincial Lord. As the Lord at that time was a member of lineage Kota, and that office, too, must rotate over the several lineages, it stood to reason that his presumable successor should *not* be a member of Kota, but of Gadong. At this point the negotiations broke down. The provincial Lord insisted on having a fellow-member of his own lineage as Shahbandar. By putting on pressure, using his personal prestige, juggling with traditional sayings and precedents he managed to block the evidently correct decision: selection of lineage Gadong. However, he did not manage to force through his own opinions to such an extent that a member of Kota was appointed. The result was a deadlock which had persisted for ten years at the time of my stay in the area. This affair had assumed the form of a sharp conflict between the provincial Lord (and his adherents among the hereditary office-bearers) and the lineage chiefs. The chiefs of the other clans, not themselves directly concerned in the matter, sided with the Biduanda lineage chiefs as they correctly interpreted the provincial Lord's tactics as symptomatic of the latter's attempts to overrule the *adat* by means of his own strong position. So we see that an existing ideal (succession by rotation) is abrogated by a group of individuals for personal reasons. A conflict arises which becomes the theme of discussions in which the ideal is explicitly stated. A situation involving an ideal will often lead to the well-known result that informants consciously mislead the investigator: they do not want him to hear of deviations from the ideal. But what is more significant, the participants themselves may also be misled; that is to say their view of their own culture becomes distorted, though for a different reason than the mere lack of interest we discussed above. An example: a genealogical survey of the village of Padang Lebar showed up a great preponderance of marriages between first cross-cousins, and a strong tendency for a girl to marry into the same lineage as her mother or her brother. However, an outright question whether there was any regular pattern of marriage relationships was always answered by an energetic denial, the informants often adding: 'How could there be any regularity, for: *rezeki, pertemuan, perkuburan – nasib kita*', a phrase that can be interpreted as 'How we make our living, whom we marry, and when and where we die is determined by *nasib*, fate, and is therefore impervious to human intervention'. Now as concerns *pertemuan*, marriage, this saying is demonstrably false: Negri Sembilan marriages are not made in heaven, but by protracted negotiations, and, as we saw, by favouring certain stereotyped relationships. So these are facts which are denied by an often quoted saying. I think the reason for this is that the saying is held to express a Muslim line of thought, a Muslim ideal. The participants attach such value to this ideal, that they refuse to register deviations from it; perhaps it would be more correct to say that they incorrectly hold the deviations they observe to be quantitatively negligeable exceptional cases. In this manner they are able to hold the ideal to be reality, and to obfuscate the reality they observe.

In both cases we have been discussing: the *adat* ideal of rotatory succession to office, and the would – be Islamic ideal of fate-determined marriage, we were dealing with ideals phrased by the participants themselves. For the observer, the ideal is of course not normative. He can study it purely as a tendency, as a 'real culture pattern'. Sometimes individuals forsake the ideal, out of self-interest or for other reasons. Once these individuals have become numerous or influential enough, a second tendency puts in its appearance. This brings us to a discussion of structure.

To what extent the participants recognize a structure in their society. We concluded that the participants' views are made clearer by contrast, and the ideals are more sharply defined by conflicts. In discussing structure we shall try to introduce the contrast ourselves, viz. by setting the participants' views in opposition to the observer's. Again we shall give two examples.

We said earlier that we held asymmetrical connubium to be one of the structural principles underlying Minangkabau social organization. The Negri Sembilan data are more ambiguous, but permit of the same conclusion. Now we saw that in Jempol MBD marriages are not infrequent, but are not recognized as an ideal by participants – actually they are not even recognized as a reality. In Rembau the situation is different: the actual incidence of such marriages is no greater than in Jempol, as far as I can judge at present, but to questions like: 'Does one ever marry one's MBD here?' one usually got the reply that such marriages were common. Spontaneously, or in reply to further questions, inhabitants often said such a marriage was *yang lebih baik*, 'the best'. The provincial Lord of Rembau answered: 'My own marriage is of that type', with an air of 'What more do you want?' They produced arguments to prove the inherent goodness of this kind of marriage, for example: because the ZS has always had MB as guardian, the latter will also be a benevolent father-in-law. Another informant immediately quoted a little rhyme after holding forth on the desirability of MBD marriages: *Usul-usul, asal-asal/asal jangan ditinggalkan /tahu usul dengan asal/tahulah salah dengan benar:* 'The origins and the principles/never forsake the origins/whoever understands the origins and the principles/can distinguish good from evil'.

In other words, this type of marriage is good, or correct, and is practised by those who know the *asal-usul*, the original institutions. On the other hand, I could never get anyone to agree that this type of marriage, if practised consistently, must lead to regular connubia. A demonstration with pencil and paper of the mechanism of asymmetrical connubium was watched as a curious *tour de force*, but nobody saw any reason for declaring it applicable to Rembau social structure. So although the observer might conclude on the basis of his field data on MBD marriage that asymmetrical connubium can be recognized as a structural principle (be it one which is anything but consistently realized), the participants do not share this point of view.

The other example concerns double descent which I also came to recognize as a structural principle in Minangkabau and Negri Sembilan, although much more hesitatingly than I accepted asymmetrical connubium. One of my reasons for accepting it was a tentative interpretation of the native terms *saka* and *baka* as matrilineal descent and patrilineal descent respectively. The proverbs in which these terms occur are rather cryptic, so I asked informants in Rembau and Jempol for an explanation. They often answered that *baka* meant *keturunan dari bapak*, 'descent from the father'. That this does not refer to the father's matrilineage nor to patrifiliation is proved by two spontaneously offered comments. One informant 'explained' the word *baka* by means of a typically Malay popular etymology, as follows: one traces back one's *baka: kepada bapak, kepada bapak* (to a father, and then again to a father), and the word *baka* is formed by contraction of these words. The other informant said: 'There are actually three kinds of descent: *saka*, from the mother; *baka*, from the father; and *pesaka*, from both parents: the language one learns as a child, for example, is *pesaka*'.

Here we have a case that the investigator rather reluctantly concluded that patrilineality is of structural importance in matrilineal Negri Sembilan, and that he later noticed that participants recognized this principle quite clearly, and found a verbal expression for it that was as unambiguous as one had any right to expect. So we find that a principle which was fairly clear-cut for the investigator, namely asymmetrical connubium, was not recognized by the participants, but another principle, much more dubious in the anthropologist's eyes, was. How is this to be understood?

It strikes a student (I shall not go into details about this) that quite a number of structural principles he considers important are not, or hardly, recognized by participants. For instance, the question what are the exogamous units: clans or lineages, elicited conflicting replies in both provinces, and the same holds for questions about the Coast versus Inland dichotomy prevalent in Rembau. Now the position is that the latter opposition has very little practical importance apart from determining succession to *adat* dignities in the 'ruling' clan Biduanda. As for exogamy, one is not greatly concerned as long as marriage is avoided with a rather fluid group of matrilineal kinsfolk. Clan exogamy is certainly not maintained, there is no sanction on its breach.

The negative or hesitant attitude of participants towards these structural principles is therefore understandable: they do not play a significant part in present-day culture, they are not upheld by any ideal. The views on MBD marriage and its final implication, asymmetrical connubium, lead to the conclusion: marriages are seen in the first place as interpersonal bonds, and this bond is appreciated. One does favour the perpetuation of alliances which have once been brought about (a girl as it were repeating her mother's or brother's marriage), and the linking of kin-groups two by two – but the resulting connubial chains, tying up greater numbers of kin-groups, are not perceived; hence they must be unimportant, and not subjected to an ideal. Finally the *saka – baka* question: this is of functional importance, as it affects election to positions of authority. There are proverbial sayings which enjoin the electors to consider both the *saka* and the *baka* of the candidate. It is not easy to do so in actual affairs, so I cannot imagine this principle having much influence in practice. That it is nevertheless recognizable to participants as a structural principle is probably due simply to its being verbalized, and thus being a suitably circumscribed subject for debate and discussion. It is linked to an ideal, be it to one of these watered-down ideals, the conventional phrases also discussed by Linton (Linton 1949: 35).

Our conclusion must be that a sense of structure appears to be closely bound up with recognition of an ideal; that participants show awareness of structure when the structural principle is supported by an ideal, and is therefore of some importance for them. The strong sense of structure reported for the Australian Aborigines may be due to their considering the very functioning of their kinship system as an ideal – and this in turn may serve to give a measure of consistency and continuity to the system. In Negri Sembilan on the other hand there is a causal connection between the lack of any pronounced structural sense, the relative weakness of ideals in this field (apart from a few special instances), and the great actual variability and tolerance.

references

P. BOHANNAN (1957) Justice and judgement among the Tiv, London.

P. E. DE JOSSELIN DE JONG (1956) De visie der participanten op hun cultuur, *Bijdragen Taal-, Land- en Volkenkunde* 112 (# 2): 149-168.

R. LINTON (1949) The cultural background of personality, London, 2nd ed.

J. VANSINA

Fieldwork is an art based on techniques. It is an art because it draws heavily on the unique personality of every researcher. It is full of uncertainties because it involves a dialogue between the temperament of the investigator and the dominant cultural patterns of the people studied. So a given person will do well in one situation and not in another less suited to his personality. No amount of technique can erase this basic fact. Techniques though are useful, essentially because they grow out of concrete experience from previous work and so it seems proper to start out by recalling our own experience during the first fieldtrip we undertook before discussing a number of practical rules which might be useful in all sorts of field situations.

Early in January 1953, I alighted from the slow train in the railway station serving Kuba country, an impatient boy of 23 with two suitcases and high hopes. My assignment was to study the culture of the Kuba people and the Kuba were an 'important' people of the Central Congo in that their works of sculpture were famous throughout the ethnographic museums of the world. An early anthropologist E. Torday had written a substantial monograph about them which described their dazzling material culture and arts and gave tantalizing hints about a complex centralized political structure. It also gave a list of 122 kings and thought the first of these to have ruled around 500 A. D. (Torday and Joyce 1910:37). This had intrigued me and I proposed in a general fashion to find out more about this. So far there was little connexion in my mind with a study of some latin oral traditions in Medieval Times which had been the major topic of my M. A. thesis. In fact the general program at my arrival was rather vague. I had read all available materials on the Kuba in Europe and summarised them (Vansina 1954). I simply wanted to add to our knowledge about them by investigating the socio-political and religious structures in the British style. The only concrete specification of the project then was its duration set at two years.

Eager I might be, but as it happened the fieldwork immediately bogged down for three months. I could not even get away from the railway station because I had no supplies, no funds and no letters of introduction for the authorities. Under the circumstances all that could be done was to read some of the archives in the district office and to walk to a nearby Kuba village to see its outlay and pick up words in a monolingual situation. It would take a whole morning work to gather the meaning of a dozen words and two or three sentences. After a week or so I found a young man who knew French and could help me in learning the language. But most of the time I had to wait for equipment. Finally it was necessary to leave for a research station 500 miles East and drive back all the way with the proper supplies. After that cardinal rule number one for fieldwork was well established: to be certain that proper introductions had been made and equipment gathered before one left for the field. The three lost months compare with the single week used ten years later on a trip to the Tio, North of Brazzaville and one where I had arrived by plane.

By April 2 I was back and able to settle on an isolated spot a hundred yards or so from a tiny village and a few miles from the capital. First I worked on the Kuba language all day long, following the outline for fieldworkers proposed by A. E. Meeussen (1946/48). I believed, and still do, that it was necessary to know the language of a people before one could really study their culture and knowing a language meant to be able to speak and understand it fluently, even if not perfectly. Later on I was to find out that for work on oral traditions this is even more a stringent requirement than for fieldwork in cultural anthropology. I also had laid out for myself an outline in anthropology. The principle was to cover the whole spectrum of the culture from gathering to value systems in a week or two and then follow the areas which seemed to be more interesting for study. The technique was later improved and used in all subsequent fieldwork. By the time I worked with the Tio the whole survey could be made in a week. The rationale was that one cannot know beforehand what is really the most intriguiging and novel part about a previously unanalyzed society and that it is therefore useless and even dangerous to arrive with a 'well-defined problem'. The latter procedure carries with it the danger of severe distortion of the reality since the investigator will focus on 'his' problem even if it is of minor importance in the culture.

In all of this early study little attention was paid to history even though a list of kings was collected from the interpreter on April 11 and again an improved one on April 13. It seems the young man had an uncle who supplied him with information. So we started going to the capital and ask the questions of the uncle himself. He turned out to be, and this was sheer luck, one of the most knowledgeable men in the capital. He could boast as he did that 'he carried all his newspapers in his head'. By April 22 he had been interviewed and so had the king and it became evident that something was fundamentally amiss with the Torday list of kings. However this did not arouse me much at the time. I simply proposed to look into it afterwards. By April 29 I discovered from Mbop Louis, the uncle, that clans had their histories just as the kingdom had, but it did not seem a very exciting discovery at the time. It was only gradually that it became clear to me that all social groups had their own oral histories with specific functions.

Then five weeks after my second arrival, on May 8 it happened. We were sitting drowsy in the hot afternoon sun, drawing figures in the sand and talking when Mbop Louis suddenly exclaimed in answer to a question:

> If I quarrel with the Kongo
> if I fight with the Mbuun
> I will not accept their cowries
> I will not eat their salt'.

It tumbled out in one jumble of words and I spent an hour or so getting the four lines down with precision. They explained to me that this was a *shoosh* poem and some of them, like this one were repositories of history. It hit me because I suddenly recognized that this was an historical text in form as well as in content and that where one has texts, one can apply canons of historical investigation. I began to compare with medieval situations, worrying about *stemma codicum*, external and internal critique etc. About half of my research time after this went into collecting *shoosh* and probing these general questions until Mbop Louis ran out of ammunition.

A week after this event it had become clear that one should collect not only the traditions of kingship but those of clanship, those of the villages and those of the chiefdoms. This came quite naturally because there were *shoosh* about all those things. At the same time I began with a little better knowledge of the language to see more and more people and by the first of July versions concerning the history of the kingdom had been collected from more than a score of elders. One other principle of fieldwork became clear: to avoid, after the initial period to build all one's observations around a few informants but to roam widely since so many differences, not only in the historical accounts, not only in the characters and appreciation of their own culture but also in the rendering of cultural norms and case studies became visible. As for the historian, the problem of variants and the reasons for variants was beginning to emerge as a major one. If one had all the variants and could explain them, it would then be possible to say which one was correct if any.

The next major break through came in July shortly after I had been able to move to the capital itself. A linguist (and others) had joined me for two weeks or so and he wanted to tape a tradition. In those days operating a taperecorder was still an Herculean task, since it needed its own powerunit and a very long line to prevent the humming of the motor to drown the text. But it was a novelty too and the king promised to tell us the tradition when he would be prepared. It had to wait a few days and then one morning we were asked to come to the royal compound where the main plaza was crammed with elders and the king was holding state. He then delivered a long speech in a formalized form and a powerful effect, describing the story of the migrations and enumerating the names of the different kings with their capitals and the *shoosh* of their capitals (Jacobs and Vansina 1956). A full translation and annotation of the text took us almost 3 weeks. It established once and for all that Torday's much longer list seemed to be wrong and it showed to all that I was collecting traditions with the approval of the king, so that it was proper for his dignitaries to tell what they knew as well. I had not realized it fully before but traditions belong to social groups and are their property. Traditions of royalty belonged to the king and could not be told without his permission. Now we had it and we also had a skeleton to start working from since the exegesis of the text covered the whole of Kuba history. In addition to the historical data a mass of valuable anthropological and linguistic material emerged as well. The whole episode shows what luck can do, rather like the one where I was told my first *shoosh*. It taught me that it pays sometimes to arrive with a spectacular device or action, if the circumstances are right.

The very same month though a major mistake was made. We had gone to look at the site of the primordial dispersion of the Kuba in this territory and found nothing but a marsh. On coming back over the plains though, we were told by villagers that there was some ancient pottery strewn about in the general area. The mistake was not to go into this, collect sherds, teach the people to report further finds and try to locate some sites. As a result of this neglect no iron age sites have come to light in this whole area. Later experience in Rwanda Burundi and among the Tio showed conclusively that when this kind of interest is expressed, people do report finds of pottery or slag and many sites can be discovered. In 1963-1964 a dozen minor sites were thus found in a few weeks time on the Tio plateau where it had been assumed before that no site existed.

In August further work developed naturally from the leads of July. Dynastic traditions, village history, clan history and clansection history were all pursued and brought our work into the analysis of villages close to the capital. One spectacular episode was the investigation of *muyum*. Muyum was the national medicine man. He had his own miniature court and lived some 15 miles out of the capital. He was said to keep the skull of one of the old kings and use it in the intronisation ritual of new kings. On arriving there we asked to see this object and brought him a gift, consisting of a raincoat which could be packaged in a mass not bigger than a cigarette box. He rather liked this but told us he could not do anything now, but advised me to meet him at midnight in the forest at an unknown point I would reach by following a certain path. So my African helper and I set out with a flickering lamp into the inkdark of a tropical forest at night. We walked for an hour before being stopped by two shadows: the *muyum* and his helper. They helped us off the path in a cleared space around a miniature hut. We sat down and immediately some people built a high wall around us with matting, enclosing us on all sides. Then the aid began to talk: 'Lashyaang, forgive us for intruding; but we have good reason . . . etc'. I couldn't make out to whom he was talking until I suddenly realized he was talking to the hut and its contents. Very vividly I learned that night that some traditions are more than dead memories; they are memories relived. He spoke thus to all the kings and then took the charm out of the hut. The skull was wrapped in pieces of cloth, one taken from the skirt of every king who had died since Lashyaang. Unfortunately I couldn't count them, under the circumstances. There were also other objects. I noticed a wooden bowl which was said to be very old and was decorated in a fashion recalling Kuba work but still different and then there was an amazing paddle. On it were inscribed the eighteen different tattoos of the different Kuba peoples and it symbolized the Kuba commonwealth. It was astonishing for it revealed a power of using symbols to synthetize ideologies and facts. This then, my most romantic experience did not teach me many new facts but it was very important for the fieldwork because of the impression it made on me. It increased my respect for the Kuba and taught me the living force of Malinowski's 'mythical charters'.

Part of the same month was spent preparing for a systematic approach to the collection of historical data, connected with villages and clans. After investigation of several villages near the capital, I thought it worthwhile to take down all the traditions of all the villages, clans and clansections. No sample would do and the job was possible because the data required were not very difficult to obtain. It was then decided to hire seven young men for short periods to collect the data. They were first trained during a few days in the art of recording in their own language, it was explained what was wanted and they set out with a very simple questionnaire. In every village they had to ask village history (successive locations, stories of war and others about the village in the past) from the village council, to list the clansections present and jot down for everyone of them: name, taboo, praisename, point of believed origin, ancestors, other sections of the same clan known to the questioned one. The only point which was to cause some difficulty was the divergent practice of different recorders in deciding what a clansection was. Some of them collected data not only on groups who were structurally clansections but even on isolated individuals of other clans. Some crosschecking resolved most of these problems though and the data were used to establish a chart for the movement of every one of the 450 Kuba clans, to show the relation between demographic movement and political stability as well as to illustrate the process of gradual and continual infiltration of foreign culture elements by the spread of foreign clansections (Vansina 1963). Apart from their historical uses the same data were of value to analyze village structures and size of population. In 1956 part of the sample was done over again and showed small changes with the 1953 results.

Towards the end of August all this was under way, the pilot runs on villages around the capital and in the South were completed and the young men had gone out. One category of sources was left which I had not started to investigate: the traditions of the chiefdoms. So I moved to the chiefdoms of the Bulaang. Arriving at the residence of the first chief I was told to wait for the council of the chiefdom to assemble. The next morning twenty or more notables assembled with the chief and myself in a fairly narrow room to start off. The session turned very soon in a free for all discussion where everybody lost control and all fourty participants gesticulated, shouted, were angry, sorry, ashamed, indignant, pressing genealogical claims and counterclaims all in the one room from sunrise to near sunset, when everybody was exhausted and the reunion broke up. It was a magnificent display of oratory temper and showed me graphically what the present impact of traditions was. In this case all the arguments had dealt with the question to know which section of the ruling clan really had the right to rule this chiefdom and the answer was to be given by historical arguments. A patient reworking of these data with individual participants of this meeting led to the conclusion that it was probably impossible to reconstruct a proper genealogy of chiefs and that no one knew the 'truth'. These men had inherited their conflicting versions from their uncles and grandfathers already and could not know anymore who of their ancestors, when and how had started to deceive! Since the whole matter fortunately revolved only about the genealogy and succession of actual chiefs it was possible though to record Bulaang tradition on many other points.

In the second Bulaang chiefdom the procedure was the same and indeed it would be in all the chiefdoms: the chief spoke in front of his council but in a spot isolated from the general public. Here what happened was that chief Nyimiloong was a very old and wise man, a highly original thinker so that his version of History – and he knew all sorts of Kuba history which he told us freely – was greatly divergent from all the others. He subscribed to the *panta rei* philosophy. 'Everything flows, there is no absolute truth and items which began as lies will become truth in time, for truth is in the believer' was one of his favorite sayings.

Apart from the concrete results a major result of this trip was the realization that in collective statements only the greatest common denominator is given to the historian: that on which all informants present can agree. In fact many of the members of these caucuses know much more and it has always paid us to question members of such bodies separately after the collective reunion had met.

Back from this trip in September I could interview a number of chiefs of different ethnic groups within the Kuba kingdom at the capital where they had been called for judicial or political purposes of the court. Valuable notes were acquired from these sources but it became gradually clear that none of these chiefs would tell all they knew, first because they were not in their chiefdom, but on foreign (and sometimes hostile) ground and second because their councils were not present. So by November it was clear that to gather the history of the chiefdoms, the only way was to visit all of them. The matter could wait because I had statements by many of the chiefs, I had notes from the territorial archives containing histories and genealogies including *procès verbaux* of collective statements for many chiefdoms.

Also research on Kuba culture was progressing and in October and November this took nearly all the time available, and took me away from the capital. By the end of November I was back and busy trying to find out how Torday had ever come to the chronology he had proposed and a list of 122 kings instead of 26. One day an old notable of the capital ushered an old man in on the veranda and said: 'This is Torday's informant'. As it turned out he was. With him and one of the best experts in the capital about dynastic tradition we then went page by page over the Torday book and he tried to explain what had happened. It appeared that they had not understood each other too well because neither one really knew a language known by the other. Then Torday had promised a reward for additional information and his interpreter-*cum*-informant apparently added much so that it grew into an Eldorado of 121 names. The whole does show the dangers of relying on one informant, on not knowing the language, on bribing one's way into information. Fortunately it must be said that apart from this caper Torday's informant had been fairly reliable so that most of the book was valid enough.

Toward November 1953 the fieldwork was interrupted by a conference with fellow researchers (anthropologists and linguists) in Rwanda and a preliminary write up of the materials took all of December. Periodic breaks are an advantage to fieldwork in that one can stand back from the data and see the forest not the trees. Also the data can be submitted to the criticism of professional colleagues, the research design can be re-examined, gaps in the material discovered and a further spell of work prepared. Later experience confirmed all of this and we would advocate very strongly meetings of colleagues or breaks in the fieldwork at intervals of about 6 months during fieldwork periods.

In 1954 we spent a total of only five months in Kuba country and collected mostly quantitative material and case studies in order to understand the culture more in depth. A very useful tool proved to be the logbook kept by a helper whose duty it was to record daily the gossip in the capital. Part of the time was lost because of ill-health induced by malaria and malnutrition. That is where I learned that food and care are really part of the fieldwork equation and should never be neglected.

It was not before April 1956 that actual work in the Kuba area could once more be resumed. In the meantime though I had worked hard at the theoretical implications of the data, I had been able to put the historical materials together in a first draft and had collected more by staying in correspondence with the Kuba. In addition my knowledge of the language was much better, because I had been reading very many texts. The planning for 1956 involved mostly a visit to all the major chiefs in their residences. Most of them I had seen in 1953 or 1954 and they knew about me. This time good transport was available with a chauffeur so I could really concentrate on fieldwork. The work went ahead at great speed and with greater ease than before. I knew what was to be expected, I knew the etiquette, I understood what was said and could ask questions without great delay. The people knew who I was, what I did, what I represented. By July the work had been done at least in its essentials, without a major hitch. It showed the real advantage of planning once the basic situation is known.

Of course, when the research was interrupted every conceivable lead had not been worked out to the fullest extent. More ought to be done with the cultural regional diversity, more data on lists of chiefs and variants therein would strengthen chronological conclusions, archaeological soundings would be very useful etc. But still the data gathered formed a whole and could be presented as such.

The basic technique used during this fieldtrip, albeit unconsciously was an approach where a first examination of culture enabled the discovery of leads which were then worked out in a pilot area after which a sample or survey was planned and perfected by new experience. The work was concluded once the results of the survey were completed. The imponderable aspects of fieldwork really lay in the rapport one was able to strike with the culture involved, in the ability to see leads and above all in the ability to amend schemes when new experience showed flaws in the existing approach.

Further fieldtrips in Rwanda and Burundi from 1957 to 1960 and a six months' stay among the Tio in 1963-1964 essentially followed the same lines[1]. The experience gained from these trips as well as experience learned from the work of others can best be integrated in a number of general conclusions.

First the fieldstay should be as long as possible, though interrupted by periodic halts during which the fieldworker should go over the acquired data and if possible assess them with scholars not personally involved. Even after the stay it is important to remain in contact with the people, not only to be able to ask subsidiary questions by mail or to remain in the 'mood' but also to acquire a sense of the changes which are taking place in the culture and maybe in its traditions and to be open for values and features which might have been completely missed during the stay.

[1] We are endebted to the Instituut voor Wetenschappelijk Onderzoek in Centraal Afrika for the research among the Kuba, Rwanda and Rundi and to the Social Science Research Council, the Ford Foundation and the University of Wisconsin for the fieldtrip to the Tio.

The preparation for the trip should be thorough and a personal study of the culture is necessary even if it is described very well in the literature. A sense for a culture comes really only from personal experience and without a sense for this no historian can write about the history of a culture. Linguistic training can sometimes be acquired beforehand, but it should be used to the fullest extent. The exegesis of traditions can be very complex and require more from the historian in the way of a practical knowledge of the language than from the general anthropologist and sometimes even than from the structural linguist. In order to absorb both culture and language and in order to establish some rapport with the people it is absolutely necessary to live among them during the fieldperiod, if possible in the same sort of dwelling, in the middle of the community rather than just outside of it and with a standard of living coming as closely as health and efficiency will permit to the local one. Failure to observe these rules always leads to weakness in the results and sometimes to disaster. One of our own projects had to be abandoned after most of the recording was done because we did not have the linguistic knowledge required to study the data and the person on whom we had relied was prevented to do it. Working a pilot area should be done leisurely and every item should be checked and crosschecked. Participant observation is possible here and should supplement questioning and listening. The pilot is the key to the whole, in that it reveals which traditions can be expected to exist, how they are tied to the culture, what sorts of survey have to be made before a sample can be drawn up, if a sample is necessary rather than a complete recording by hand or on tape of all the the traditions.

Once this stage is finished the survey can be made. Very often its size is formidable and help is required. Now participants in the culture can be trained in a short time to collect data and in many countries high school boys are very useful for this purpose, because they have the literacy, the time during their vacations, and very often they understand what it is all about and find satisfaction in the job. However if a questionnaire is used it should be very simple. If need be several questionnaires can be drawn up for different situations. The questionnaire should be open ended and more of a memo or checklist of things to do than of a form. E.g. one we used in Rwanda would state: 'ask the name, lineagename of a person, inquire in his local reputation as a storyteller, ask the titles of the stories he knows, let him tell the stories, ask for any commentary on parts you do not understand'. It is our belief that if the oral data for history extant in Africa and Asia primarily are going to be collected in this generation it can only be done by amateur societies of persons belonging to the cultures or nations involved and that they can do it after minimal training, and then at a much higher speed and with greater accuracy than we can because language and culture are known to them since their infancy.

A further major element in fieldwork is the building of a sample or more generally the research design which takes shape after a few months of residence. This always exists even if no surveys or samples are being planned and it often is partly unconscious. It must constantly be recalled and compared with the data acquired to see if it fits or not. The more flexible the design and the more adapted to the experience from the fieldsituation the better the results will be. On the other hand just going by hunches or leads, which is hugging field-experience as closely as can be done will not be enough for these indicate that the researcher may have gone by some of the important materials available without ever wondering if these existed or not.

A systematic approach is necessary in addition to sheer intuition.

The scholar should also remember that oral traditions are often living things which may harm or profit and he should honor the confidence of people and respect their reluctance. The latter is especially difficult to do but it is unwise to try to force information. The cause of the reluctance should be understood before any attempt at reasoning with the reluctant informant is undertaken and bribing in a case like this should never be done. The temptation is too strong to take the bribe and tell something inaccurate to placate the scholarly Nemesis! Ultimately it is only through gaining the confidence the under-standing and the respect of people that a good job can be completed.

Then one should also keep in mind that every situation is different, that no matter how much fieldwork one has done every new trip adds to one's ex-perience and that one must remain open all the time for new experiences. The dogmatic person is just as much of a pest as the inspired one, and the essential quality here is the awareness that seemingly non educated people are apt to be right when they differ of opinion with the foreign investigator and indeed that every child in a given culture knows more about it than the most learned and highly trained anthropologist or historian from the outside. The advise of people, their opinions, their discussions are always extremely valuable.

So far we have dealt primarily with the historian whose concern is the collection of oral traditions. But this is only a part of his interests. More and more historians will be concerned with archaeological sites and with the gathering of cultural data for the purpose of diffusion and invention studies. For them the techniques to be used are those of the anthropologist. But they must often be concerned with minutiae and weigh off delicate balances of functional pull and traditional drag. Therefore they must rely on even more thorough contact with cultures, a constant appraisal of what they are looking for and why, so as not to be lost in details.

The techniques for using cultural evidence as sources for history are as yet not fully developed and therefore fieldwork in this area will be more difficult. We suggest that in practice this sort of research be done in conjunction with collection of traditions and the search for archaeological sites, preferably at a later stage of the fieldtrip when it is possible to assess already the other data collected before.

History in the field is exciting. It is demanding in that it poses problems both of personal adaptation and of organisation in the research. Although it leads to the recovery of many data, requiring painstaking efforts to collect these, its results can often be expressed in a modest number of pages. But if the accumulation of knowledge is an ideal sound results will always be worth the effort.

references

J. JACOBS and J. VANSINA (1956) Nshoong atoot: het koninklijk epos der Bushong, *Kongo Overzee* 22: 1-39.

A. E. MEEUSSEN (1946, 1947, 1948) Hoe een inlandse taal te beschrijven, *Kongo Overzee* 12-13: 216-220; 282-286; 14: 37-41; 223-235.

E. TORDAY and T. A. JOYCE (1910) Notes ethnographiques sur les peuples communément appelés Bakuba, ainsi que sur les peuples apparenteés. Les Bushongo, Bruxelles.

J. VANSINA (1954) Les tribus Ba-Kuba et les peuplades apparentées, Tervuren.

J. VANSINA (1963) Geschiedenis van de Kuba, *Annalen Koninklijk Museum voor Midden Afrika, Wetenschappen van de Mens* no. 44, Tervuren: 215-252.

7

the restudy as a technique
for the examination of social change

G. K. GARBETT

In this chapter I consider the restudy as a technique for the examination of the processes of social change. Social change has become a central concern in modern social anthropology and a number of techniques have been applied to its study with varying degrees of success. For a number of reasons, which I elaborate, I consider the restudy to be the only way that the processes of social change can be studied satisfactorily. As I see it, we must begin to work towards obtaining a planned series of restudies for each society and attempt to avoid the rather haphazard way in which restudies have come about so far. Eventually we shall have for each society a number of restudies which will form a firm foundation upon which to build an adequate theory of social change. In this account I discuss the theoretical as well as the practical considerations involved in the restudy and make some assessment of it as a technique for the study of social change.

At the outset, I distinguish between the restudy and the replication study. The restudy involves the re-examination of a previously studied community after the lapse of a period of time. It may be carried out by the investigator who made the initial study, or by others, but the techniques and conceptual framework used may well be different from those used in the first study. In a replication study, on the other hand, all the circumstances of the first study are reproduced as exactly as possible even to any errors which the conceptual framework or the techniques may have contained. In the natural sciences there may be value in replication, but in the social sciences, because circumstances can never be exactly replicated, the technique seems of very little value, though it has been attempted.

Lewis (1954), in considering the possibility of establishing controls and experiments in anthropology, has discussed the restudy in some detail. He lists four types of restudy: the first, in which the purpose is the revaluation of an earlier study; the second, where the purpose is to assess 'cultural' change; the third, in which an aspect of a society not previously studied is examined; the fourth, where some aspect of a society previously studied is re-examined from a different point of view, or more intensively.

Lewis considers, as I do, that the second type – where the object is to assess cultural or social change – is the most important (Lewis 1954:468). The third and fourth types which he identifies, are met with fairly frequently now that the two or three year field expedition, broken by a period of preliminary analysis and reflection, is becoming the rule rather than the exception. The first type, in which attempts are made at revaluation is only successful, as Lewis and others have pointed out (Tax 1954), when the period of time between the two studies is very small and where the rate of social change is slow or where the restudy is carried out independently in the same area and at the same time by another anthropologist. If these conditions are not met the restudy is valueless as a means of establishing areas of bias and for checking errors since it becomes impossible to establish whether observed differences are due to errors in the first or second study, to conceptual differences, to social change, or to combinations of all three.

Before it became feasible to study a community for a second time anthropologists had examined the effects of the passage of time upon social structures by three methods (cf. Reader 1964). A brief consideration of these methods will help us more easily to assess the additional contribution which the restudy might make. I consider each method separately though they are not mutually exclusive and have often been used in conjunction.

In the first method, which Reader (1964:26) terms sociological history, the anthropologist uses his own field material as a base mark and then works back from this to examine what he considers to be earlier forms of the society he is studying by using whatever documentary sources are available. Barnes (1954) in his account of the Ngoni state did this, as also did Gluckman (1958) in examining the establishment of the Zulu nation.

Barnes traced the development of the Ngoni state over a period of 130 years. He begins his account with a brief description of the Ngoni and then traces the migration of the horde under Zwangendaba from South Africa to what are today Zambia and Malawi. He shows how the horde which formed the core of the state drew to itself bodies of people who had been overrun or captured. He then examines the effects of the defeat of the Ngoni by the Imperial powers and the establishment of the colonial administration up to the time when he made his own field study. Of the Ngoni state he writes (Barnes 1954:1). 'It is an enduring group with a history. The same forms of social organisation have endured despite changes in space and despite biological discontinuity; and where these forms have changed there has been continuity even in change'. For the purposes of his study he worked solely from historical documents for he found that 'it was impossible to tell whether similarity between an informant's account of a past event and a previously published version was due to common origin, independent invention, or good teaching in school' (Barnes 1954:4). Barnes's account, then, was more or less a straight political history. On the other hand, Gluckman's account of the Zulu state had somewhat different aims. Gluckman relied on oral traditions as well as documentary sources (Gluckman 1960:158). He writes, 'I used historical data, variously acquired, to reconstruct past equilibria. The purpose of these reconstructions . . . was to provide the same analyses as those we apply to data collected in the modern field . . .' (Gluckman 1958:50). In the absence of synchronic field studies made at crucial points in Zulu history, Gluckman attempted to reconstruct his own (v. also Reader 1964:26). He then examined the changes which occurred from one (reconstructed) equilibrium situation to the next to produce what is in effect a dual-synchronic (v. infra) study.

Given that the anthropologist *qua* historian will exercise the same care and critical judgement as a historian, the main difficulty arises in the historical study because he is at the mercy of his sources. Documents, particularly for earlier periods in what were pre-literate societies are often non-existent or scanty. Even when they exist in relative abundance as, for example, for the period of Portuguese occupation of southern Africa, or for the 19th Century colonial period, they frequently relate to administrative matters and, with few exceptions, are only helpful in giving the major outlines of gross changes and some indication of the rate of change. This applies also to oral traditions which may provide, if carefully collected and analysed, another source of historical evidence as Vansina (1965) has recently indicated. But oral traditions at best can give only a fragmentary view of past events because people tend to retain in their traditions only those aspects of their history which have contemporary relevance for them. In general, such traditions relate to political history rather than, say, to the development of religion or of kinship arrangements.

The second method which has been used to give time-depth to anthropological studies depends upon the use of oral evidence from eye witnesses of past events. One of the most effective uses of this type of evidence was made by Turner (1957) in his study of an Ndembu village. In what he terms 'an experiment in diachronic micro-sociology' he traces the vicissitudes of a village, from informants' accounts, through a period of some twenty years to show how 'the general and the particular, the cyclical and the exceptional, the regular and the irregular, the normal and the deviant are interrelated in a single social process' (Turner 1957:328). This 'extended-case method' as it has been termed (Gluckman 1961) is carried out in two stages. First, a systematic analysis of the structural principles which underlie the institution being studied is made based on data from a synchronic field study. Secondly, the institution is traced through time, using eye witness accounts, to show how the structural principles are affected by chance occurences such as death, illness, misfortune, personality factors, and so on. The 'extended-case method' is an extremely exciting technique and has presented us with a new mode of analysing social process but in its present form it has two drawbacks, both of which, as I suggest, can be corrected by the use of the restudy.

Firstly, the norms and values by which the extended case is interpreted and analysed are derived from the anthropologist's own synchronic study. This applies also, by and large, to the structural principles. The assumption is then made that the normative framework current at the time the synchronic study was made can be used to understand people's actions in a social situation which occurred, say, some twenty years ago. Obviously this assumption is fraught with difficulties, particularly when social change is rapid. However, this assumption need not be made if one has two studies, one at the beginning and one at the end of the period being considered. The position would be even more improved if there was a series of studies at appropriate intervals throughout the period considered. I return to this point later.

The second drawback with the extended-case method concerns the reliability of informants' memories of past events. There are two aspects of memory which need to be distinguished here, the psychological and the social. Bartlett (1932) and other psychologists have demonstrated how during recall, past events become distorted and how this can be related to some degree to a person's own psychological make-up. What I have termed the social memory can be related closely to structural principles and social processes. The way in which genealogies become telescoped and maintain a constant depth has received considerable attention (cf. Evans-Pritchard 1940:199 ff). Barnes (1947:52) draws attention to the ease with which those who do not attain importance in the social structure are forgotten. Turner (1957:98) writes of one episode he presents, which was constructed from informant's accounts recorded *only four years* after the events had occurred, that 'it is impossible to get any closer to the actual facts for the events are no longer susceptible to enquiry and the account has acquired a mythical character'. Turner explains that the account of these past events had become a 'mythological charter' giving social justification to the exclusion of a particular person from the succession to a village headmanship. Here we see that 'social amnesia' and the interpretation of a past event in terms of present values may be interrelated.

For the anthropologist the problem of recall is an important one. Not only is the actual reliability of recall important in itself if one is using the extended-case method but, as I have indicated, the areas where memory is vague or blurred may be related to social processes. What is remembered and how it is remembered as well as what is forgotten may illuminate significant social processes. The restudy may prove a valuable tool for investigating this aspect of memory. Mead (1956) and Harries-Jones (1963) in their restudies make some comments upon the reliability of recall. Mead writes that during her first study of Manus in 1928 she made no attempt to use oral evidence to 'reconstruct the past', for 'there was no way of checking whether it would be accurate or not' (Mead 1956:496). During her restudy in 1953 she specifically checked the ability of her informants to recall events she had witnessed herself in 1928. She also constructed a 'memory test' based on a series of photographs which she had taken in 1928. Mead remarks that the 'extremely high accuracy of recall was the principal point demonstrated' (p. 496). This encouraged her to explore the history of the period before her first study and she found that the early history of the village of Peri, in which she stayed during both studies, revealed a much greater degree of instability and mobility than she had originally supposed. However, there were areas of recall which were blurred. These seem to be related to periods of intense social disturbance. Thus, Manus were able to recall easily the pre-Christian period and the events which followed the disturbances created by a millenarian movement, but their recall of the early period of Christianization and the turbulent events which surrounded the millenarian movement itself were blurred (p. 220).

Harries-Jones, who restudied the Bemba village of Kasaka twenty-eight years after it had been studied by Richards, writes that the accuracy of Bemba memories 'extended not only from the intervening years between Richards's visit and our own, but at least ten years before the study was made . . .' (Harries-Jones 1963:61). However, he comments that for the problems he was examining – the causes and processes of Bemba village fission – the crucial data were lacking (p. 7, 10) so that he was unable to either prove or disprove an argument which Richards's had advanced about the causes of fission based on her earlier synchronic study. Here again, it would appear that memories of a significant period of social disturbance had become blurred. Further restudies might explore this whole problem further and give us some insights into the social value of forgetting and its relationship to social process.

The final technique I wish to consider has underlain a great deal of modern social anthropology though rarely has its use been made explicit. In this technique an abstract structural time is used. For example, let us suppose that an anthropologist is undertaking a synchronic study of a society and that he has become interested in village structure. He will no doubt record villages of various sizes. He may find on further investigation that there is some direct relationship between genealogical depth and complexity of kinship ties within a village and its size. Some villages he will examine may exhibit conflicts among their members. In some cases certain members of such a village may say that they are about to leave their old village because of the conflicts. The anthropologist may witness their departure and the events surrounding it, and observe the establishment of a new village. Now, by assuming that certain villages are at the beginning and others at the end of a developmental cycle, whilst the remainder represent various intermediary forms, and by assuming that similar structural principles are operating in all villages, the anthropologist can piece together logically the different forms and create a model, set in an abstract structural time, of the developmental cycle of the village. Such a model will enable him to examine the way in which various structural principles work themselves out through time. It is in this way that accounts have been produced of, for example, the segmentation of lineages, political cycles and the developmental cycles of families. These have been obtained, by and large, from synchronic studies with little or no recourse to the past history of the societies being studied.

The use of this technique has been particularly illuminating and has made a significant contribution to the theoretical development of social anthropology but, in some circumstances, it has decided weaknesses. Firstly, it is difficult with material derived from a synchronic study to separate what is accidental and non-repetitive in a social system from what is regular and repetitive. Secondly, the method is inappropriate for societies experiencing rapid social change since developmental cycles, of whatever kind, may themselves be undergoing change. Thus, to cast what appear to be aspects of the same social form into a developmental cycle may be to put together into one cycle, forms which in fact belong to several different cycles. It is in the case of such societies which are undergoing rapid change, that the restudy can make what is perhaps its most significant contribution. It enables what is accidental and haphazard to be more easily separated from what is cyclical and repetitive and, what is more important, it enables developmental cycles presented in abstract structural time, derived from an initial synchronic study, to be reexamined in historical time. What appeared to be a chance, deviant form in the first study may appear, after the passage of time, as part of a new cycle. Conversely, a social form which appeared to be a new feature in the first study may turn out to be a chance deviant in a regular cycle. I illustrate this point further from three restudies of societies which have experienced rapid social change at various periods.

Redfield (1957) first studied the Maya Indian village of Chan Kom in 1931. He made a restudy of the village in 1948, seventeen years later. For a number of political economic and social reasons which Redfield relates, the villagers of Chan Kom in 1931 firmly intended to set their faces against their old way of life. They had a passion for education, for introducing new forms of relationship between men and women, for scepticism, for new buildings, for new forms of agriculture and for the development of communications. The leaders of this 'new' movement were young and vigorous; they appeared to want to revolutionize the traditional way of life and to espouse many of the ways of their sophisticated urban neighbours. At about the same time as this movement began to develop its leaders were influenced also by evangelists and, except for a very small faction, were converted from Catholicism to Protestantism. A year after Redfield had left the field, in 1932, almost all the community had been converted to the new faith. The adoption of Protestantism appeared to coincide 'with the period of greatest enthusiasm for change in Chan Kom' (Redfield 1957:113). To Redfield, and no doubt to many of the villagers, it appeared that Chan Kom was on the threshold of a radically different way of life. However, when Redfield returned to Chan Kom in 1948, the Catholic faith had been reestablished and the pressures for radical change were spent. The leaders, bold and vigorous in their youth, had become, in their old age, with few exceptions, traditionalist and conservative. 'To one who returns to the community in 1948, the conservative temper of the people is apparent. No radical change in viewpoint has occurred. The bold and critical talk of 1930 is now not heard. Today the visitor listens to leaders who speak with satisfaction of the old religion, and who deplore the more extreme changes in costume and custom. The radicalism that prevailed seventeen years ago is forgotten or ignored' (p. 114). Thus, the pattern of behaviour which had existed prior to the radical movement of the early thirties was, in large measure, reestablished. What had appeared to the anthropologist at the time as a movement heralding radical and far-reaching changes seems, after the interval of seventeen years, to have been a temporary aberration in a cyclical pattern involving the rebelliousness of youth and the conservatism of old age which soon reasserted itself. Even in the field of material culture, Redfield writes, 'much more is unchanged than changed' (p. 44). There were indeed some important changes in Chan Kom but the restudy revealed the resilience of the 'old' social system in the face of change – a resilience that was under-estimated very considerably during the first study.

Mead's restudy of Manus (Mead 1956) presents a contrary example: rapid social change where only slow and gradual change was expected and predicted. The astonishment of Mead at the extent of the changes which had occurred between 1928 and 1953 in the Manus village of Peri provides a salutary lesson to all anthropologists on the dangers of prediction from a single synchronic study. The Manus 'a mere two thousand nearly naked savages, living in pile dwellings in the sea, their ear lobes weighed down with shells, their hands still ready to use spears, their anger implemented with magical curses, their morality dependent upon the ghosts of the recently dead', had become, in the short space of twenty-five years, 'potential members of the modern world, with ideas of boundaries, in time and space, responsibility to God, enthusiasm for law, and committed to trying to build a democratic community, educate their children, police and landscape their village [now built on land], care for the old and sick, and erase age-old hostilities between neighbouring tribes' (p. 21).

Mead could not have anticipated the events of the Second World War, during which the Manus and neighbouring peoples came into contact with some one million American soldiers who passed through bases on the Admiralty Islands. Nevertheless, Mead feels that the far-reaching changes which occurred cannot be explained solely in terms of this traumatic experience. 'The occupation' was a necessary condition of change but not a sufficient condition. Other peoples have experienced similar periods of intensive contact, and for longer periods. Why was it that Manus reacted in the way that they did and much more vigorously than some of their near neighbours? Mead asks herself what aspects of Manus culture she misunderstood or ignored during her first study which might have enabled her to predict the possible responses of Manus to rapid and intense change? Thus, a historical accident provided an experimental situation which enabled Mead, because she had two studies on which to base her analysis, to advance our understanding of why some peoples are able to respond to change whilst others are less able. As she herself writes, 'without the record of 25 years ago, this . . . would be a shallow record of a people who appeared interested in modernization or, less christianly interpreted, of a people who had been upset by contact with World War II armies . . .' (p. 11). Harries-Jones's restudy of Kasaka (Harries-Jones 1963) illustrates another and related point: how a prediction based on a synchronic study may underestimate the time needed for structural processes to work themselves out. Richards, from her observations, had assumed that the fission of Kasaka village would be complete in only a few months. In fact, as was revealed by Harries-Jones's restudy, the process took seven years and, furthermore, did not follow the regular pattern which Richards had supposed that it would. As Harries-Jones himself states (p. 56) the essentially diachronic emphasis of his analysis 'avoided the confusion of imposing a synchronic model on a constantly fluctuating situation and shows the importance of taking into account the whole life history of a village rather than deducing principles from only one part of the cycle'.

These examples illustrate how the restudy can contribute more fully to our understanding of the processes of change and, as I have indicated, enable us to separate out in the social process what is haphazard and accidental from what is regular and repetitive. In addition, the restudy may give us some indication of the time required for structural processes to work themselves out from one society to another.

The restudy then, can be considered as an additional technique to be added to the three which I have outlined but, to be successful, it must be used in conjunction with them. Historical and oral evidence, as well as the analytic use of structural time are still important for the successful restudy. What we have to aim for is the diachronic study as opposed to what Firth (1954:14; 1959:22) has termed the 'dual-synchronic' study.

In the 'dual-synchronic' study a society is examined at two points in time. The differences between the two points are charted but no attempt is made to trace through from the first point to the second the social processes by which the changes were produced. My own restudy (Garbett 1960) of five villages in a Shona Ward was largely dual-synchronic. I gathered the quantitative data relating to formal village structure similar to that which Bernardi (1950) had collected ten years previously and then drew attention to the differences between the two sets of data. Firth also writes of his highly detailed restudy of Tikopia, that 'it is a dual-synchronic, not a strictly diachronic study' (Firth 1959:2) although he explains that from oral evidence a great deal of the interim sequence of events could be recovered. Firth in fact states that he feels that the dual-synchronic study is all that most social anthropologists can manage.

The question is raised therefore, as to what actually constitutes a diachronic record. Presumably by a 'complete diachronic record' Firth (1959) has in mind a complete account of the processes of change over a period of time based on observational data and documentary sources. Accepting that no complete description of a society is possible then the diachronic study in this sense becomes something of a chimera. It is not possible for anthropologists, historians or anyone else to achieve such an objective but this does not mean that a diachronic study in a more limited sense is impossible.

For the anthropologist a diachronic study is not simply a historical study. Bohannan (1953) in his review of Barnes' *Marriage in a Changing Society* discusses the necessity of separating history from social process when making a dia- chronic study. History appears as a logical sequence of events, each event arising from its predecessors. But in the diachronic study, as I see it, we are not seeking only to establish a sequence of events. This is but one part of the exercise and, given the data, may be fairly easily accomplished. What we are trying to ascertain is how people come to choose between a number of alter- native courses of action determined by a particular institutional framework and how the institutional framework itself is altered when these alternative courses of action no longer suffice to meet new situations (cf. Firth 1954:4). This, in fact, constitutes the social process.

'The extended-case method', as I have indicated, has already been used with some success to examine problems of social process. As I pointed out its weaknesses can be corrected by the use of the restudy technique. If, now, instead of trying to plot every type of change and so obtain some kind of 'complete' diachronic record, we were to use the extended-case method in conjunction with a restudy to trace through time the vicissitudes of a particular institution as, for example, Turner did for an Ndembu village, then, with this more limited objective, a diachronic study is possible. Used in this way the restudy technique would become a very powerful one for the study of the processes of social change.

To achieve this objective, heavy reliance would have to be placed upon eye-witness accounts. Firth, I consider, underestimates the value of eye-witness accounts, carefully collected and critically analysed. In his own restudy Firth does make some attempt to trace through processes of change as, for example, when he discusses the changes which have occurred in the Tikopia political system (Firth 1959:279 ff). Mead (1956) and Harries-Jones (1963) all use eye-witness accounts in their restudies to trace out how certain factors changed through time. Of course, wherever this type of evidence can be supported by documentary evidence, even if this is only fragmentary, the result is obviously enhanced, bearing in mind the fallibility and partiality of memory which I considered earlier. Lewis (1951) made effective use of documentary material as well as eye-witness accounts and observational data in his restudy of Tepotzlán. He succeeded in tracing significant patterns of change not only for the period between Redfield's original study of 1926 and his own of 1943, but also for the prior period which had its roots in the Mexican revolution.

If we allow that the restudy can make an effective contribution to our understanding of social change we must, I think, move away from the rather haphazard ways in which restudies have come about in the past and begin to plan for them. This involves a number of problems as to the kind of data to be collected, the period of time which should elapse between one study and the next, the conceptual framework and, finally, whether or not the same person should undertake both studies.

Since the original study provides the foundation for the restudy it is important that it should be as thorough as possible and contain quantitative as well as qualitative data. If we are to study social process diachronically small changes which may be significant can only be shown by quantitative data. Colson (1954:48) writes 'Even where a single anthropologist makes a return visit to a society which he studied ten to twenty years ago, he cannot be certain that the implicit standard against which his qualitative description was made have remained the same. The anthropologist who follows another into the same field has even more of a problem unless his predecessor has made his yardstick explicit' and, she continues, 'some method of measuring trends must be developed, and I suspect that for this, quantitative information is again necessary'. Some early studies suffered because they relied too much upon impressionistic, qualitative judgements and upon statements that such and such a phenomenon was 'rare' or 'frequent', without providing quantitative data to support these statements.

Lewis (1951), in his restudy of Tepotzlán, faced considerable difficulties because Redfield's original study was written largely without any quantification and was impressionistic in its approach. For example, when discussing land ownership in Tepotzlán, Redfield conveyed the impression that each family had its own land. Lewis subsequently found, in 1944, that only 64% of families owned land and he argues that here was no reason to suppose that the position was significantly different in 1926 (Lewis 1951:125). Lewis himself considers that one of the major positive functions of quantification is to provide a solid basis for future restudies (Lewis 1954:467).

Firth (1954:11) shows the usefulness of quantitative data in revealing what he terms 'latent structure' (cf. also Fortes 1949:83). By latent structure Firth refers to regularities within a society which cannot be inferred from any rules or norms stated by people themselves. For example, Firth shows that the proportion of clans among the Tikopia has remained constant over a period of some forty years. This fact could only be ascertained by quantitative data since the Tikopia have no rules of preferred marriage nor do they make overt statements about the situation. Similarly, in my restudy of a Shona Ward, I showed (Garbett 1960:30) that though the formal structure of villages had remained remarkably constant over a ten year period, the latent structure and economic organization of the villages had changed considerably because of the increase in the number of married men away at work in the towns.

What we must work towards, I think, is the development of a series of indices which will enable us to assess the rate of change in different sectors of society. Firth, for example, constructs from his two sets of data, what he terms 'Indices of Identity and Partial Change' which together give an 'Index of Continuity' –

'that is the degree to which a house as a social locus persisted over a generation' (Firth 1959:191). Mitchell (1954; 1963) has also developed a series of indices for examining the processes of urbanization in Zambian towns. One of these indices, for example, 'The Index of Commitment to Urban Residence' aimed at providing some measure of the stability of the African population in the Copperbelt towns of Zambia. The index was derived from seven factors: the proportion of time spent in town during adulthood; the period of continuous residence in town; presence or absence of wife; occupation; level of education; attitude to town life; wage level (Mitchell 1963:7). This index was a much more sophisticated measure than the 'Index of Stabilisation' which Mitchell (1954:15) had computed in an earlier study which was simply the number of years spent in town since age fifteen against the number of years over age fifteen expressed as a proportion. Already some of the towns covered by Mitchell's Copperbelt Survey of 1951-54 are being restudied and such indices as these will prove invaluable as indicators of change. It is also possible, as Durkheim (1933:64) pointed out long ago, to develop indices to measure indirectly social phenomena which at first sight appear to be capable of only qualitative evaluation. In addition, the development of indices of this type would reduce considerably the element of subjective judgement which is always a component of qualitative evaluations (cf. Firth 1959:25).

In considering the period of time which is allowed to elapse between one study and the next there are a number of considerations. In an earlier account (Garbett 1960:31) I suggested that a period of ten to fifteen years would appear to be the maximum amount of time which should elapse between one study and the next. I suggested this because I was concerned about the problem of failing memories and how this might affect one's ability to trace through the intricate processes of change from one period to the next and thus prevent the production of a diachronic account. If the time interval is too large many of the informants used during the first study will be dead and the memories of others begin to fail. Lewis (1954: 467) makes much the same point. Thus, one would not be able to apply the tests of memory which I suggested earlier, nor fill in the intervening time interval satisfactorily. Harries-Jones (1963:61) criticised my suggestion because, from his own experience, he found it possible to produce a diachronic account even though the time interval was twice that which I suggested. Indeed, most of the restudies to which I have referred, were based on time intervals considerably longer than that which I proposed. However, the point at issue seems to me to be not what is possible, but what is optimal. I also suggested that in many cases ten to fifteen years might be too long a time interval – particularly for societies where the rate of change is rapid. I would add now that we must also consider the different structural times which various social processes may have. For example, significant changes might occur in social networks in towns over only a few months, in family cycles over perhaps a generation and in political cycles possibly over fifty years or more. I would suggest, therefore, that if we are to plan for restudies we ought to take into account such factors as the rate of change, the fallibility of memory, the availability of documentary material, and the structural time of the social processes in which we are interested. The ultimate aim should be to produce not only one restudy of a society but a considerable number, spaced out at intervals of time, each diachronic in character and all contributing to our knowledge of social processes in that society.

Finally, if restudies are to be planned, is it necessary to have the same person carry out all the studies? Mead considers that it is better for the same investigator to carry out the studies otherwise 'the new field worker luxuriates in commenting on his predecessors deficiencies' and so is distracted from assessing improvements in technique and theory (Mead 1956:481). This view has some support from Lewis (1954:467) particularly 'if', he writes, 'the investigator is sufficiently aware of the problem of methodology to make explicit the changes in his outlooks between the two studies'. However, there are often considerable practical difficulties which prevent a person from finding the time to undertake a restudy of a society which he originally studies. It seems to me that it does not matter unduly if another person carries out the restudy provided that his conceptual framework is not vastly different from that of the original investigator. It would have been most difficult, for example, for Mead's study of Manus to have been replicated by someone trained, say, in the British 'structural school' because his interests would lie in quite different directions. On the other hand, Spillius was able to continue Firth's restudy of Tikopia within much the same frame of reference (Firth 1959:23, 24). Lewis's conceptual framework was somewhat different from that of Redfield's and he was much opposed to Redfield's concepts of 'folk-culture' and 'the folk-urban continuum' (Lewis 1951:432ff; 1954: 468). However, Lewis was able to some extent to replicate Redfield's study though, because of its deficiencies, he had to present a great deal of new material (Lewis 1951: xi).

In assessing the contribution which the restudy may make to social anthropology I have indicated some of the difficulties involved, both practical and theoretical, in the use of the technique and outlined some of its strengths and weaknesses. I have suggested that it is the only means by which the problem of social change may be satisfactorily tackled. The strength of the technique lies in providing sets of comparable data, separated by intervals of time, for a given society which may enable us to develop both our knowledge and our theory of the processes of social change. Its weaknesses, some of which may be ameliorated along the lines I have indicated, stem from the difficulties involved in producing a diachronic account and not one which is simply 'dual-synchronic'. It is not enough to know that a society has changed: we must be able to show the processes by which it has changed. The most satisfactory way to do this and produce truly diachronic accounts, I have suggested, is to couple the restudy technique with that of the extended-case method.

references

J. A. BARNES (1954) Politics in a changing society, Cape Town.

F. BARTLETT (1932) Remembering, Cambridge.

B. BERNARDI (1950) The social structure of the Kraal among the Zezuru in Musami, S. Rhodesia, Communication from the School of African Studies XXIII, Cape Town.

P. BOHANNAN (1953) Review of J. A. Barnes, Marriage in a changing society, *Man* 8: 13-14.

E. COLSON (1954) The intensive study of small sample communities, in: R. F. Spencer ed., Method and perspective in anthropology, Minneapolis.

E. DURKHEIM (1933) The division of labour in society (translated by G. Simpson), New York.

R. FIRTH (1954) Social organisation and social change, JRAI 84 (# 1): 1-20.

R. FIRTH (1959) Social change in Tikopia, London.

M. FORTES (1949) Time and social structure: an Ashanti case study, in: M. FORTES ed., Social structure: studies presented to A. R. Radcliffe-Brown, Oxford.

G. K. GARBETT (1960) Growth and change in a Shona ward, Occasional Paper no. 1, Department of African Studies, University College of Rhodesia and Nyasaland, Salisbury.

M. GLUCKMAN (1958) Analysis of a social situation in modern Zululand, Rhodes-Livingstone Paper no. 28, Manchester.

M. GLUCKMAN (1960) The rise of a Zulu Empire, *The Scientific American* 202 (♯ 4).

M. GLUCKMAN (1961) Ethnographic data in British social anthropology, *The Sociological Review* 9 (♯ 1): 5-17.

P. HARRIES-JONES and J. C. CHIWALE (1963) Kasaka: a case study in succession and dynamics of a Bemba village, *Human Problems in British Central Arica* 33: 1-67.

O. LEWIS (1951) Life in a Mexican village: Tepotzlán restudied, Illinois.

O. LEWIS (1954) Controls and experiments in field work, in: A. L. Kroeber ed., Anthropology today, Chicago.

M. MEAD (1956) New lives for old, London.

J. C. MITCHELL (1954) African urbanization in Ndole and Luanshya, Rhodes-Livingstone Communication no. 6, Lusaka.

J. C. MITCHELL and J. R. H. SHAUL (1963) An approach to the measurement of commitment to urban residence, Paper presented to the Second Central African Scientific and Medical Congress, Lusaka.

D. H. READER (1964) Models in social change, with special reference to Southern Africa, *African Studies* 23 (♯ 1): 11-33.

R. REDFIELD (1957) A village that choose progress: Chan Kom revisited, Chicago.

S. TAX ed. (1954) An appraisal of anthropology today, Chicago.

V. W. TURNER (1957) Schism and continuity in African society, Manchester.

J. V. VANSINA (1965) Oral tradition (translated by H. M. Wright), London.

8

orientation and research methods in african urban studies

P. C. W. GUTKIND

In fact the whole picture of African society has altered more rapidly than
the anthropologist's technique. (Richards 1935: 20)

Introduction. Although urbanization in Africa is a very recent development,
there is no longer any doubt that in future years an increasing number of
scholars will carry out research in Africa's old and new towns. The reasons
for this are at least three fold. Firstly, the steady growth of towns is one of the
most significant and obvious features of the transformation of Africa. For
example, Mitchell, writing in 1951 about the Copperbelt says (1951:20):

We in Northern Rhodesia today are living in a revolution, the intensity of which, as far as we can
judge, has not been equalled in thousands of years. This revolution, which has been going on for
about a generation, is in the lives of Africans and arises from the impact of Western industrialism on
their traditional way of life.

One aspect . . . as yet relatively unstudied, but nevertheless of singular importance, is urbanization.

While the social scientists working in Africa in the period 1920 to 1945 mostly
ignored both African and non-African life in the towns because (if they were
anthropologists) they were told that urban life did not fall within their disciplinary interests (Richards in Gutkind 1963: ix), in the Africa of the 1960's
it would be wholly impossible to ignore the significant drift to the towns and
rural-urban interdependence (Apthorne 1958). Since the independence of over
thirty African countries between 1951 and 1964, both small and large urban
areas have assumed greater importance in the social, economic and political
life of Africa – it seems to be a case of 'Over-Urbanization and Underdevelop-
ment' a common feature in the low-income countries. The larger urban areas
in particular act like a magnet in drawing Africans into an urban-based wage

economy. In this and other respects the urban areas act rather like catalysts: the new towns of Africa are certainly the focal point of change. This is not to suggest that before long Africa will be as urbanized a continent as Western Europe or North America. Far from it – Africa remains the least urbanized continent. While the percentage of the population defined as urban varies from under 1% to almost 40%, for the continent as a whole probably less than 10% of the population are resident in urban areas of 5000 people and more. The rate of growth for towns of 100,000 inhabitants and over has been accurately estimated at 3.9% per annum for the period 1940-52. The United Nations has more recently calculated an annual growth of 5% in 28 cities in Africa during the period 1948-60. This compares with Asia's 3.8% and South America's 3.7%. Some specific examples will illustrate the point: Dakar's population has risen from 185,000 in 1948 to 383,000 in 1960; Accra from 136,000 to 326,000; Lagos from 230,000 in 1950 to 380,000 in 1960; Ibadan from 459,000 in 1952 to 620,000 in 1960; Nairobi from 195,000 in 1955 to 250,000 in 1960; Mogadishu from 61,000 in 1953 to 140,000 in 1961 and Bulawayo from 130,000 in 1953 to 183,000 in 1958 (United Nations 1962b). But the point made here is very simply that a statistical index of urbanization does not reflect the importance of Africa's new and older urban centres.

Secondly, Africanists are showing considerable interest in the urban areas as laboratories for the study of new and/or changing social systems, their specific structures and their particular features. It is, therefore, in the area of social theory that we are presented with a unique situation for documentation and analysis (Hauser and Schnore 1965). To Africanists, who have devoted most of their time to rural-based tribal communities, these new urban structures might hold the key to a better understanding of African culture and social systems as a whole (Forde 1963: 1-6; Mitchell 1963; Epstein 1964). For example, Simms reviewing the field of urbanization in West Africa, observes (1965: xiii):

West Africa is more than a locale for urban studies; it is a frame of reference for exploring non-industrial, agricultural, and commercial-based cities. It allows examination of urban social organization outside the confines of advanced industrial societies. It permits analysis of the social and cultural effects of a change of urban base, i.e. from simple agricultural [sic] for export to major commercial and industrial centers.

To argue this way is to suggest that the changes to which Africans are now exposed might reveal features of traditional African life which were imperfectly analysed and understood. This might be so because urban life brings Africans face-to-face with a wide range of new values and the need to incorporate these, or to reject them, in the context of traditional values and social organization. Furthermore, a good many social anthropologists have held certain unwritten assumptions about African societies (and for that matter about other tradition-based groups elsewhere) such as their cultural homogeneity, their tradition-boundness, a kind of stable cultural equilibrium and their inability to withstand some of the consequences which have resulted from contact with non-Africans and alien Africans, i.e. numerous other tribal groups. In this respect those who have an interest in African urban research, have largely turned to this area in the hope that they might find data which would throw more light on the basic ingredients of social systems, group life and collective and individual adjustment to change.

Thirdly, African urban studies are likely to occupy us increasingly in the next few years because acute social tensions and social problems are building up all too rapidly. Not only has the social theoretician cast an eye on the urban areas, but also students interested in social policy, applied studies and practical affairs (United Nations 1962c; Soret 1962; Riby-Williams 1962; Chinn 1962). It is possible that urban research can harmoniously combine theoretical and applied approaches. A very large number of studies have been carried out with a practical object in view and have also significantly contributed to theoretical knowledge (Marris 1961). This applies particularly to various studies carried out on African housing estates and on the characteristics and organization of African migrant labourers with particular reference to the problem of labour stability – all of which have not only provided governments and agencies with basic descriptive material but also contained much that was both analytically and theoretically useful. Special mention might be made of the most politically explosive issues facing African countries, namely rapidly increasing unemployment, mainly prevalent in the towns, and which poses particularly acute social and economic problems. Demographers are also turning increasingly to the urban areas, gathering not merely vital statistical information but also engaging in analytical studies.

In short, a very large number of Africans are moving into the cities – some for brief periods but an increasing number for longer periods (Gutkind 1965a), and a good number will likely stay for very many years. This is primarily true for the already fairly large urban areas, as those in West Africa; in East Africa, however, this development is more recent. There is also a rapid population increase in the smaller towns. This in turn has led to an increased interest in rural-urban migration patterns (Kuper 1965) and in the study of towns as particular social structures. As a social process urbanization and urbanism are viewed by some writers as both independent and dependent variables, i.e. urban life influences 'the social structure and changing patterns of relations on one hand, and it may be influenced by changes in social relations on the other'. (Simms 1965:19).

Approaches to urban research methods. What urban research has been carried out in Africa thus far has been conducted primarily by social anthropologists, sociologists and geographers (Hamdan 1964: 239-53; 1959a:89-120; 1959b; Mabogunje 1962:56-77; 1965:413-438; Nyarko 1959:3-8; Mitchell 1963: 279-302; Steel 1961:249-276; de Blij 1963). I know of no research worker who, as a trained urban sociologist, has studied in, and published on, urban Africa. Thus the methodological traditions brought to this field of research are mostly those acquired by social anthropologists working in rural areas. It is this background which for long fostered the view that we were studying tribesmen in town and not townsmen in town. This is born out by the view that 'ethnic groups must be observed in the first instance in their traditional environments, which must be thoroughly known for any useful study to be made of the processes of change among representatives of such groups settled in towns' (Lebeuf 1960:108). In 1959 Professor Clyde Mitchell pointed out (1959:2):

The danger of working with the idea of a tribal culture in change is that the set of tribal norms too easily become standards against which urban behaviour is measured. Urban life therefore tends to be looked upon as departures from established patterns rather than as *new* patterns with different norms. Urban behaviour is thus seen in terms of 'detribalization' where tribal standards are unconsciously set up as desirable and departures from it in towns as deplorable lapses from it. This approach, of course, must overlook the new patterns of behaviour which have emerged to accommodate the changed social environment and therefore must prevent a deeper insight into the dynamics of the behaviour of African townsmen.

This warning was followed by Professor Gluckman who incisively pointed out that 'the starting-point for analysis of urbanization must be an urban system of relations' (1961: 80) and that 'an African townsman is a townsman, an African miner is a miner' (1961:69). This did not lead Gluckman to place any less emphasis on the importance of a 'tribalistic' tradition. Rather he pointed out that 'tribalism in towns is not that it is manifested by tribesmen, but that it is manifested by townsmen' (1961:68).

Most of us who have worked in African towns have in fact been reared on a 'rural tradition' which led us straight into the constricting view of 'detribalization'. Thus our past conceptual ideas, and important parts of our methodology, were simply transferred into a context wholly unsuitable for the characteristics and conditions of African urban life. It therefore took some time before it was recognized that research methods might differ in urban areas from those used in rural areas (Cooper 1959:135-139). Africans in towns were viewed as no more than the wayward who had strayed from the fold.   When between 1953 and 1955 the East Africa Royal Commission studied 'Conditions for Urban Development', they reported that all too many administrators had taken 'the view that the town was not a suitable habitat for a permanent African society' (East Africa Royal Commission 1955:201). Anthropologists did not go quite that far; nevertheless, certain important assumptions did influence their views of what they felt constituted African urban life.

There is the question of whether social anthropologists viewed urban life as constituting 'a system of relations'. Did urban social organization and social structure exhibit clearly predictable regularity so that systematic interconnections between groups and individuals could be traced? After all, this was the assumption behind much anthropological research in the rural areas. Was there, in fact, an 'urban system'? Or were those Africans resident in Africa's towns a hodge-podge of amorphous groupings which could not be sorted out. In any case, the vast majority of Africans in towns did not stay long enough; there were no similar groupings as in a village with its continuity despite its changing composition over time. Also, African urban life brought together peoples from far and wide, all with very different cultural and social patterns, which made it difficult for the anthropologist to find the kind of cultural and social homogeneity which generally prevailed, or was thought to prevail, among rural people. Naturally, as a result, it was difficult to locate the institutional underpinning of urban social life; behaviour, it was assumed, had no reference to traditional sanctions. The 'kinship system', beloved by the anthropologist, was in shreds and pieces. The urban African was there, to be sure, but he presented so complex and different a life that it was best to leave it alone. What was not as clearly recognized was that in taking this view, the anthropologist cut himself off from an important feature of social change, namely the influence, and the reciprocal relations, of the city on the countryside and the countryside on the city. In a recent work edited by James L. Gibbs on the *People of Africa* (1965), fifteen writers on contemporary African societies relegate the nature and operation of social change to a maximum of four pages. The majority did away with the matter in one page. Yet even in this cursory presentation they fill their meagre paragraphs with enough evidence to suggest that 'their' tribe no longer persists in as pure and abstract a fashion as they outline. Dr. Audrey Richards, for example, writes as follows (1935:20):

Anthropological theory was evolved very largely in Oceania, where the relative isolation of small island communities provided something like 'typical' primitive social groups. Most of Rivers's hypotheses were based on Melanesian material, and Malinowski's functional method, the inspiration of most modern field work in all parts of the world, originated on an island off New Guinea with only 8,000 inhabitants. The anthropologist who embarks for Africa has obviously to modify and adapt the guiding principles of field work from the start. He has probably to work in a much larger and more scattered tribal area, and with a people that are increasing in numbers rather than diminishing. ... More important still ... most of the tribes in Africa are facing a social situation which is, in effect, a revolution. In fact, the whole picture of African society has altered more rapidly than the anthropologist's technique.

This was written in 1935!
With this 'tribalistic' background how have research workers tackled the tasks of African urban research? Before an answer can be given, some further considerations are appropriate. Firstly, and this is not a contradiction of all that has been asserted above, those research workers who have ventured into urban areas have done remarkably well. By and large, as their studies have

evolved, lively descriptions (Leslie 1963; Southall and Gutkind 1957) have been matched with reasonably sophisticated theorizing. Until recently, the level of theory might be placed in the 'middle' range, but in more recent studies, particularly those by Mayer (1961), Epstein (1957:67-70; 1958; 1961:29-62) and Mitchell (1956; 1960a:169-172; 1959; 1963), both theory and methodology are quite sophisticated. The reasons for this seem to be at least twofold.

In the first case years of exposure to the peoples of the rural areas has taught the social anthropologist that people organize their activities in a far more complex manner than was at first thought. This is so quite irrespective of the environmental setting, be it an urban-based or a rural-based society. As such it was gradually recognized that urban African society was unlikely to be an incoherent and haphazard composite of unrelated activities and organization. If certain important institutional arrangements, and the structural principles underlying these, gave us the key to the understanding of traditional, rural-based societies, would this not be equally true of those new human groupings which had been established away from the direct influence of tribal life? Thus, and this *is* the point I wish to make, while some social anthropologists had a difficult time in accepting the fact that there were important communities outside the traditional tribal framework, the orientation used in rural fieldwork could be, and was, transferred to urban-based societies. The anthropologist had a view of the principles and structure of social organization even though the methodological tools used in studying urban-based societies were lacking – and still are to a large extent. The disadvantage which accompanied the transfer of the anthropologist's approach was the assumption, mentioned earlier, that urban-based societies were merely bastard and hybrid extensions of rural societies – tribesmen in town.

Secondly, the anthropological approach rests heavily on the documentation of the cultural and societal characteristics of different societies. Rather like the theory of cultural relativism, which compels us to avoid value judgements about a people's way of managing their affairs, the methodology of the comparative method, without its emphasis on evolution and 'progress', is deeply embedded in anthropological orientation and research technique (Radcliffe-Brown 1951; Evans-Pritchard 1963). Both as an approach and as a technique, social anthropologists seek their data from highly diverse cultures which clearly, in more recent years, have included urban societies and other complex large-scale societies such as those of India, China, Western Europe and North America (Mandelbaum, in: Thomas 1955). The comparative study of social institutions, the backbone of anthropological research, led some research workers into urban areas. Among some, their curiosity was aroused and they wished to find out how certain institutions, such as marriage and family life, operated when they were removed from the direct influence of tribal institutions and norms. This 'look over the fence' did not mean that anthropologists as a whole had accepted that they had a research role to play in urban studies; but rather the comparative approach eventually compelled them to add studies of urban life to the field of social system analysis. It was as impossible to ignore urban studies as it was to ignore studies of the Bushmen or the Dyjaks. In terms of theories of culture and society, it was impossible to set aside the fact that an increasing number of Africans left their rural habitat, for short or long periods, to take up new occupations in a new environment which they fashioned in a new and particular way.

An interest in urban Africa was strongly stimulated by the growing recognition, which crystallized in the years between the first and second world war, of the importance of analysing the characteristics and processes of social change and culture contact. While rural life was itself gradually changing, the urban areas were the most visible expression of change. But this recognition did not in itself bring the importance of urban studies any closer to realization. In West Africa, for example, where large urban centres have for a long time been part of the social and cultural life of some important tribal groups, social anthropologists virtually ignored the existence of towns such as Lagos, Ibadan, Freetown and Kano despite the fact that most of them were predominantly African and had large populations, i.e. 100,000 and more. It is extraordinary that social anthropologists considered it possible to write, for example, about the Yoruba of Western Nigeria although they paid very little attention to Ibadan, Ife or Oyo. Studies about these towns did not appear until after the second world war – but then urban studies generally rapidly became fashionable – when the authors told us how interdependent town and country always had been, particularly in West Africa.

Probably the first analytical literature on urban Africa, other than the accounts

of travellers, missionaries and administrators, came from South Africa. Here
we have the excellent monograph by Monica Hunter who, in her study of the
Pondo, first published in 1936, saw the need to include three chapters on the
urban community. We are also reminded of the pioneering work by Hellmann
in *Rooiyard*, carried out in 1934 but not published until 1948. Likewise, Hellmann is probably the only social anthropologist who wrote about 'Methods
of urban field work' as early as 1935. A little further north, in Northern
Rhodesia (now Zambia), Godfrey Wilson published his work (in 1941 and
1942) on Broken Hill. I am not aware of any analytical literature on the West
African towns as early as this.[1]

Anthropologists, therefore, took an interest in urban Africa largely because
they could no longer ignore the old and the new towns of Africa. Yet to this day
there are a number of anthropologists whose theoretical interests are formulated
in such a way to make it possible for them to ignore the direct influence of the
towns. Of course many tribal groups, it is true, are only remotely touched by urban life – but these are relatively few. For, of course, to be influenced by urbanism
one does not have to live in a town. Many anthropologists also felt that their
research techniques were not adequate for the tasks demanded by urban
research. This view was based on the fact that rural communities, by virtue of
their alleged homogeneity, were less complex entities, or at least more integrated systems which could more readily be analysed. Rural groups were small-
scale groups whereas urban groups were amorphous and large-scale and tied
to external agents which were not a proper field of study for the anthropologist.
For example Malinowski writing on the Dynamics of Culture Change (1945),
and in the papers published in *Africa*, collectively re-issued under the title of
Methods of Study of Culture Contact in Africa (1938), made only the most
cursory reference to urban life. To be sure, these authors wrote at a time when
the towns of East and Central Africa were small and inhabited predominantly
by non-Africans. Yet increasingly in the 1930's and 1940's labour migration
was a fact and many Africans filled the lower levels of the urban wage workers.
More significantly then, as now, the model set by urbanism as a distinctly

---

[1] Virtually all the literature cited by Simms is dated from 1950 onward.

different way of life was filtering back to the rural areas. In East and Central Africa rural-urban interdependence was no doubt significant then, although we lack the precise documentation to prove this. Certainly the process of culture contact and change greatly accelerated in the 1950's; yet it is significant that a good many studies during this period indicate that major changes had started at an earlier period.

Hellmann, writing in 1935, suggested that it was 'inevitable that work among the urban natives should concern itself greatly with culture contact, and it is just from this urban research that the most fruitful data dealing with culture contact can be anticipated'. Turning to methodological problems Hellmann found that the functional method 'has proved itself in its application to field work among integrated tribes' but in an urban area, 'Native society does not form this integrated whole to which an analysis according to functional method can forthwith be applied'. The functions of the urban field worker are to observe and record 'the gradual adapting of the rural Native to urban conditions and his gradual assimilation of Western culture . . .' (1935: 186, 188). The 'culture contact' approach has, of course, come under critical analysis particularly by Gluckman, who has rejected the approach of 'detribalization, which had to be analysed and measured as the tribesman slowly changed' (1960: 57) from one cultural tradition to another. In fact, however, in recent years the 'cultural model' has been replaced by a 'social relations' model which sets out clearly that townsmen pattern their behaviour and relations appropriate to an urban system and tribesmen to a tribal system. In relationship terms, many urban Africans alternate between systems.

Urban research method. In the light of what has been said so far, it must be clear that there has not developed a special research technique, or techniques, which can be clearly presented in African urban studies. Yet, urban sociologists working in Western cities have developed very sophisticated techniques for the analysis of urban demographic and social data (Gibbs 1961). Many of these techniques, however, are those employed by sociologists generally but have been specially adapted and refined for urban research. I am thinking particularly about survey techniques, such as the questionnaire, which are widely used by sociologists with very diverse interests and increasingly by social anthropologists working in African urban areas (Silverman 1954:279-99; Lebeuf 1960).

In African urban research the need for special techniques does not appear at first sight as absolutely essential. Firstly, as most African urban research is still being carried out by social anthropologists, trained in the special techniques of their discipline, they use them in urban studies as they have used them in rural studies. It is only at a specialized level of urban research that the traditional techniques, and conceptualizations, of social anthropology may appear inadequate. It is generally only when it is recognized that urban communities are very particular aggregates that particular research techniques are needed. Powdermaker (1962: xv), for example, sums up her methodological approach as follows:

My study [in Luanshya, Zambia] was exploratory, and therefore methodology had to be flexible. As the problem expanded or deepened, so did the methods. I used any methods which had potentialities for securing relevant data which I was capable of handling, which fitted into the time and financial limits of my study, and which was feasible within the power structure, European and African. Some methods were based on current anthropological practices and my previous field experiences; others were devised on the spot to meet the particular situation. There were problems which lent themselves to quantification, while others excluded it. The ideal of narrow exactitude may lead to good surveys and statistical data but sometimes excludes the formulation of other significant problems.

Secondly, anthropologists have by and large restricted themselves to those studies of African urban life which are particularly amenable to the use of their traditional research methods. This is of course the result of their view that African urban areas have not really taken on the particular characteristics of urban life as conventionally defined. In short, anthropologists have adapted their traditional research techniques in the context of urban studies. Beneficial as this has been in the sense that we have a number of studies which take us right into the life of an urban community, or a particular segment of it, its composition and the main features of individual and group activities, the disadvantages are also clearly evident. For example, far less attention has been paid to those Africans who have been resident in urban areas for a considerable length of time, and such communities exist both in West Africa, Central Africa as well as in South Africa (Pauw 1963; Wilson and Mafeje 1963), than to migrants and those less committed to urban life. McCullock (1956a: 30), for example, found in her Livingstone survey using 1952 data that out of a sample of 832 Africans, 35% had resided continuously in the town for ten years and over, and Thompson (in McCullock 1956a: 30), using 1947 Lusaka data, found that 43.3% of a sample of 266 Africans had had ten years and over length of residence. Other urban areas indicate similar data yet we have paid extremely little attention to this vital urban African group. Likewise Mayer (1962: 576) considers that the 'ongoing nature of the urban social systems has been successfully distinguished from the temporary or shifting nature of the migrant personnel'. Studying African urban areas from the perspective of migrants has resulted in explaining 'town-located phenomena by reference to tribal systems located outside the towns'.

Yet another limitation has been that few anthropologists have paid much attention to the non-African urban communities in Africa, i.e. particularly the Europeans (Sofer and Sofer 1955: 23-24, 52-54, 73-76, 99-101, 105-106, 110-111; Gussman 1963; Tanner 1964: 319-27). What we know about them is exceedingly limited, the result of the view that anthropologists did not generally study such communities and that, in any case, they lacked the training and the techniques to do so. The result is that we lack really comprehensive and comparative studies of African urban areas which reveal the total composition, structure and organization giving adequate descriptions of the various racial and tribal groups and how they stand in relation to one another. Thus far our studies have been either too generalized or too specialized to achieve this objective.

Those who have ventured into the urban areas have had to face some particular difficulties. Although the anthropologist very soon asks himself the question, 'What particular way of life prevails here?', the urban setting forces him to seek some important preliminary data.

The first problem is one of definition: what is a town? What is distinctly urban and what is not? Should size of population determine this question, or is it a question of whether the inhabitants are engaged in primarily non-agricultural activities? It is possible to have huge agricultural villages and very small non-agricultural settlements. One way to get out of this dilemma is to define urban areas as those with populations of 10,000 or over on the assumption that when an agglomeration reaches such a size a large percentage of the inhabitants are in non-agricultural occupations. This is not entirely a satisfactory approach because small localities may have a large percentage of non-agricultural occupations. The first research task the anthropologist faces, therefore, is to arrive at a satisfactory definition which should combine the characteristics of size with characteristics of urbanism, i.e. such features as heterogeneousness, class structure and political and administrative organization (Mitchel 1955: 1-13). Size of groups and their functions should provide a better basis for a clear distinction between urban and rural. Secondly, urban aggregates are usually, but by no means always, substantially larger than rural village communities. So that an other task is to define and limit the population of greatest interest to the urban researcher. This cannot be done effectively without precise demographic information: how many people live in the town, or a segment of it, and who are they. What are the limits of their distribution? What language or languages are spoken there? What is the mobility of the population – will they be there tomorrow or the next day? The occupation and residential instability of African urban populations are still very great with the result that it has been very difficult to collect precise statistical information. What statistical data is available is usually of limited value and lacks the kind of refinement which is badly needed. The result is that much urban research lack in definition and methodological precision.

Most urban research workers have to turn themselves into enumerators and untrained demographers although they lack the skills to perform these specialised tasks (Richards 1935:32). Yet there is little alternative. As a result most studies are preceded by large or small scale surveys of the areas selected (Flegg and Lutz 1959:1-24). Such survey work can of course produce valuable information forming the basis for a more precise formulation of the research problem. Pauvert (1960:84) summarises this technique as follows:

The various surveys carried out in towns have been directed largely to the study of new types of groupings and of the community ties resulting from the new family, ethnic, occupational or political affiliations which urban life promotes. In many cases these surveys have been based on statistical data obtained by means of questionnaires, thus constituting a quantitative approach; nearly all are concerned first and foremost with the demographic structure of the centres considered, without however forming a complete census. The surveys are almost always based on sampling.

But survey techniques also have their limitations. They do not generally reveal the complex processes whereby groups were or are set apart. As a method they help to set out the broad patterns of the socio-economic structure of an urban area but do not easily reveal the factors involved in the development of a network of individual and group relations.

Schwab (1962:6), discussing his research orientation and research techniques in Oshogbo (Western Nigeria) and in Gwelo (Rhodesia), has pointed out very clearly how urban research methods must differ depending on the nature of the community to be studied. In Gwelo a census type of survey could be carried out because:

the life of an African in Gwelo is regulated and largely determined by a seemingly endless series of forms, questionnaires and passes. He was accustomed to them and intimidated by them. It seemed that he saw this census as just one more inevitable and incomprehensible form against which there was no defense, if he was to remain working in town.

The reaction to the census in Oshogbo . . . was quite different. The people had many concerns and fears which they articulated. They did not understand the sampling procedures, superstitions, such as those relating to the enumeration of children, were mobilized against the census, fears about taxes or conscription into the army or labor gangs, among many others, were varied.

Schwab considers that the 'critical problem' in his urban research was 'to find techniques which would assure representativeness of the data and at the same time penetrate deeper into the fabric of the society than statistical sampling ordinarily does'. He concluded that the questionnaire was 'inadequate in any situation which involved complex material and could not, for example, reach such problems as the changes in norms and values that are crucial to the understanding of much in the Oshogbo social system'.

Yet much can be done. Occupational distribution, prestige and social status ratings and measures of urban 'commitment' (Mitchell 1964a; Mitchell and Epstein 1957:13-26; 1959:22-40; Mitchell and Shaul 1963), certain aspects of marriage, family life and differential fertility (Mitchell 1957:1-30; 1964b:195-211) such as the patterns and stability of marriage and size of family (Gutkind 1962:149-217), household composition or family budget studies (United Nations 1962a), adult and juvenile crime surveys (Stenning 1962); all these can to a large measure be obtained by survey techniques. In more recent years, survey techniques have been coupled to more precise statistical analysis although as yet these techniques are not very sophisticated (Southall 1956: 578-90; Mitchell 1964a). Yet, as Professor Southall has pointed out, statistical analysis of African urban data is particularly important because in an urban community:

Members of it are not able to visualize their social system in any coherent way which has general validity, and the behaviour of different individuals and groups may be so variable that no description of them can be relied on in forming a picture of the whole. Hence the necessity for some statistical definition of behaviour frequencies and their interrelationships (1956: 580).

The importance of this orientation, and the use of statistical research techniques, lies in the fact that in urban research 'some of the assumptions usual in anthropological field research cannot be entertained' because 'there are few regularities of behaviour which can be taken for granted' (Southall 1956: 578-79). Whether or not the variability and frequencies of behaviour in an African urban area are greater than in a tribal society is exactly the kind of hypothesis which needs comparative testing. Urban research methods should therefore make it possible to reveal the extent of variability involved in African urban life. In this respect, survey techniques either need considerable refinement or more traditional anthropological techniques need modification. A prerequisite to the latter approach is to eliminate the ambiguity of theoretical and conceptual models. To commence with models which are based on the assumption that in tribal societies, in contrast to urban societies, 'variability within any institutional complex is often comparatively low' (Southall 1956: 579), is to structure both orientation and research techniques in such a way that the documentation and analysis of the urban system *as a whole* might never be revealed. The very fact that this duality of models has arisen indicates that so far we lack studies of African urban areas which might indicate that there is an essential structural similarity between urban and rural systems, i.e. that the multiplicity of variables within any institutional complex is just as great in many rural systems and that there are as many regularities of behaviour in urban systems as there are said to be in rural systems (Geertz 1959: 991-1012; Brown 1962: 57-69).

The use of the survey technique is applied both on a macro and on a micro level; both to obtain information of a broad general nature and of specialized activities. As a method, to obtain both preliminary information, and information in depth, the survey technique itself gives rise to the particular research methods which are eventually adopted (examples of all these uses of the survey method will be found in Forde 1956). Frequently, basic survey research methods have been used in order to refine definitions and conceptual tools. This is particularly so in regard to the literature on urban Africa which deals with detribalization and stabilization of the urbanite. The question asked is: how long do Africans remain in town and what is the relationship between length of residence, urban commitment and social patterns? The concept of urban commitment can be sociologically and demographically refined by means of survey and statistical techniques (Mitchell 1956b: 693-711; McCulloch 1956a: 57-65; Mitchell 1951).

The survey technique has been used in a number of different ways and with different objectives in mind. On the one hand it is used to obtain broad outlines of the socio-economic features of an urban area and on the other as a tool to obtain exhaustive and detailed data. It has already been suggested that when used with the first objective in mind its usefulness is generally considerable. It is however questionable whether the survey technique can reveal the underlying principles of social organization, their structure and function, and the complex network of individual and group relationships (in the context of African urban studies, see particularly: Schwab 1962; Silverman 1954:279-99). At the same time Whyte and Williams have recently shown how the questionnaire survey method, and the more traditional anthropological methods of observation and interviewing complement each other when applied to communities which are clearly undergoing far reaching changes. They conclude that the questionnaire survey technique 'can provide measures that will help focus problems for anthropological research' and that 'previous anthropological research suggested to us a number of items that went into our questionnaire'. (1964).

An urban area is basically a system within which there are innumerable and overlapping sub-systems. How these systems develop, how precisely they overlap and on what occasions and for what purposes are the vital questions to ask. Of course we have to take into account that we are still in the early stages of African urban research. Some recent literature has been instructive not only from the point of view of substantive content but also method, although very few urban research workers have been particularly informative on the latter. Some of the most instructive discussions are those by Gamble (1963:254-68), Hellmann (1948), Bettison (1958 and 1959), Powdermaker (1962), Mayer (1961 and 1962), Wilson and Mafeje (1963), Banton (1957), Marris (1961), Leslie (1963) and Southall and Gutkind (1957). Most discussions on method are very meagre while some important writers on urban studies have told us virtually nothing of how they did their fieldwork, i.e. Acquah (1958), Epstein (1958) and Comhaire-Sylvain (1950; n.d.). No doubt there are others in both categories which could be added.

New guidelines for african urban research. A look at this literature suggests that some authors have attempted a comprehensive documentation of a particular problem, of particular features of African urban life, and others have attempted a broad documentation of what they consider to be the most important characteristics of a particular urban area. While all of them express a good deal of dissatisfaction with the survey research method, and its haphazard mixing with more traditional anthropological research techniques, they nevertheless expect to gain more from either method than is actually possible under urban conditions.

If we accept the view that African urban life comprises a system, with regular recurring patterns of individual and group relations, then our orientation and method should not contrast rural and urban ways of life but focus on the concepts of social system and social structure. This has a number of implications for African urban studies. The first of these is that we do not restrict our observations to one particular group or groupings in an urban area. Every tribal group, every occupational and status category, is part of a socio-economic and political network – a situation which is often only accidentally revealed when a survey and questionnaire technique is used. Of course, to concentrate on one particular group might be the only way out of a difficult practical and/or methodological situation. In such a case the study of even one segment of an urban system will reveal the network of the total society. Nevertheless, it is important to investigate as many tribal, political, occupational and status groupings as possible, as these are part of one social field.

When we speak of one social field we imply that urban Africans are linked in a complex pattern of inter-dependent and multiple relations which, unlike those in a rural social system, are progressively tied into a widespread network of economic and political relations whose boundaries reach far beyond the kin and specific non-kin groupings. Gamble (1963:254-55), for example, brings out very clearly how differentiated even a small town in Sierra Leone is:

In village studies one is normally dealing with people of only one tribe. In towns one meets people from a dozen different tribes in the course of a day ... In Lunsar were to be found ministers of religion, Muslim teachers, primary school teachers, civil servants, bank clerks, dispensers, native doctors, 'cowboys' (idle young men), thieves, police informers, good time girls ('rah rah girls'), traditional blacksmiths, skilled artisans dealing with Euclid earth-moving equipment and diesel locomotives, laboratory assistants, self-confessed witches, rich traders who owned lorries, characters who earned a few pennies toting loads to and from the long park, peasant farmers, diamond dealers, and beggars. There were men from the villages for whom Lunsar was a big town, men from Freetown who looked on it as a 'bush place' without amenities, men who had visited England and men who had been on pilgrimage to Mecca.

With such a range of people multiple forms of segmentation and stratification emerge – age, religion, education, occupation, kinship, tribe – all playing a part ...

The practical problems in terms of research method which are posed by such an approach, and such conditions, are no doubt considerable, but no real alternative approaches come to mind. What other approach or technique would reveal the network of social relations which cut across the heterogeneous groupings so typical of African urban life (Epstein 1961:29-62; Banton 1961: 113-125)? Merely to note that many urbanites are not just members of specific tribes, trade unions and particular voluntary organizations, produces no more than an enumeration of categories to which men and women belong. What we need to know is how membership in diverse groupings fit into a total social order. This approach is well demonstrated by Professor Mitchell who has suggested that African urban social structure might best be analysed in terms of structural relationships, egocentric relationships and categorical relationships. Each one of these types of relations does not exist *in vacuo* but only assumes functional purpose in relationship to the other categories of relations (Mitchell 1959).

The work by Mayer goes a long way towards these objectives although it also raises the problem of the use of rather a rigorous typological analysis and its applicability to urban areas generally. Thus Mayer's stimulating contribution is to see the total urban system in terms of a clear-cut dichotomy between true urbanites and those who live and work in the town of East London but are not of the town (1961). This line of inquiry is also followed by Powdermaker (1962). The limitation of drawing so sharp a dichotomy seems to be the almost complete absence of a continuum between the two categories. In this sense each category is studied *in vacuo*, and in a synchronic frame of reference, but not as part of a much larger urban system of which either category is an integral part.

On the other hand, the work by Epstein, which avoids both the synchronic and this typological approach, gives us a very comprehensive view of the town of Luanshya on the Copperbelt of Zambia (1958). While Epstein tells us virtually nothing of his particular research method, in his research orientation, which by reference is also a research technique, he follows the method outlined by Professor Gluckman (Gluckman 1958).

It is this method and approach of situational and social network analysis, coupled with Southall's small group analysis (1961:25-30), which appears to me the most comprehensive and penetrating technique to be applied in African urban research (Gutkind 1965a; 1965b). Van Velsen has applied all these techniques in a rural tribal study (1964) and Mitchell in an African urban area (1956a). Situational analysis, as an approach has been defined by Van Velsen as follows (1964: xxvii).

Where agents in the system are not so much corporate groups as individuals linked through continually changing alignments in small and often ephemeral groups . . . with opposed interests and apparent lack of unity.

This characterization of a certain type of social system seems to me to define adequately, for the time being at least, the African urban situation. The emphasis should clearly be on the words 'apparent lack of unity' simply because there is order and regularity in African urban areas, however heterogeneous they are, but integration takes place around variables which in the past we have not associated with structural regularity. Structural analysis seeks to demonstrate relations between formal social positions whereas emphasis on situational networks brings to light the social morphology of particular sets and events.[1] Like Van Velsen, but more than twenty years earlier, Schapera pointed out (1933:406):

... culture is not merely a system of formal practices and beliefs. It is made up of individual reactions to and variations from a traditionally standardized pattern; and indeed no culture can ever be understood unless special attention is paid to this range of individual manifestations.

Most of the literature on African urban areas seems to me to support the view that 'particular' actions, i.e. variation and diversity of social forms and relations, can be fitted into a general frame of reference which allows us to use the concept of social system. The literature further indicates that African urban systems are composites of overlapping, yet distinct, social networks. As any institutional arrangement, these networks, which have regularity over time, although their composition and form change as fluid urban conditions demand, are designed to assist the individual and the group to both meet traditional and new needs. In this sense the particular network of which an individual or a group is a part, at any particular time and place, reflects the degree of urban commitment as well as the extent of participation in the matrix of a traditional social order. The fact that segments of the urban social system stand opposed to one another is no more surprising than the observation that this is also so among people living in the rural areas. However, while a number of urban studies have demonstrated this, the implications for urban research techniques have still to be spelled out. Possibly the most useful technique is situational analysis which Gluckman has described as follows:

Social situations are a large part of the raw material of the anthropologist. They are the events he observes and from them and their inter-relationships in a particular society he abstracts the social structure, relationships, institutions, etc., of that society. By them, and by new situations he must check the validity of his generalizations (Gluckman 1958: 2).

This technique (Gluckman 1958; Van Velsen 1964) leads us not only to understand the form and structure of specific social situations in which individuals and groups are involved but also becomes the instrument for documenting and

[1] Radcliffe-Brown, for example, has rejected the analysis of the particular as not giving an 'account of the form of the structure'.

analysing the structure and functions of the various sub-systems. As a technique Epstein has shown how much can be achieved when the researcher follows through the activities of a single urbanite and his daily activity (Epstein 1961).

The concept of social network has received considerable attention in recent years (Barnes 1954:39-58; Bott 1955: 345-384; Jay 1964:137-139; Srinivas and Béteille 1964:165-168) and as a model it has been thought particularly suitable for the analysis of mixed and complex groupings. The concept of social structure postulates numerous but interdependent enduring groups and highly specific categories, groups and classes. Srinivas and Béteille suggest that the distinction between social structure (enduring groups – those with 'a high degree of consistency and constancy') and networks 'is primarily one of boundaries. A group is a bounded unit. A network, on the other hand, ramifies in every direction, and for all practical purposes, stretches out indefinitely... The character of a network... varies from one individual to another'. (Srinivas and Béteille 1964:166).

Such a formulation allows more adequately for description and analysis of many semi-independent social situations which result from the complex adjustments which need to be made and the disturbances and struggles so much a feature of African urban life. In this sense a network:

... has a dynamic character. New relations are forged, and old ones discarded or modified. This is particularly true of rapidly changing societies in which individual choice plays an important role (Srinivas and Béteille 1964: 166).

The objective then of network analysis is to:

... chart the type and the channels of interaction between persons and the extent of regularities which give a minimum of order and coherence to social life in communities which have no clear structure of discrete groups (Southall 1961: 25).

Seen from a methodological point of view, this analysis leads to the techniques of small group research – of microanalysis – whereby small neighbourhoods and groupings are seen within the framework of a macro system (Gutkind 1965b). Here Southall points out (1961:25):

Work on small groups has two important aspects. Most obviously, it concerns social groups which are small in size, but also constitutes a special approach to the study of face to face relationships in small clusters within larger populations which seem to lack corporate structures except as a wide impersonal framework. The object is both to study small groups for their own sake and to see how the wider corporate structures impinge upon those who compose them, that is, how continuous chains and interlocking networks of role relationships link the members of small groups to the structures of the wider society and the persons who play key roles in them.

This approach, which calls for a series of small group and neighbourhood studies, is likely to reveal not only the micro world of specific groupings and the behaviour of individuals who are part of these groups, but also the macro world of African urban society. This is so because each small neighbourhood is part of a larger urban system. 'In fact each neighbourhood only enjoys its semi-autonomous existence because *it is* part of a far larger urban community'. (Gutkind 1965a). This approach utilizes the 'anthropologists framework of theory [which] helps him to look at people's actions in contexts as part of a system of action into which other people also enter' (Firth 1954:2). As societies change they take on a new and different kind of complexity – a complexity which is increasingly the outcome of the way individuals manipulate a variety of traditional and new situations and social relations. New groupings and new types of relations are the result of an ever widening field of choices which individuals and groups can make in social, economic and political life. This is the essence of change and modernization which gives rise to new networks which in turn cut across and involve change over the entire system (Mair 1963:11-31).

Of course there are practical difficulties involved for the anthropologist carrying out a series of small group and neighbourhood studies. Hence it becomes vital to select carefully those neighbourhoods and those groupings whose members straddle a number of networks. The approach of the urban anthropologist, and the methods he employs, are concerned 'with the behaviour of individuals acting within a framework of a situation determined by political, administrative, demographic, economic and other external determinants' (Mitchell 1963). It is these external determinants to which particular attention must be paid in African urban studies because they largely determine the particular and unique social matrix of urban life. Mitchell, writing about southern Africa, puts it this way (1960a:171):

... we must approach the study of African behaviour in towns by recognizing that a series of external conditions set the framework within which urban Africans must interact. These are the external imperatives of the social system. Political and legal provisions, for example, limit behaviour by determining where Africans shall work and live, where they may own land, which occupations they shall follow and so on. Demographic features such as the disproportionally large number of young adult males in the urban areas, the instability of residence and perhaps more than anything else, the heterogeneity arising from the variety of tribal hinterlands from which the towns drain their populations, provide the limiting framework within which Africans must solve the problems of giving meaning to actions.

Closely linked to this approach is the view that anthropologists need to use the heuristic device of describing the 'total society', an approach which has come about because the anthropologist has been reared on the traditions of the small, self-sufficient local tribal community. Today, communities are rarely any longer self-sufficient or isolated. Instead, we see them as 'a social system and then demonstrate how and in what way certain aspects of behaviour and beliefs are logically linked in such a system' (Michell 1960a:172). Or, as Epstein has put it (1964:26):

... we have to view the town as a single field of social relations in which the different, and sometimes opposed, sections of the urban population are also closely linked by ties of interdependence.

African urban research, in short, really compels the anthropologist to raise his 'sights beyond the immediate level of the local community being studied' (Epstein 1964:26) as urban life is fitted into a wider economic and political system. It is at this point, Epstein has reminded us, that 'we become most acutely aware that we are approaching the limits of our anthropological competence, and exposing ourselves to the charge of naiveté' (Epstein 1964:26-27). The anthropologist venturing into the African urban areas will have to handle a new field for which he has not been prepared. Orthodox anthropological approaches and techniques may not do as the anthropologist seeks concepts and techniques from other disciplines (Southall 1959:17-34) or is compelled to refine and to modify those concepts which he has used in the past (Balandier 1956:495-510).

Methodologically, some anthropologists have insisted that the complexity of urban life and organization is such that traditional anthropological techniques are useless. Thus, some of them have concluded that only statistical techniques can hope to get at the uniformities and regularities which are assumed to exist in urban life. ('Quantitative studies', A. F. Wells writes, 'inspire the reader with much more confidence than do studies of the other type' [qualitative accounts] (1935:84)). Banton, with some reservations, has expressed this view (1957: xiv-xv):

The relatively simple life of a tribal village can perhaps be adequately described in purely verbal terms but the uniformities found in urban life can for the most part be expressed only statistically. In the town few generalizations of any validity can be obtained without the use of social survey techniques – taking a sample of the populations and showing the variation of behaviour and circumstance in numerical form.

However he almost immediately qualifies this when he notes (Banton 1957: xv):

Important as survey techniques may be, much that is real and important in the social life of an urban population is likely to fall through the net of any statistical classification. So before surveys are undertaken in these circumstances, it is desirable that there should be an anthropological investigation to plot the cultural patterns, the manner in which one way of life may be entwined with another, the clusters of things that are meaningful for the people, and the significance which the items to be surveyed posses in their eyes.

Fortes, in his 'Ashanti Case Study' suggests that 'more systematic methods are necessary' because in a 'highly diversified society there will be a large number of . . . principles [influencing individual and group relationships] none of them general'. In these societies 'norms cannot be discovered by inspection or haphazard comparison' (Fortes 1949:59). Hence, he has suggested that the 'application of statistical concepts will show that the concept of 'structure' is most appropriately used for the kind of abstract or generalized description which Radcliffe-Brown calls 'structural form''. (Fortes 1949:59). Fortes sees the use of even 'elementary statistical analysis [as] indispensable for the elucidation of certain problems of social structure that arise in a society which is in process of becoming socially diversified'. The advantage of using these concepts and techniques is 'to reduce apparently discrete 'types' or 'forms' . . . to the differential effects of identical principles in varying local, social contexts' (Fortes 1949:83-84).

Likewise some authors insist that 'because of the complexity of urban life most of those who have done intensive research in this sphere have found it necessary to combine social surveys with quantitative studies' (McCulloch 1956b:55). Mitchell rejects this view of complexity and asks whether 'the relationship of a man to his wife [for example] in town [is] more complicated than in the rural area . . . ?' He does not feel that it is. In fact he suggests that it might be simpler 'being hedged around with fewer relationships with affines and ritual practices'. He rejects the complexity argument on the ground that it is merely evidence of 'a lack of theoretical concepts available' (Mitchell 1963:7) for analysis. Quantitative methods, Mitchell suggests, should 'be used to refine and deepen the generalizations which have been derived from anthropological methods or to bring to light regularities which might otherwise have escaped notice' (1963:8).

This approach can best be implemented within the framework of situational and network analysis. Here the question of perimeters and of frequencies of specific types and ranges of behaviour does not initially arise. The starting point for urban African research should be the actions and activities of an individual, a townman, or the membership activities and programme of a voluntary association or the composition of neighbourhoods. In all cases hypotheses can be tested by following through the activities of individuals or groups. As in rural tribal studies, so in urban studies, the starting point of analysis should lead to an opening up of the total network of relationships extant in the system. Once significant relationships are established, quantitative method should be used to give precision and frequency measures to the generalizations made. However it is equally important that the student of an African urban area enters the system *at a number of points*, preferably from the very beginning of the research work or at least over a period of time. This is important because of the diversity of groups and the possibility of more multiplex roles acted out by individuals and groups. Yet another justification is the rapidity of social change in urban areas.

In this respect Southall sounds a warning when he writes: 'It is important to distinguish the rapidity of change in a system or a situation from the rapidity of change in persons'. (1961:18). I believe this conceptualization of change points to the view that when analysing urban systems we are face-to-face with a more dynamic or changeable social structure than in rural areas, while at the same time individual norms change at a far slower rate. The important point is that an urban system produces a vast range of different *situations* in which individuals and groups are caught and which they handle with varied objectives in mind. It is from this point of view that the fieldworker must devise a research technique which will allow for observations of a number of groups, neighbourhoods and distinctly urban situations. The pitfalls of this approach are well set out by Mitchell who cautions us not to embark on rural-urban comparisons in situational analysis lest we inadvertently analyse African urban data in terms of 'culture change' rather than 'situational' change. There is a clear place for 'historical' or 'processive' change, as Mitchell designates non-situational change, but such studies need to be carried out over a considerable time span so that major institutional changes can be documented. However this conceptualization introduces a typological distinction which is difficult to apply, in as much as all situational analysis leads to a demonstration, eventually, of 'historical' and 'processive' change. (Mitchell 1962; 1963:9-12). A given urban type of relationship, behaviour, act or attitude, while distinctly urban, nevertheless can be fitted into an institutional referant which need not be the rural system. This is, I believe, shown most clearly in the analysis of urban voluntary associations and in particular of the syncretistic cults (Little 1965: 35-46). In suggesting this modification of Mitchell's approach, I do not ignore Gluckman's warning that tribal origins of the new townsmen are of secondary importance. But the urban system *has* its links to the rural hinterland in the same way as the latter reaches out to the urban area. A migrant arriving in town must act as a townsman in those situations which demand it. Some situations however demand that he act otherwise – at least for the time being. This does not produce an uneasy mixture of rural and urban life but rather selective situational contact and behaviour. The concentration should rather be on the urban social system *as a system*, or as Gluckman and others have suggested, on a specific 'social field' which demands that we describe and analyse 'the pattern of social interaction within it and the values and beliefs in terms of which this interaction takes place' (Mitchell 1963:12-13).

In the past, African urban studies, not of the general survey type, have concentrated on specific parts of the urban social system. In this respect anthropologists have merely had to face the same problems as they experienced in rural tribal studies. A tribal study selects a village, or a set of identifiable units, as a focus of study. The assumption is, of course, that the particular unit for observation is representative of a particular 'tribe' or a particular society or of a particular segment of either. At the same time, or at a later stage, comparisons are made with other tribes, other societies or other segments in the context of a hypothesis to be tested. Those working in an urban situation cannot proceed in quite the same way.

Although theoretically the study of even one African urban neighbourhood, or of a distinct 'social situation' that has arisen should reveal much of the social fabric of the total urban society, the larger and more complex the town the greater the possibility that each neighbourhood bears distinctive features. This approach could be modified if we study a very small town which is still in an early stage of growth, development and differentiation. But, certainly, if the town is large, and has been in existence for a considerable time, a number of neighbourhoods, associations and groupings of all kinds must be examined. However, in either case it is important to treat the urban social system as one 'social field' which 'may be thought of as a series of inter-connecting relationships all of which in some way influence each other'. Whether it is appropriate for us to conceptualize our thinking, and the analysis of our (urban) data, in terms of a single social field is a matter which needs separate and particular treatment. The important point is, as it bears on methodology, that urban Africans are 'involved in a number of different sets of social relations which stem from forms of social organization distinct from, and in many respects opposed to, one another' (Epstein 1958:46). The various subsystems, referred to, are 'interdependent, but they are not synchronized' (Epstein 1958:234).

It is, therefore, by means of such a conceptualization that the student of African urban life might most usefully proceed in gathering and ordering his data. However it is clearly evident that the approach in this presentation needs refinement in many respects. Certainly a number of other important features of African urban studies have not been treated adequately or have been wholly ignored. One of these is the relationship of social change to urban research techniques. Whatever the multiple facets of this relationship are, the need for longitudinal studies is now very pressing.

Urban studies in Africa have suffered from the same handicap as rural studies: the need for greater time perspective. Researchers have lived among a people for a limited time. Thus they reported on the life of a particular community as it was at a particular moment in time. True, this does not result in a static presentation because most students have shown how institutions and values have changed over time. But the transformation in urban areas is particularly rapid with the result that urban institutions are, or seem to be, in a constant state of flux. The concept of social structure sprang from the work of social anthropologists who were in relatively static and ethnically homogeneous communities. But as societies change they take on a new and different kind of structure and complexity – a structure which is increasingly the outcome of the way individuals manipulate a wide variety of situations and social relations not hitherto part of rural life. This in turn is the result of an ever widening field of choices which the individual can make in social, economic and political life (Mair 1963:11-31). This is the essence of change and modernization which gives rise to new networks which cut across and involve change over the entire system. The same process, no doubt, gives rise to what appears to be, at first sight, a large number of relatively unstructured situations but which, on closer inspection, might turn out to possess a large measure of structure and regularity. Gamble, for example, refers to the variety of the urban situational networks as 'social encounters'. He writes (1963):

New situations are constantly arising, and rights and obligations are more rarely formulated, a greater number of alternative patterns of behaviour presenting themselves.
Social encounters, too, tend to be more casual – on the level of men meeting in the same bar for a drink, walking to and from work together; drifting to the same street corner to associate with friends and acquaintances; renting rooms in the same house; supporting the same football team; or acknowledging a feeling that one has something in common with a man who comes from the same part of the country. Among women informal groups are formed by meeting at the same stream for washing clothes, or at the same stand pipe for drawing water.

Furthermore, no place in this presentation has been given to the presence of conflict and its integrative or disjunctive consequences. The daily activities of individuals, be it in a rural or an urban context, bring to light basic inconsistencies of the normative and the institutional system. Any social and cultural system is a delicately balanced – and as such integrated – system of opposed groups. It is possible that in the urban context there is a greater tendency for these groups to proliferate while at the same time membership in any grouping can be changed more readily, thus providing a larger measure of opportunity for individual role performance than in a rural system (Mayer 1962; Southall 1959:17-34). Urban research techniques, therefore, must take into account the need for approaches and methods which will reveal these conditions.

Conclusion. Theory and method must be closely geared together. The new areas of interest to which social anthropologists are turning demand from them not only the need to re-work traditional anthropological techniques, but also an acceptance of the research techniques of other disciplines. For example, no mention has been made of such standard techniques as participant observation, intensive interviewing and special questionnaire techniques as these are conventionally used in social anthropology and sociology (Richards 1946: 272-316). Special attention should also be paid to the orientation, and the techniques, formulated in more recent years, pertaining to the study of traditional, yet large-scale societies, i.e. India, South Asia, Puerto Rico, Mexico and the like (Gillin 1949:392-399; 1957:24-39). A direct outcome of this development is the 'community study method' (Arensberg 1954:109-124; Taylor 1947: 416-441) which is likely to have considerable relevance and usefulness for African urban studies.

Yet another dimension which clearly needs further exploration, as it relates to methodology, is the political and racial contexts in which the urban African research worker invariably finds himself. For example, Powdermaker (1962: xix) discusses a barrier that was hard to overcome although it was essential to do so:

I lived in the European part of the municipality [of Luanshya in Zambia], and it would have been impossible from either the European or African point of view for me to have lived on the segregated African township. Although I drove to it almost daily, I was missing the intimate knowledge and feeling – tone of daily life which comes from actually living in a community, seeing and hearing much that goes on, and participating in daily life, all of which is so essential to an understanding of any society.

Non-African research workers are increasingly subject to 'surveillance' by African government officials, trade union leaders and other political leaders. It is not unusual for research workers to be held up to public ridicule (Nyasaland Protectorate 1964:44-45). In pre-independence days the research worker worked under the protective umbrella of the colonial officials[1] and much of their work reflected the ideology of colonialism, i.e. the subordinate status of Africans. Indeed, the Sofers write, primarily in respect to the African community in Jinja, Uganda, that the 'most effective single point of entry into a community is through the top levels of status, authority and prestige', presumably being a European vis-a-vis Africans! Yet they likewise caution the researcher 'not [to] be too closely associated or identified with the group in authority'. From what the Sofers tell us it appears that the suspicions of urban Africans were such that their role of independent researchers was never wholly accepted by the African population. They write about 'occasional onrushes of anxiety that we might after all be government officials who would somehow use the research information against Africans' (Sofer and Sofer 1955:8). In this respect, all anthropological research has to 'live down' a past which is often condemned by present-day African leaders. It is therefore wise for those working in towns of Africa to proceed with caution and to obtain the understanding and support of the local leaders. It is in the towns that a minor mismanagement, or an error of judgement, can seriously interfere with the orientation and the field methods of the research worker. Rumour spreads rapidly and suspicions are raised immediately. Most towns are filled with aspiring politicians who are willing to latch on to any issue which places them in the public eye; newspapers are ever ready to report on the activities of research workers. Tense racial and political situations limit the activities of research workers (Mayer 1961:297; Wilson and Mafeje 1963:11-12; Bettison 1959:112-114; McCulloch 1956a:13-14).

[1] This is brought out clearly by Sofer and Sofer (1955: 7) who write:
We arrived in Jinja as academic research workers attached to the East African Institute of Social Research, and working with Government backing. On our arrival the administrative officer [a European Protectorate Uganda Government official] then in charge of the town, showed us round the area and introduced us to certain European officials, businessmen and African chiefs with whom the research was likely to bring us into contact.

Nor has any attention been paid in this paper to the problems raised by the use of enumerators and research assistants in African urban research. Generally urban studies rely more extensively on such junior personnel. Their use raises special problems for field work methods. It is not always easy to find assistants who have had some training in field work. The way out of this is to give brief and supervised training using the learn-by-doing approach (Acquah 1958: 8). For example, Powdermaker writes (1962:xvi-xvii):

Finding good assistants was not easy. After a period of trial and error, I found seven students in their late teens who were home on vacation from the Munali Secondary School in Lusaka. I employed them for five weeks for a survey of the use of the mass media . . . The young male assistants were bright and receptive. I gave them some initial training, and then they met with me every morning when I reviewed and discussed the interviews they had handed in the previous day. They quickly caught on to the goals of the study and to the method of asking open-ended questions to elicit attitudes, as well as specific questions for factual information.

Most urban studies gloss over the problems posed by inadequate training of field assistants. Some research workers have considerable difficulties in explaining to their assistants not to take anything for granted. Supervision of untrained interviewers is important. Gamble, for example, writes as follows (1963:264):

Checks on the work of interviewers were made either by comparing work of different men, by comparing the work done by an interpreter working on his own with results obtained by the author, and by checking a proportion of the interviews to see that the persons mentioned had actually been seen. This led to the discovery on one occasion that an interpreter had not bothered to interview people, but had filled in the forms himself at home.

Bettison in Blantyre-Limbe seems to have developed what might be termed the 'group study method' which he describes as follows (1958:2-3):

A team from six to ten . . . Research Assistants put through a questionnaire in each village [in the peri-urban area of Blantyre-Limbe]. The Research Assistants comprised a number of experienced men with five or more years research experience and a number of local recruits. The latter underwent both theoretical and practical training prior to being put into the field. The practical training was supplied concurrently with the piloting of the questionnaire. There is reason to believe that the work was done carefully and reliably.
The questionnaire . . . was devised by the group method, i.e. the Senior Research Assistants went together to villages . . . and there talked, drank beer and so became broadly acquainted with the

type of social structure in the villages; concurrently the Research Officer made contact with local officers of Government, examined any written material on the local area and devised a preliminary draft of the questionnaire . . . thereafter the whole team met round a table to discuss . . .

This group method has several advantages. It unites the theoretical knowledge of the Research Officer with the practical experience of the Assistants before any piloting of the draft is attempted; it encourages a team spirit towards the task ahead; it elucidates points through argument and discussion which neither the Research Officer nor the Assistants had previously foreseen; it is the product of the team as a whole rather than of any one individual; and speeds the work by ensuring that every team member knows the exact meaning of words used in the questions . . . It is possible that the method is satisfactory only where both Research Officer and some Assistants are experienced in field research.

The problems raised by the extensive use of research assistants are particularly applicable to all those urban studies investigating living conditions, consumption patterns and standards of living. The study by Mersadier of the town of Thiès, Senegal might be cited as an example (1956:535-545).

The approach taken in this paper is that theoretical orientations in African urban studies are closely related to field work methods (and, in some measure to field relations, a subject in need of special exploration) which are likely to differ from those employed by anthropologists working in the rural areas. By itself this is hardly a significant observation but what is possibly more important is the need to explore more fully the complex urban social system in such a manner and by such techniques that we obtain more than a descriptive presentation and a catalogue of characteristics. Research in African urban society might lead to a more comprehensive analysis and understanding of those significant characteristics which have been seen in a static rather than dynamic context. As pointed out earlier, certain assumptions and propositions have been made about major normative and institutional patterns. It is likely that the value and significance of these propositions can be re-evaluated in urban studies. Towards this end, refined research techniques are essential.

references

I. ACQUAH (1958) Accra survey, London.

R. J. APTHORPE ed. (1958) Present interrelations in Central African rural and urban life, Eleventh conference proceedings, Rhodes-Livingstone Institute, Lusaka.

C. M. ARENSBERG (1954) The community study method, *AJS* 60: 109-124.

G. BALANDIER (1956) Urbanism in West and Central Africa: the scope and aims of research, in: D. Forde ed., Social implications of urbanization and industrialization in Africa south of the Sahara, Paris: 495-510.

M. BANTON (1957) West African city: a study of tribal life in Freetown, London.

M. BANTON (1961) The restructuring of social relationships, in: A. W. Southall ed., Social change in modern Africa, London.

J. BARNES (1954) Class and committees in a Norwegian island parish, *Human Relations* 7: 39-58.

D. G. BETTISON (1958) The demographic structure of seventeen villages, Blantyre-Limbe, Nyasaland, Rhodes-Livingstone Communication 11, Lusaka.

D. G. BETTISON (1959) Numerical data on African dwellers in Lusaka, Northern Rhodesia, Rhodes-Livingstone Communication 16, Lusaka.

E. BOTT (1955) Conjugal roles and social networks, *Human Relations* 8: 345-384.

P. BROWN (1962) Non-agnates among the patrilineal Chimbu, *Journal of the Polynesian Society* 71: 57-69.

W. H. CHINN (1962) Social problems of rapid urbanization with particular reference to British Africa, U.N. Conference on the Application of Science and Technology for the benefit of the less developed areas, Geneva, E/CONF. 39/G./3.

S. COMHAIRE-SYLVAIN (1950) Food and leisure among the African youth of Leopoldville (Belgian Congo), Communication from the School of African Studies, New series, 25.

S. COMHAIRE-SYLVAIN (n.d.) Migration, in: S. Stanley ed. (1960) Social Survey of Addis Ababa, Addis Ababa.

K. J. COOPER (1959) Rural-urban differences in responses to field techniques, *HO* 18 (# 3): 135-139.

H. J. DE BLIJ (1963) Dar es Salaam, Evanston.

EAST AFRICA ROYAL COMMISSION 1953-1955 REPORT (1955) Cmd. 9475, London, H.M.S.O.

A. L. EPSTEIN (1957) African townsmen, *Human Problems in British Central Africa* 22:67-70.

A. L. EPSTEIN (1958) Politics in an urban African community, Manchester.

A. L. EPSTEIN (1961) The network and urban social organization, *The Rhodes-Livingstone Journal* 29:29-62.

A. L. EPSTEIN (1964) Urban communities in Africa, in: M. Gluckman ed., Closed systems and open minds, Edinburgh.

E. E. EVANS-PRITCHARD (1963) The comparative method in social anthropology, London (L. T. Hobhouse Memorial Trust Lecture No. 33).

R. FIRTH (1954) Social organization and social change, *Journal of the Royal Anthropological Institute* 84 (I & II):1-20.

H. FLEGG and W. LUTZ (1959) Report on an African demographic survey, *Journal for Social Research (South Africa)* 10:1-24.

D. FORDE ed. (1956) Social implications of urbanization and industrialization in Africa south of the Sahara, Paris.

D. FORDE (1963) Background and approaches, in: Urbanization in African social change, Centre of African Studies, University of Edinburgh: 1-6.

M. FORTES (1959) Time and social structure: an Ashanti case study, in: M. Fortes ed., Social structure: Studies presented to A.R. Radcliffe-Brown, Oxford: 54-84.

D. P. GAMBLE (1963) Sociological research in an urban community (Lunsar) in Sierra Leone, *Sierra Leone Studies, New series* 17: 254-68.

C. GEERTZ (1959) Form and variation in Balinese village structure, *AA* 61 (# 6): 991-1012.

J. L. GIBBS ed. (1965) Peoples of Africa, New York.

J. P. GIBBS ed. (1961) Urban research methods, Princeton.

J. GILLIN (1949) Methodological problems in the anthropological study of modern culture, *AA* 51 (# 3): 392-399.

J. GILLIN (1957) The application of anthropological knowledge to modern mass society, *HO* 15 (# 4): 24-39.

M. GLUCKMAN (1958) Analysis of a social situation in modern Zululand, *Rhodes-Livingstone Papers* 28, Lusaka.

M. GLUCKMAN (1960) Tribalism in modern British Central Africa, *Cahiers d'études africaines* 1:55-70.

M. GLUCKMAN (1961) Anthropological problems arising from the African industrial revolution, in: A. W. Southall ed., Social Change in modern Africa, London.

B. GUSSMAN (1963) Out in the midday sun, London.

P. C. W. GUTKIND (1962) African urban family life: comment on and analysis of some rural-urban differences, *Cahier d'études africaines* 3 (# 10): 149-217.

P. C. W. GUTKIND (1965a) African urbanism, mobility and the social network, *International Journal of Comparative Sociology*, in press.

P. C. W. GUTKIND (1965b) Network analysis and urbanism in Africa: the use of micro and macro analyses, *Canadian Review of Sociology and Anthropology* 2 (# 3), in press.

G. HAMDAN (1959a) Some aspects of the urban geography of the Khartoum complex, *Bulletin de la société de géographie d'Egypte* 32:89-120.

G. HAMDAN (1959b) Studies in Egyptian urbanism, Cairo.

G. HAMDAN (1964) Capitals of the new Africa, *Economic Geography* 40 (# 3): 239-53.

P. M. HAUSER and L. F. SCHNORE eds. (1965) The study of urbanization, New York.

E. HELLMANN (1935) Methods of urban fieldwork, *Bantu Studies* 9 (# 3): 185-202.

E. HELLMANN (1948) Rooiyard: a sociological survey of an urban native slum yard, *The Rhodes-Livingstone Papers* 13, Lusaka.

M. HUNTER (1961) Reaction to conquest, London (2nd ed.).

J. E. JAY (1964) The concepts of 'field' and 'network' in anthropological research, *Man* 64:137-139.

H. KUPER ed. (1965) Urbanization and migration in West Africa, Berkeley.

J. P. LEBEUF (1960) An outline of survey methods for the study of urbanization in Africa south of the Sahara, in: Housing and Urbanization, Second session of the Inter-African Conference, C.S.A., Nairobi, January 1959, 47, London, C.C.T.A.: 106-113.

J. LESLIE (1963) A survey of Dar es Salaam, London.

K. LITTLE (1965) West African urbanization: a study of voluntary associations in social change, Cambridge.

A. K. MABOGUNJE (1962) The growth of residential districts in Ibadan, *Geographical Review* 52 (# 1): 56-77.

A. K. MABOGUNJE (1965) Urbanization in Nigeria – a constraint on economic development, *Economic Development and Cultural Change* 13 (# 4, I): 413-438.

L. MAIR (1963) New nations, London.

B. MALINOWSKI (1945) The dynamics of culture change, P. M. Kaberry ed., New Haven.

B. MALINOWSKI et al. (1938) Methods of study of culture contact in Africa, Memorandum 15, International Institute of African Languages and Culture, London.

D. G. MANDELBAUM (1955) The study of complex civilizations, in: W. L. Thomas ed. (1955) Yearbook of Anthropology, New York: 203-225.

P. MARRIS (1961) Family and social change in an African city, London.

P. MAYER (1961) Townsmen or tribesmen, Capetown. Oxford University Press (for Institute of Social and Economic Research, Rhodes University).

P. MAYER (1962) Migrancy and the study of Africans in towns, *AA* 64 (# 3): 576-592.

M. MCCULLOCH (1956a) A social survey of the African population of Livingstone, *Rhodes-Livingstone Papers* 26: 57-65.

M. MCCULLOCH (1956b) Survey of recent and current field studies on the social effects of economic development in inter-tropical Africa, in: D. Forde ed., Social implications of industrialization and urbanization in Africa South of the Sahara, Paris: 53-225.

Y. MERSADIER (1956) An experimental investigation into urban African standards of living in Thiès, Senegal, in: D. Forde ed., Social implications of industrialization and urbanization in Africa South of the Sahara, Paris: 535-545.

J. C. MITCHELL (1951) A note on the urbanization of Africans on the Copperbelt, *Rhodes-Livingstone Journal* 12: 20-27.

J. C. MITCHELL (1956a) The Kalela dance, *Rhodes-Livingstone Papers* 27, reprinted 1959, Lusaka.

J. C. MITCHELL (1956b) Urbanization, detribalization and stabilization in southern Africa: a problem of definition and measurement in: D. Forde ed., Social implications of industrialization and urbanization in Africa South of the Sahara, Paris: 693-711.

J. C. MITCHELL (1957) Aspects of marriage on the Copperbelt of Northern Rhodesia, *Rhodes-Livingstone Journal* 22: 1-30.

J. C. MITCHELL (1959) The study of African urban social structure, Paper presented at the C.C.T.A. Conference on Housing and Urbanization, Nairobi, January 1959, C.A.S. mimeographed. (Summary in Housing and Urbanization, 47, C.C.T.A., London, 99-101).

J. C. MITCHELL (1960a) The anthropological study of urban communities, *African Studies* 19 (# 3): 169-172.

J. C. MITCHELL (1960b) Tribalism and the plural society, London.

J. C. MITCHELL (1962) Social change and the new towns of Bantu Africa, in: G. Balandier ed., Social implications of technological change, Paris: 117-130.

J. C. MITCHELL (1963) Theoretical orientations in African urban studies, Paper presented at the Meeting of Association of Social Anthropologists, Cambridge (U.K.).

J. C. MITCHELL (1964a) Aspects of occupational prestige in a plural society, Paper presented at the Sixth International African Institute Seminar on social class and elites in contemporary Africa, Ibadan.

J. C. MITCHELL (1964b) Differential fertility amongst urban Africans in Northern Rhodesia, *Central African Journal of Medicine* 10 (♯ 6): 195-211.

J. C. MITCHELL and A. L. EPSTEIN (1957) Power and prestige among Africans in Northern Rhodesia, *Proceedings and Transactions (Rhodesia Scientific Association)* 45:13-26.

J. C. MITCHELL and A. L. EPSTEIN (1959) Occupational prestige and social status among urban Africans in Northern Rhodesia, *Africa* 29 (♯ 1): 22-40.

J. C. MITCHELL and J. R. N. SHAUL (1963) An approach to the measurement of commitment to urban residence, Paper presented to the Second Central African Scientific and Medical Congress, Lusaka.

N. C. MITCHEL (1955) The Nigeria town: distribution and definition, *Research Notes* 7:1-13 (Dept. of Geography, Ibadan University College).

N. C. MITCHEL (1961) Yoruba towns, in: K. M. Barbour and R. M. Prothero eds., Essays on African population, London.

K. A. J. NYARKO (1959) The development of Kumasi, *Bulletin of the Ghana Geographical Association* 4 (♯ 1): 3-8.

NYASALAND PROTECTORATE (1964) Proceedings of the first meeting of the first session of the National Assembly, second day, 27th May 1964, Zomba, Government Printer: 44-45.

J. C. PAUVERT (1960) The process of urbanization in French West and Equatorial Africa and Cameroon, in: Housing and urbanization, Second session of the Inter-African Conference, C.S.A. Nairobi, January 1959, Pub. No. 47, C.C.T.A. London: 80-92.

B. A. PAUW (1963) The second generation, Capetown.

H. POWDERMAKER (1962) Copper town: changing Africa, New York.

A. R. RADCLIFFE-BROWN (1951) The comparative method in social anthropology, *Journal of the Royal Anthropological Institute* 81 (I and II): 15-22.

J. RIBY-WILLIAMS (1962) Social problems of development and urbanization, U. N. Conference on the application of science and technology for the benefit of the less developed areas, Geneva, E/CONF. 39/G./36.

A. I. RICHARDS (1935) The village census in the study of culture contact, *Africa* 7 (♯ 1): 20-33.

A. I. RICHARDS (1946) The development of field work methods in social anthropology in: F. C. Bartlett et alii eds., The study of society: methods and problems, London.

A. I. RICHARDS (1963) Foreword, in: P. C. W. Gutkind, The royal capital of Buganda, The Hague: IX-XIII.

I. SCHAPERA (1933) The BaKxatla BaxaKxaefla: preliminary report of field investigations, *Africa* 6 (♯ 4): 402-414.

w. b. schwab (1962) Comparative field techniques in two African urban towns, Typescript.

l. silverman (1954) The urban social survey in the colonies, *Zaire* 8 (# 3): 279-99.

r. p. simms (1965) Urbanization in West Africa: a review of current literature, Evanston.

c. sofer and r. sofer (1955) Jinja transformed, *East African Studies* 4, Kampala.

m. soret (1962) Sociologists and town planning problems [Brazzaville]. Geneva, U.N. Conference of the application of science and technology for the benefit of the less developed areas, E/CONF. 39/G./33.

a. w. southall (1956) Some problems of statistical analysis in community studies, illustrated from Kampala (Uganda), in: D. Forde ed., Social implications of industrialization and urbanization in Africa south of the Sahara, Paris: 578-90.

a. w. southall (1959) An operational theory of role, *Human Relations* 12 (# 1): 17-34.

a. w. southall (1961) Introductory summary, in: A. W. Southall ed., Social change in modern Africa, London.

a. w. southall and p. c. w. gutkind (1957) Townsmen in the making: Kampala and its suburbs, *East African Studies* 9, Kampala.

m. n. srinivas and a. beteille (1964) Networks in Indian social structure, *Man* 64:165-168.

r. w. steel (1961) The towns of tropical Africa, in: K. M. Barbour and R. M. Prothero eds., Essays on African population, London.

d. j. stenning (1962) Documentary survey of crime in Kampala, Uganda, United Nations, Economic commission for Africa, Workshop on urbanization in Africa, Addis Ababa, SEM/URB/AF/13.

r. e. s. tanner (1964) Conflict within small European communities in Tanganyika, *HO* 23 (# 4): 319-327.

c. c. taylor (1947) Techniques of community study and analysis as applied to modern civilized societies, in: R. Linton ed., The science of man in the world crisis, New York.

united nations economic commission for africa (1962a) Family living studies in Africa, Workshop on urbanization in Africa, Addis Ababa, SEM/URB/AF. &/ADD. 1.

united nations economic commission for africa (1962b) Introduction to the Problems of Urbanization in Tropical Africa, Workshop on urbanization in Africa, Addis Ababa, SEM/URB/AF. 1/ADD. 1.

united nations economic commission for africa (1962c) Workshop on urbanization in Africa, Addis Ababa, SEM/URB/AF, 1-28, mimeographed.

j. van velsen (1964) The politics of kinship, Manchester.

a. f. wells (1935) The local social survey in Great Britain, London.

w. f. whyte and l. k. williams (1964) The use of questionnaire surveys for community studies of culture change and economic development, Paper delivered at the annual meeting of the American Anthropological Association.

g. wilson (1941, 1942) An essay on the economics of detribalization in Northern Rhodesia, *The Rhodes-Livingstone Papers* 5 (# I) and 6 (# II), Lusaka.

m. wilson and a. mafeje (1963) Langa: a study of social groups in an African township, Capetown.

9   *the anthropologist in government service*

J. W. SCHOORL

Introduction. The position of the anthropologist in government service will be discussed in the light of an investigation carried out by the author among the Muyu people of West Irian, which at the time was still a part of the kingdom of the Netherlands. In 1954 the then Governor, Dr. J. van Baal, himself a cultural anthropologist, charged me with an investigation to be carried out during a period of 6 months in the Muyu region. I was an administrative officer, but for the duration of the enquiry I was exempted from all administrative duties. After the investigation was concluded I was appointed head of the Muyu subdivision.

Since an important part of the enquiry was concerned with existing administrative problems Dr. van Baal selected me, as an administrative officer cum anthropologist, for this assignment.

For a better understanding of the situation the reader will need to know something about the Muyu people and their culture.

The Muyu tribe inhabits the hilly country along the border of Australian New Guinea between the central highlands and the plains of the south coast. A small part of this tribe resides in the Australian area. At the end of June, 1955, the Administration counted 12.223 members of this tribe in the Muyu region of West Irian.

The first contacts between the Muyu region and the west date from some military explorations between 1907 and 1915. More intensive contacts came about through the bird of paradise hunting expeditions, carried out from Merauke between 1914 and 1926. Chinese and Indonesian hunters penetrated deep into the interior of the Muyu region. The Muyu assisted the hunters, in return for western goods – especially axes and knives. Many Muyu, particularly younger men, went along with the hunters to the Merauke sub-division. In this way a knowledge of western culture, such as it existed in the sub-division of Merauke, was introduced in Muyu society.

In 1933 the Order of the Sacred Heart opened a mission post at Ninati. The Administration followed in 1935. Soon after their arrival, the Mission attempted to concentrate the population into villages with a minimum of 100 to 150 inhabitants. This was connected with the fact that the mission used schools as an important medium in missionary work, another reason being the subsidy allotted by the Government for schools with at least 15 pupils. Concentration in villages thus became desirable, and this endeavor was supported by the Administration.

Western education was promptly accepted by the Muyu. There was no resistance against schools on account of the new religious beliefs taught there. Their easy acceptance of the schools was due to their knowledge concerning schools in the Merauke sub-division. School was to them a means towards acquiring 'progress': western material welfare.

Although the people themselves wanted to be taught, the formation of villages met with difficulties. Attachment to the way of life in the original settlements, economic reasons, especially pig-breeding, individualism and strong individual rights to land, all led to resistance against the forming of villages and permanent residence in the latter.

A lack of mutual kinship relations could not be the reason for a lack of integration within the village, since nearly all villagers were related to each other in some way. Village chieftains and their assistants, appointed by the Administration, had but little authority.

Originally the Muyu lived together in small patrilineally related groups or lineages. The number of members of forty-two lineages investigated varied from 2 to 61.

The lineage was a territorial group with a territory of its own. Although the dwellings of individual families might be scattered, they were always situated on the territory regarded as belonging to the lineage. The importance of the territorial element in this institution is indicated by the Muyu term for the lineage: *nuwàmbíp*, which literally means 'our dwellings'. The territory belonging to the lineage was called *nuwàmbípkím*, literally 'the place of our dwellings'.

The lineage is attached to its territory by traditional and religious bonds. On this territory there is a sacred spot called *kètpòn* which is *àmòp*, that is, taboo. It is preferably avoided. There is a story or myth attached to each *ketpon*. Most of these myths are the exclusive property of the lineage on whose territory the *ketpon* is located but some of them are more general property. In a few cases a *ketpon* belongs jointly to two or more lineages. Such situations may be the result of residential changes or splitting up of lineages. In spite of this, land tenure is not communal within the lineage, but individual.

The Muyu depends on his garden for an important part of his diet. Bananas and tubers are grown as principal crops. Fish is not abundant. Pigs are bred, not to provide meat for home consumption but as a means of obtaining cowry-money. Women occupy an important position in economic life by the part they play in gardening and above all in the care of pigs.

The cowry shell (*òt*), may be regarded as money among the Muyu. It serves as a medium of exchange, a standard of value and a store of value. Trading expeditions range 40 to 50 kilometers from the place of residence. The pig feasts are also aimed at acquiring cowry-money while at the same time these feasts have the function of markets.

Four features strike us in this culture when compared with some other primitive cultures. These salient features are:

1 Individualism: the relatively great independence of the individual with respect to the groupings to which he belongs.
2 Mobility: the Muyu is often away on trips to keep up friendly relations and, in particular, for trading purposes.
3 The atmosphere of fear, distrust and circumspection: this atmosphere is the result of such factors as personal justice, a strong compulsion for revenge, the explanation of sickness and death as due to sorcery and the methods of discovering who is guilty.

4 the main interest of the Muyu: the acquisition of property in the form of *ot* and other valuables.

The anthropologist's position with regard to the administration. I had been with the New Guinea administration for two years when I was asked to carry out this anthropological enquiry. In view of the necessity of taking administrative measures for the Muyu region an intensive investigation was not considered advisable, since the results of such an investigation would not be available for two or three years. The enquiry, moreover, was to concentrate on specific administrative problems.

For administrative purposes it is often necessary that data of this kind be obtained at short notice. Administrative work continues even if no detailed information is available and often, unfortunately, decisions have to be made on the basis of insufficient knowledge. The information and advice supplied by an anthropologist may furnish the administrative officer with a sounder basis for these decisions.

But even in those cases where extensive anthropological reports have been published, the administrative officer does not always have the time and/or schooling to work through them. And if he does, he will not always find an answer to his specific problems. Every investigation is concerned with particular aspects, whether scientific or 'practical', and often otherwise detailed reports pay no special attention to specific administrative problems. What the administrative officer needs is a concise but very lucid discussion of the particular problems that concern him in determining administrative policy and in carrying it out. The selection, for this particular enquiry, of an administrative officer trained in anthropology was based on the consideration that the investigator should be alive to the specific problems of administrative work and that his recommendations should be feasible within the administrative framework. All administrative work has to take place within a framework of existing ideas, traditions, laws and regulations, and available means. An administrative officer will quickly see what possibilities are afforded by this framework in combination with factors of time and place. An anthropologist not familiar with administrative work will need more time for this. There is a danger, however, that the administrator – investigator will not be able to detach himself sufficiently from existing administrative practices and that consequently his mind will not be sufficiently open to new possibilities.

The administrative officer, moreover, is a member of a bureaucratic organization and as such he is involved, whether consciously or unconsciously, in the competition for higher posts. A temporary assignment outside the actual administrative apparatus does not mean that the influence of this competition is altogether absent. This raises the question of objectivity. Will his report and his recommendations be influenced by the fact that he is a member of this organization? The anthropologist carrying out an investigation in behalf of the administration, without having worked as an administrator himself, will of course be subject to similar influences but they are less likely to affect his work since his aspirations are of a more academic nature, making him more independent, with regard to the administration. The administrative officer will need to be aware of this danger and, on the basis of his personal responsibility as a scientist, be prepared to take the risk of making unpleasant remarks and unpopular recommendations. My situation in this respect was favourable since the Governor himself attached great importance to an objective report, the results of which might help to determine a suitable administrative policy.

The acculturation situation in the Muyu region at the time of the enquiry. Various factors were involved in the changes that took place in the culture of the Muyu as a result of western influences. Such factors were, in the first place, the nature of the western culture which exerted these influences and the nature of traditional Muyu culture. Other important factors were the location of the Muyu region, climate, the nature of the soil and so on. The process of change was determined by an interplay of factors some of which were conducive and others impedimental to the acceptance of certain elements of western culture.

The western influence of the Muyu region took place through two important channels, western administration and mission. These consciously worked towards the introduction for certain changes. For the mission, schools were the first means to this end. Since the government subsidized schools with at least 15 pupils, the mission endeavoured to concentrate the population in villages with a number of inhabitants that would guarantee this number of pupils. The spreading of education was limited by the number of qualified teachers available. At first these teachers were Kaiese or Tanimbarese. After World War II the training of Irian, including Muyu, teachers was taken in hand. In those villages where no qualified teachers were appointed, instruction was limited mainly to the teaching of the Indonesian language, prayers, the catechism and church liturgy. Since the school was an important instrument in the missionary method, the mission was averse to anything that interfered with its smooth operation. One such element was village-absenteeism, which was regarded as the cause of school-absenteeism, and which also impeded the conversion of older persons.

The primary aim of the western administration was the pacification of and maintenance of order in the Muyu region. A subsidiary aim was to civilize the population and to promote the activities carried out in this respect by the mission. This meant that the administration also favored the formation of villages of sufficient size and the setting up of schools. School attendance and residence in the villages were supervised by the administration. The supervision of hygiene in the villages and medical work were also considered a part of civilization work.

These western institutions, administration and mission, worked together to bring changes in Muyu culture. Certain conditions were considered essential for this purpose. The administration employed coercion, if necessary to obtain these conditions. Such coercive measures were taken with the approval or on the advice of the mission.

On the part of the mission there was little or no direct interference with the religious practices of the Muyu. In sermons and conversations the missionaries did express censure, but no systematic action was taken, even in the case of Christians. The Christian religion was more or less placed side by side with the old religion. The mission expected that the old religious notions and practices would gradually disappear. In the sphere of social organization their main objection was, as we saw, to the scattered system of residence. Apart from this, by addressing themselves in the first place to the young they interfered with the traditional authority of older people. No attempt was made to alter the system of kinship relations or marriage, except the practice of polygyny.

The administration, too, did not interfere directly with many aspects of Muyu culture. As far as social organization was concerned it disapproved mainly of scatterred residence, the system of personal justice and forced marriages. In the religious sphere the administration only took steps against the practice of delaying burial, since this was contrary to western norms of hygiene. In addition measures were taken against any messianic movements that came to light, for these movements constituted a threat to law and order.

The western culture with which the Muyu were confronted by no means displayed the great diversity that the term may denote. Initially the mission regarded education exclusively as a means of Christianization. It was not till after World War II that they realized the importance of more extensive education which might help the Muyu to obtain certain functions. The limitedness of western culture as it presented itself to the Muyu was further due to the fact that the school teachers were mainly Indonesians or Irians who themselves had only a limited knowledge of western culture.

Muyu notions of western culture were also limited by the fact that non-Irians and especially whites held leading positions in their community. Whites were hardly ever known to do any manual work and as a rule they were well-paid. This gave the Muyu an incomplete and therefore distorted picture of the western world. The west was personified in the wealthy white who did little or no manual work and held leading positions. Apart from this the Muyu saw only the products of the western world: a multitude of western goods and a profusion of western money. They had no opportunity of observing the background of all this wealth or the effort expended in producing it.

Prerequisites for the success of a short-term investigation. A short-term investigation is by no means always profitable. Conditions need to be favourable for such an investigation to produce results of any value. Although these conditions vary with time and place it may be useful to mention here several factors which contributed to the success of my investigation.

1 Language. A first requisite is some previous knowledge of a language with which the people studied are familiar or which at least enables one to com-

municate with informants and interpreters. Within a period of 6 months one cannot be expected to learn a language in addition to carrying out the investigation and writing the report.

In my case the Indonesian language could be used. This language had been introduced in West Irian by Indonesian and Chinese traders, by the Government and by the missionaries. Many Muyu had a fair knowledge of Indonesian. My training as an administrative officer and my two years in West Irian had taught me sufficient Indonesian for this work.

2   Personal experience. All the problems that face an anthropologist when starting an investigation in a strange country, which often take much time to solve, did not exist for me, or at least to a much less extent, because of my experience as an administrative officer. I knew the way to travel in this country and I needed no time to get acquainted with the subtle relationship between mission and administration.

3   Access to records. A study of records and documents must be considered important for every investigation concerned with change. It helps to distinguish trends in development. Such a study, however, is not only important for the historical perspective it provides for social and cultural changes. It may also help to provide a starting-point for subsequent field-work. In particular I wish to point out the significance of court sentences. The records of courts of justice may contain interesting information concerning customary law. They may show, too, to what extent the people's notions of justice disagreed with those of the administration. They illustrate not only the conflict between the system of personal justice in a small society and the system of public justice in the larger society, but also the tensions and antagonisms within the native community.

The administration archives of Tanah Menah, the only station in West Irian where the complete pre-war archives had been preserved, were an important instrument in my investigation. I stayed at Tanah Menah for two weeks, waiting for a boat connection with the Muyu area. Thanks to the cooperation of the administrator I had access to all records that might be of importance for my enquiry.

My study of these records proved to be especially important for the making of certain recommendations. I was able to point out, for instance, the great uneasiness that had arisen among the population, even leading to the murder of a policeman, when they thought the administration intended to withdraw the cowry-money from circulation.

4 The 'ripeness' of the region for this type of enquiry. In my opinion a brief enquiry is possible only when foreign influences have sufficiently penetrated the region for a number of people to have acquired a certain openness towards the investigation.

The Muyu were highly receptive to western culture, particularly western goods. Their traditional interest in in the acquisition of property (including cowry-money) as well as their individualism and mobility contributed to this attitude. Although some of them, especially among the older people, still regarded every stranger with suspicion, a large part of the population cherished great expectations of what the foreigners might bring them. Many persons, especially among those who had become Christians or who had had prolonged contacts with foreigners elsewhere, were prepared to supply information about their way of life even if the desired information concerned some aspect about which they generally preferred not to speak before strangers.

The investigator's position with regard to the population. It is an anthropologist's ambition, when doing fieldwork, to avoid being identified with administrators, missionaries or traders. In my case this ambition was threatened when the administration intended to charge me with certain administrative duties. Administrators on the whole are not very sensitive to the desirability for the investigator to dissociate himself as much as possible from the authorities. Fortunately the Governor intervened to prevent such direct connection with the administration during the enquiry. Nevertheless I did not completely succeed in realizing the above-mentioned ambition. In the first place the missionaries in Mindiptana – centre of the administration of the Muyu region – organized an official welcome for me. The schoolchildren sang the Dutch national anthem, as they usually did for a visiting Dutch administrator. On my first orientation tour the school-teachers in each village I visited followed this example. No wonder, then, that the village headmen and their people could not regard me as quite unconnected with the administration. In some villages, moreover, I met Muyu who had known me as an administrative official in Merauke.

As a matter of fact my work could not but be associated with the administration. The European official had introduced me at a meeting of all the village headmen and on that occasion had told them that I would, among other things, investigate possibilities of development for the region. Some Muyu, too, had their own opinions about my investigation, connecting it in their minds with specific administrative problems. To get their cooperation I myself repeatedly pointed out that suitable measures for the desired development could only be taken if the administration knew and understood as much as possible of their customs and way of life. On the whole I consider such a justification of an anthropological or sociological investigation appropriate, except, of course, in those cases where the population expect nothing but ill from the government. For many Muyu, however, it seemed to me a reasonable argument, since they really wished for 'progress', i.e. development in the Muyu region.

All the same I tried to keep the typical picture of the administrator in the background. On my tours I was not accompanied by policemen, as the administrator always was. I issued no orders and inspected nothing, did not exercise power in any way. My prolonged stay in the various villages, my visiting people in their own houses, listening to their stories, taking no action against practices prohibited by the administration, all this gave me an 'image' of my own with the Muyu, sufficient to get the necessary information from them.

The local officials, missionaries and most of the schoolteachers, however, continued to regard me as an administrator with all the authority attached to that office. Their willingness to supply information was partly determined by this fact. As a former colleague I enjoyed the complete confidence of the administrative officials in the district. We have noted that as an anthropologist the former administrator is liable still to identify himself too much with the administration, even in his relationship with the population. If he recognizes this danger, however, he is in the favourable position of being able to see the administration through the people's eyes. Between the Roman Catholic missionaries and the administrative officials there were various differences with respect to administrative policy. In some cases these differences had developed into more or less open conflicts which were, of course, reflected in the reports of the missionaries and officials involved. The fact of my being a Protestant was perhaps a further reason for the unwillingness of the local missionaries to let me see more than one or two reports from the Mission's archives. In all other respects, however, my contacts with the missionaries in question were excellent.

Procedure of the investigation. Every anthropologist is faced with the same sort of problems in selecting one or more villages for more detailed study. Because of the short period of time available it seemed advisable to study only two villages intensively. I wished in any case to study more than one, because of the cultural differences within the Muyu region. Although we may speak of one Muyu culture, some differences are to be expected among a group of 12.000 people, scattered over c. 80 villages. A study of two villages will not, of course, give a complete picture but it does afford some impression of the magnitude of such differences and of the amount of conformity.

In order to arrive at an authorized choice I made an orientation tour, from 18 May to 5 June, visiting eighteen villages, selected in consultation with the local administrator. To visit all eighty villages would have taken too much time. The most important factor determining the choice of these eighteen villages was the presence of suitable informants. The distance between these villages was no more than a few hours' walk in each case, which made it possible to visit one village every day. Previously I had gathered as much information as possible on Muyu culture, to give me something to start from in my first interviews with informants.

Since I could not spend much time on winning the confidence of potential informants I tested their willingness to supply information in the course of my first interviews with them by bringing up subjects that are preferably not discussed with strangers. Although this is rather a rough method it suited me quite well in the circumstances. Obviously it can only be used if one has sufficient previous knowledge of the culture. It has certain drawbacks, too, since a potentially good informant may be put off by this method. In view of the circumstances, however, I believe I only profited by it, as willing informants were noticed straightaway.

This way of selecting a suitable village with good informants and interpreters also has its disadvantages. The first selection of 18 villages, followed by a fairly superficial contact with the inhabitants of each village meant that some undoubtedly interesting villages were left out and some potentially good informants were not noticed. In view of the available time this drawback had to be taken into the bargain.

Before visiting these 18 villages I had asked both the district official and the missionaries about suitable Indonesian-speaking informants. Their information proved valuable in many cases, although, of course their advice could not be blindly followed. Here the opposition between mission and administration came to the fore again.

My most important informant, Cornelis Kubun, was the village headman of Kawangtet. He had done a lot of travelling, having visited many islands of the Moluccas and was one of the few Protestants among the Muyu. His reputation with the Roman Catholic Mission was not so good, but the administration considered him an excellent headman. At our first encounter he told me that everything should be brought into the open, be 'turned upside down' for a change. To demonstrate this attitude towards his own culture he proceeded to give me all sorts of information about various forms of witchcraft, a subject on which the Muyu were, as a rule very secretive. On later checking his information proved to be completely reliable.

My principal informants in both villages were the village functionaries. They were accustomed to not being able to take part in the daily activities of the family on account of 'official' duties. Although I am convinced most of them enjoyed giving information they regarded this, too, as a sort of official duty. This was partly due, of course, to the fact that they still saw some connection between me and the administration. Their great readiness to cooperate was partly a result of the prestige this gave me in their eyes.

In addition to my interviews with the principal informants I interviewed, as much as possible, any other informants who happened to be available. In this way I wanted both to check previously acquired information and if possible obtain supplementary data. In Jibi I often talked in the evenings with some young informants, the principal among whom was a former policeman. These younger people proved to be far more willing than the older informants in this village to supply information about matters in the 'amop' (taboo) sphere. Although the brevity of the investigation limited the possibility of observing things actually taking place, I tried to do so as much as possible. For instance, I arranged to have the interviews in such a way that I could keep an eye on what was happening in the village. If necessary the interviews were interrupted or discontinued. In this way I was able to watch an ordeal (*awonatuk*) that I had not been told about. Even my otherwise very helpful informant Kubun, who had told me about the *awonatuk* in general, had not mentioned this one to me. The institution was frowned on by the administration and perhaps, being the headman, he did not want to admit that the *awonatuk* was still held in his village.

Only two months were available for collecting the material in the selected villages Jibi and Kawangtet, as I had to allow time for working out notes and writing the report. Even for a limited enquiry with a definite aim two months is a minimum, since the phenomena investigated should be studied in as wide a context as possible. The knowledge necessary for administrative purposes cannot be isolated from other aspects. This became clear in the course of the investigation but was already inherent in my instructions. These asked for information on:

1   The principal elements of social structure, that is kinship structure, kinship terminology and inheritance;
2   Land tenure;
3   Territorial organization, with data concerning the size of territorial groups and their leadership;
4   The sources of the troubles with the administration;
5   Possibilities of breaking down the supremacy of cowry-money;
6   Possibilities and difficulties in connection with the introduction of a development project.

The enquiry was held alternately in the two villages, twice a period of a fortnight in each village. This change of village after a fortnight had the advantage of giving the villagers a 'rest'. Another advantage consisted in the confrontation of the informants of one village with the information obtained in the other. The informants in Jibi knew that the subject on which I questioned them would also be discussed with those of Kawangtet and vice versa. This undoubtedly contributed to the accuracy of the information offered. The same effect was obtained by checking every piece of information as much as possible with other informants in the same village. The material already acquired also helped to stimulate the informants in the other village to supply more data, especially on subjects that were more or less 'amop' (taboo). When they found that I was already informed about certain 'amop' matters, new informants were less reluctant to give me more particulars. The existence of cultural differences also had a stimulating effect on the informants' interest in my investigation. As it proved, they often did not know about these differences themselves. When such differences came to light they made no attempt to adjust their information to my previously acquired material, which reinforced my impression that they did their best to provide me with accurate information.

Social structure. In both villages I started with a complete registration of the population. The villagers were used to registration since the administration registered the whole population regularly once a year or every two years (one of the reasons being the government's duty to report annually to the U.N.O.). My way of carrying out this registration, however, was radically different from the customary method. I did not summon all the inhabitants to the school or church but visited each house separately to take away some of the official aura surrounding the practice of registration. On these visits I was always accompanied by the village-headman or his assistant.

I believe that there are considerable advantages attached to beginning in this way in the case of small village communities (in my case respectively 286 and 382 inhabitants), provided the people are accustomed to registration and have no objections to it. I shall list some of these advantages.

a   While doing this registration work I was able, at the same time, to draw up a map of the village. This immediately provided an insight into the system of residence of kinship groups (the lineages), which formerly each lived on a territory of their own and now proved to have formed separate quarters in the village. In addition I was able to note any residents in these houses who did not actually belong to the lineage.

b I could directly place any villager who happened to be mentioned in the further course of the investigation.

c I was able to observe dwellings, furnishing and any changes in these as a result of foreign influences.

d Different types of kinship relations within the kinship groups were immediately noted. (It became apparent that the knowledge of genealogical depth was limited).

e It was possible to determine in what way the village headman was related to the various villagers and what kinship terms were used. Thus the great complexity of kinship relations was revealed.

f 'Strangers' in the village were remarked straightaway. The reasons for their presence could be traced later. At the same time I could inquire about any village members who were temporarily absent and find out the reasons for their absence.

g In the course of this registration I could look out for potential informants.

h Special types of marriage (such as sister exchange) could be noted and the people concerned could be asked what they thought of it.

i Through this registration I met practically all the inhabitants of the village. They could see that I did not have the habits of a typical administrative official, for I went to the trouble of visiting them in their own houses, I sat on the floor by the fire with them and I neither gave orders nor inspected anything. The enquiry showed that an important aspect of kinship relations is their concomitant function as trade relations. The extensive way of reckoning kinship relations is connected with this function.

Apart from providing trade relations, kinship relations also meant resting places on the trading-route. People travelled from one relative to another. Similarly, one's relatives might help by accompanying a traveller to relatives of his own who lived further on. A man from another village, a clever talker, was said to be an expert at working out all sorts of possible and impossible relationships. In this way he managed all over the Muyu region either to find relatives or to convince people that they were related to him. Thus he could travel everywhere without having to carry food. He found food and shelter in every village he visited and meanwhile dexterously disposed of his goods (tobacco etc.).

The reckoning of kinship relationships and the use of kinship terms thus proved to be notably a means of acquiring trade relations. In other words, the kinship system served other purposes besides the regulation of marriage relations. The Muyu do know a relationship outside kinship relations (*kam-barim*, i.e. acquaintance), but such a relationship is often later consolidated by arranging a marriage.

This possibility of extending relations through marriage is due to the fact that the bride-price is a dominant factor in the marriage system. It consists of a number (24-84) of cowry shells, *ot*, and of other valuables. A portion of the bride-price is returned in the form of other goods but an important part of it serves as a compensation for the rights acquired over the wife. This enables the Muyu to obtain another woman for the one ceded. This indirect system of exchange leaves a great freedom of choice in selecting a mate. Thus it is possible for the Muyu to increase his relations as much and as far as he likes through marriage (his own, his daughter's or his sister's).

Administrative problems: village formation and pig-feasts. As a result of their forced move to the villages founded by the Mission, many families lived a long way from their sago-plantations, gardens, and hunting and fishing grounds. The consequent lack of supervision of their property and the trouble resulting from the destruction of other people's property by their pigs caused them much damage. The Muyu found a good solution: they could take a second wife, so that there would be one to care for the children in the village while the other could look after the pigs at the forest-dwelling. This solution, however, met with fierce opposition on the part of the Mission. The latter believed a solution should be found in a gradual decrease of pig-breeding, since on the whole pigs were not bred for home consumption but only to be sold for cowry-money.

The pig-feasts are the principal feasts of the Muyu region. The feastgivers are members of one lineage or of a number of lineages combined. Preparations may take months or even years. Participants are invited from many different and distant settlements. The feast-givers sell the pigs they have slaughtered for a cash payment of cowry-money, usually to old exchange relations. By such a feast they succeed in collecting a large sum of money (cowry shells) on a single occasion. At these feasts markets were held, where all sorts of goods were sold or exchanged. Neither Mission nor administration were very happy with these feasts. The preparations took place outside the village, in a part of the forest that belonged to one of the feastgivers. This meant a prolonged absence from the village for the feastgivers and their families. During this time they did not take part in village work, did not go to church and their children often stayed away from school. During the actual feasts, some villages were practically deserted.

On their own initiative, (without instructions from higher authorities) the local administration had tied the feasts to a system of licences. A licence was granted only if in the feastgivers' village, village work was carried out properly and the children duly attended school. One of the questions asked by the Governor was whether it was advisable to continue the licence system and if so, on what conditions licences should be granted. The result of my investigation led me to recommend the cessation of the licence system. I found that in most cases the feastgivers could not exert sufficient influence on the village as a whole to realize the conditions necessary for obtaining a licence. Pig-feasts were only rarely the concern of the whole village. These lineages were too independent and the headman's influence too limited to expect a collective effort. In many cases the feastgivers' plans were upset by the negligence of fellow-villagers or the carelessness of schoolchildren. There was a danger, when a licence had been refused once or several times, that the injured party might take revenge on 'guilty' villagers or else would have no more to do with the administration and retire into the forest. This advice was followed and as far as I could see, in my later function as administrator, it had a favourable effect on the relations between people and administration.

The problem of personal justice. The Muyu have a highly developed system of personal justice. When a wrong or harm is inflicted the wronged individual himself takes action. He will often try to kill the offender or one of his next of kin. Reconciliation may be effected through exchange or payment of valuables. It is possible to hire assassins to carry out the retaliatory murder.

To make the vengeance complete, it was customary in former times to eat the victim's remains. If hired assassins were employed the employer received a previously stipulated part of the body. By beating the slit drum (wong) and the walls of the house in a special way people in neighbouring houses were notified that the victim's body was going to be eaten. Other persons who for some reason also harboured a grudge against the victim, could buy a part of the body in exchange for cowryshells, ornaments or stone axes. Various relatives were invited to take part in the eating of the victim. The victim's own next of kin were not allowed to eat his flesh. It would make them ill. For the same reason the eating of human flesh was considered dangerous for children. The eating of the victim's flesh made vengeance complete. In cases of war, therefore, it is certainly not true that all those killed were eaten. The person who was eaten was always the object of vengeance and not, for instance, a relative of his, except perhaps his wife. The aim was not merely to eat human flesh. On the contrary, the Muyu had a certain aversion to killing and eating human beings. In cases of adultery, the adulterers might both be killed and eaten. The wronged husband and his relatives would eat the woman and the woman's relatives the man. According to Muyu notions this makes for complete satisfaction.

Not many deaths are attributed to natural causes. Most deaths are ascribed to murder by witchcraft. Illness, as a prelude to death, is viewed in the same light. After the death of a kinsman, his relatives attempt to find the guilty person by means of an ordeal. The Muyu seeks his enemies in the near surroundings. People living far away, he feels, will attempt nothing against him unless they are hired as assassins. Due to the method of investigation, few relationships are free from suspicion and mistrust. Fear and mistrust are the dominating factors in Muyu society and have a disintegrating effect on social life. Lineages break up and relations are severed for such reasons. On the other hand crime is limited because of this atmosphere of fear.

The administration does not believe in the effectiveness of witchcraft and therefore does not take action in cases where the population ascribes an unexpected death to witchcraft. The same administration, however, does punish a person who takes an in Muyu eyes justified revenge in cases of rape or adultery. No wonder many older Muyu feel that the administration often acts in an unfair or at least very arbitrary fashion. In their opinion the fact that no action is taken against witchcraft is the cause of many deaths in the Muyu region. According to them there were considerably fewer deaths before the coming of the administration. Witchcraft was less common then for fear of revenge on the witches pointed out by the oracle.

But now that killing for revenge is prohibited, while the administration itself takes no action against witches, witchcraft makes an unnecessarily high number of victims.

The cowry-money. The acquisition of wealth in the form of valuables occupies an important place in Muyu life. The principal of these valuables are the *ot*, or cowry-money. Other valuables are ornaments (*wam* and *inam*) and utensils (such as stone axes), but *ot* are exclusively used as exchange-objects. The value of other goods is expressed in *ot*. Cowry shells thus have the typical functions of money. Accumulated wealth is stored in the form of *ot*. In a special dance, called *anotang*, the Muyu can display his wealth in *ot* at a particular moment (after a pig-feast or before paying a bride-price). Although other valuables may also be used as a means of exchange and a store of value, the *ot* exceeds these by far in importance. The *ot* may therefore be referred to as money. For small change, in payment of goods of less value than the *ot*, the traditional culture uses dogs' teeth. These, however, are much less important than *ot*.

Traditionally, the acquisition of *ot* and other valuables is one of the principal ambitions of the Muyu. Many aspects of their culture are touched by it. An extensive trading system has been developed. The essentially peaceful attitude of the Muyu towards members of other groups and tribes is directly connected with the importance of trade. So is the extensive way of reckoning kinship relations and the marriage system through which, as we have seen, relations may be extended, consolidated or renewed. For the woman's family, marriage also means the acquisition of valuables. This is the basis of the asymmetrical marriage system, part of the bride-price serving as a compensation for the woman ceded and as a means of obtaining another. Pig-breeding, which occupies such an important place in Muyu economy, is one of the principal sources of *ot*. The pig-feasts are aimed at acquiring the greatest possible number of *ot*. The *ot* itself and its acquisition are not confined to the purely secular sphere. Important religious practices and beliefs are connected with it. According to the myth the *ot* originated in primeval times. No additions are made to their total number. Lengthy religious ceremonies are carried out at the pig-feasts to ensure good sales and cash payments. One of these ceremonies is the killing of the sacred pig. The Muyu believes that deceased kinsmen, who were rich during their lifetime, will watch over and increase his wealth. At the time of the messianic movements of 1951-1953, great wealth in *ot* was expected from contacts with the spirits of the dead.

The records showed that in the past both Mission and administration had repeatedly advocated the disappearance of cowry-money on account of the part it played both in the bride-price institution and in the pig's meat trade. The opinions of Mission and administration differed on such subjects as whether or not *ot* currency should be abolished and polygyny prohibited, and the policy adopted varied with circumstances of time and persons involved. For a long time the mission believed the administration ought to abolish cowry-money, since in their opinion it led to all sorts of abuse such as retaliatory murder, witchcraft, forced marriages, polygyny and pig-breeding with all its undesirable consequences. The records, however, showed the great risks attached to any measures tending towards abolition of *ot* currency. The frequency of non-attendance at school led an assistant administrator to impose high fines on families staying at their gardens away from the village. In this way he withdrew so many *ot* from circulation that the people were disturbed at the monetary consequences. This ultimately led to the killing, in 1942, of a policeman by a village headman. After this the administrator was replaced by another.

Since that time no actual attempt was made to withdraw the *ot* from circulation. The desirability of doing so, however, was regularly mentioned by both missionaries and administrators to the people as well as to their own superiors. My investigation, too, was thought by some to be connected with this. In the course of it I found that several informants had a distinct opinion on the possibilities of replacing cowry-money. Some of these opinions showed a very good insight into the problems this would involve. In addition to sounding opinions I looked for objective indications to confirm them. In recent times, I found, some Muyu had been asking for government money instead of *ot*, both as a part of the bride-price and in connection with the pig's meat trade. My recommendation to the Government was to stimulate a gradual development by:

a   providing the Muyu with a regular income in western money, by the introduction of commercial crops in as large a part possible of the Muyu region,

b   (promoting) the establishment of a shop in this area,

c   promoting temporary paid employment of adult Muyu elsewhere, that they might become familiar with western money and its possibilities,

d   active Government participation in the pig's meat trade, including the possibility of exchanging western money for cowry-money and vice versa,

e   the same with respect to the goat-trade, once goats were introduced, as planned,

f   advising the Muyu about the possibilities offered by western money.

On the basis of this report the Governor decided to take no steps against cowry currency and to leave it to 'die out' as stone axes had died out.

The attitude of the Roman Catholic Mission changed radically after this report, which they, too, were given to read. One of the missionaries even told me in 1955 that the Mission would have serious objections if the administration were to abolish the *ot*. This change of attitude was mainly the result of a better understanding of the function of the bride-price, in which cowry-money played a prominent part. My investigation showed that the bride-price made for great freedom in choosing a mate and had a stabilizing effect on conjugal relations. The payment of a bride-price did not mean that the bride was purchased, as was until recently believed in missionary circles. It is an extension of the principle of reciprocity. A group that wants to survive must be sure that there is an incoming woman for every outgoing one. Maybe the simplest form of this is sister exchange. Somewhat more complicated is the arrangement by which two groups have a fixed mutual relationship as bride-givers and bride-takers. With the Muyu, the bride-price serves as a guarantee to the bride-giving group, in that the valuables acquired will enable them to obtain another woman from any group they choose.

Conclusion. As the above, I hope, has shown, a short investigation concentrated especially on problems of administration may be of great help in the determination of administrative policy. Unnecessary interference with the way of life of the people concerned may thus be prevented and consequent disturbances and suffering avoided. The same is true in the more limited sphere of so-called community development. The administration of West Irian aimed among other things at the introduction of modern education and modern health care, both of which activities may be considered more particularly a part of community development.

What has been said above, therefore, applies in particular to the situation in the so-called developing countries, where a small elite is trying to carry out a rapid modernization programme.

The combination of anthropologist and administrator or leader of a development programme, as the case may be, seems to me a happy one. Such a combination can be of great help in formulating an appropriate administration or development policy. The situation would be ideal if such functionaries were to carry out an anthropological/sociological investigation personally, before starting on their task. The time given to such an investigation would be more than compensated by the gains of better insight and consequently better founded policy.

I refer here only to those situations where the two roles are taken in succession. Investigation does not only require time for collecting data and placing them in the widest possible cultural context. It is equally necessary that the investigator at the time of the enquiry should be as far as possible removed from the atmosphere of authority. An administrator in office will find it difficult to obtain data concerning certain practices that are frowned upon or even prohibited by the administration. Even for an anthropologist who is totally unconnected with the authorities it is not always possible to investigate customs of this nature.

Of course an investigation of this sort is practicable only if the administrator or development leader in question has sufficient anthropological/sociological schooling – which, in my opinion, is an indispensable part of his training. Obviously the administrator or development leader will not always be in a position to carry out the investigation himself. It will be useful for him, however, to have carried out such an enquiry once at least. Mostly he will have to rely on the work of pure anthropologists or sociologists. Sufficient anthropological/sociological schooling, however, supported by experience in fieldwork will enable him to appreciate the work of others.

reference

JW. SCHOORL (1957) Kultuur en kultuurveranderingen in het Moejoe-gebied, Den Haag.

some ethical problems in modern field work[1]

J. A. BARNES

Introduction. Many people maintain that social anthropology and other empirically-based social sciences would advance faster if they were modelled more closely on the natural sciences or on mathematics. There are two parts to this view. On the one hand we are urged to use concepts and methods of analysis closer akin to those of the natural sciences, on the other we are told that we should collect our empirical data in what is thought to be a more systematic and objective way. Here I am not concerned with the first issue, whether mathematics or atomic physics are better analytical models for social science than history or geology. My point of departure is the second issue. Can we behave in the field in essentially the same way as we would in a laboratory, looking down a microscope or watching through a one-way screen; or, since this is generally admitted to be a policy of perfection, should we in the field at least try to get as close as possible to laboratory conditions of work? I hope to show that this aim can lead to poorer, not better, research and that effective fieldwork in part depends on realizing how the field situation differs from the natural science laboratory.

Any empirical inquiry is likely to have several objectives, some theoretical, others practical, but usually one objective has precedence over the others. My discussion is restricted to scientific or academic research, where the main commitment of the investigator is to his discipline, to the acquisition and

---

[1] An earlier version of this paper was published in 1963 in the *British Journal of Sociology* 14:118-134.

dissemination of knowledge. The problems I shall discuss present themselves in different guise when the primary research goals are administrative, thera-peutic, educative or ameliorative, and their examination under these conditions lies outside the scope of this paper.

I refer to the field investigator as an ethnographer, a convenient neutral term, whether the people he is studying are tribesmen or townsmen, pre-literate or industrialized, and whether he thinks of himself as sociologist or social anthropologist or both.

Colonial and post-colonial conditions. Many decades ago ethnographic fieldwork did usually take place under conditions similar to those met with in natural science. For example, when Haddon and his colleagues on the Cambridge expedition worked on the islands of the Torres Straits in northern Queensland in 1898 their methods of investigation were similar to those used in the natural sciences in which many of them had been trained. The field of inquiry was perceived as exterior to themselves, something which could be observed by an outsider without significant distortion. The lives of the islanders were thought not to be seriously disturbed by the presence of the ethnographic team, though in its reports the effects of prolonged missionary activity are discussed briefly. Information was collected mainly in interviews, using 'jargon' English as a medium. Ceremonies were observed in essentially the same spirit as artifacts and physical characteristics were measured and depicted. Some attention was paid to European influence and somewhat unexpectedly there is an account of the courts set up by the Queensland government; but it is clear from the reports that European administrators, traders and mission-aries did not form part of the field of study. They constituted, as it were, boundary conditions of the area under investigation. The research work was not aimed at influencing the future of the Torres Straits islanders. The islanders were not expected to read the reports of the expedition, nor, I think, was the Queensland government expected to be interested in them except as a disinterested contribution to knowledge; in any case, thirty-seven years elapsed before the last research report appeared. The names, marriages and totems of the islanders were given in the published genealogies (Cambridge expedition

1901-1935). In brief, the Torres Straits islanders were under the microscope and Haddon and his colleagues were looking down the tube at them.

These methods and assumptions are typical of ethnographic work done by avowed anthropologists until, say, 1925. Even Malinowski, despite the tremendous changes he brought about in fieldwork methods, still regarded the Trobriands as though it was a laboratory. The effects of missionary and administrative contacts on the Trobriands were marginal to his work and he was not much concerned with any influence his published work might have on the islanders or on the Papuan administration. He wrote:

On the islands of the Pacific, though I was pursued by the products of the Standard Oil Company, weekly editions, cotton goods, cheap detective stories, and the internal combustion engine in the ubiquitous motor-launch, I was still able with but little effort to re-live and reconstruct a type of human life moulded by the implements of the stone age, pervaded with crude beliefs and surrounded by a wide, uncontaminated open stretch of nature. (Malinowski 1930:406).

Nowadays the picture is different. The ethnographer is usually greatly interested in the relationships existing between the community or system he is studying and the wider world. He knows that his own presence will affect the behaviour of people round him and he seeks to minimize or control this effect. He may discuss his manuscript with some of his informants before he publishes, and he knows that his published works may be read not only by government, missions and other outsiders but also by the people he has been studying. He is aware that what he writes may well become the basis for action designed to alter what he describes and will therefore either take special steps to prevent this happening or, alternatively, he will seek consciously to influence and even to take responsibility for such action (cf. Chapple 1952; Mair 1957). Typically, in the old days informants and other actors in the ethnographic picture were given their real names, even though some of their actions might be described in Latin, whereas nowadays informants and others are given disguised names but their actions are described in plain English. The innocent daughters of the metropolitan reader, if they still exist, are no longer considered. Instead, regard is paid to the susceptibilities of people who may see their own private lives in print, and to the law of libel, the provisions of the Official Secrets Act and similar legislation.

Fieldwork during what we might call the colonial period was based on several assumptions that have been abandoned. The boundaries of the field of study were clear, and for the most part only non-Western peoples were studied. Inquiries were aimed at increasing knowledge rather than prompting local action, and although the knowledge acquired might have practical applications, these were ancilliary. It was quite legitimate to seek support from governments, both metropolitan and colonial, as appropriate patrons for disinterested research. The ethnographer took for granted that the observations and records he made did not significantly disturb the behaviour of the people studied. In the classical mechanics of the nineteenth century it was assumed that physical observations could be made without affecting the objects observed and in much the same way ethnographers assumed that in their researches there was no direct feed-back from them to their informants. Published research reports were intended to interest professional colleagues and the metropolitan public rather than the colonial administrator, and only rarely reached members of the tribes concerned.

These assumptions are now obsolete. Firstly, the ethnographer's field of study is enlarged so that even when focusing on an illiterate tribe he gives some attention to outside agencies. Secondly, the focus of study is no longer always an illiterate tribe but may be a community many of whose members can read, write letters to the newspapers and learned periodicals, and even sue the ethnographer if need be, and who may be his fellow-citizens. Thirdly, the ethnographer hopes not only to publish generalized statements about customary behaviour but also to describe the actions of individuals whom, for purposes of exposition he must identify in some way; and these actions may be, in some eyes, reprehensible or illegal. Fourthly, administrators and others realize that ethnographic publications may include statements construable as criticism of their activities, and hence are more cautious about giving information.

This last change was impressed on me early in my own fieldwork in Rhodesia. I went with a colleague to call on the bishop of an area where there were many European planters. We were both firm believers in non-directive interview techniques and keen to make the best use of our first bishop as an informant. As the interview progressed non-directively, the bishop grew puzzled, until finally he asked, 'And where do you intend to farm?' I answered, 'We are not planters. My friend is a psychologist and I am an anthropologist'. The bishop smiled with comprehension and replied, 'Then we must be very careful what we say'.

In brief, the division between those under the microscope and those looking scientifically down the eyepiece has broken down. There may still be an exotic focus of study but the group or institution being studied is now seen to be embedded in a network of social relations of which the observer is an integral if reluctant part (cf. Lévi-Strauss 1950: xxvii). Significant action in this social field is not restricted to the period the ethnographer spends working in the field. It begins when he first makes plans to visit his field location and continues at least until the time when his published work is discussed by the people he has studied.

Sponsors. In this new situation the ethnographer faces problems of right conduct that were absent in the colonial period. One serious problem is what attitude the ethnographer should adopt towards those in authority. Before fieldwork can be begun almost anywhere in the world, permission must be obtained from some authority or other. Sometimes permission is required from a plurality of mutually antagonistic authorities. It is commonly believed that ethnographers experience more difficulty in this matter than do their colleagues in the natural sciences. If we assert that ethnographic research can be of value to an enlightened administration, we should not be surprised that less enlightened administrators exaggerate its dangers. Some fieldworkers treat the establishment of relations with government as merely a necessary formality, even if a lengthy one. Thus Keesing, writing about fieldwork in Oceania, says:

... The prospective investigator does well not only to have his institutional credentials in order, but also to stress them in applications for visas, special entry permits, and any other needed approvals. Clearances, as well as courtesy, often require a complex series of contacts by correspondence, to be followed by personal calls. The anthropologist should be able to curb his impatience here because of his professional awareness of the importance of ceremonious behaviour, and of the functions of elaborate hierarchical and other patterned social structures. (Keesing 1959:16).

This formulation gives cold comfort and misses the point. The investigator's professional training should enable him to realize that what is more important than the ceremonial or bureaucratic delays of the administration is its power to prevent him from doing any work at all in its territory. And here the dilemma comes. In the colonial situation it was well realized that, for example, in a tribe with a chief, his co-operation was necessary to ensure the success of fieldwork. Usually this was not a serious problem. Behind the ethnographer was the support of the colonial administration, so that it was difficult or dangerous for the chief to resist the ethnographer openly. Appropriate gifts could smooth the way, for in the main the ethnographer's activities, if incomprehensible to the chief, did not threaten his position in any way. Though the ethnographer might not approve of, say, the arbitrary power wielded by a chief, or of the tribal subjection of women, or of the moral code and religious ideas of the people, he did not try to alter what he saw. Instead, he tried to understand and explain without passing moral judgments of his own. For the most part, this is still the accepted style of working, but now we are not sure over how wide an area we have to suspend moral judgments and to refrain from action. If it is wrong to influence the tribesman, it is wrong to influence the administration? For research purposes we want to study some at least of the actions of the administration; must we, therefore, treat the administration as though it were another savage tribe? Or is the administration a body to which we can appeal in the name of science; or again, is it a constitutional body in which we have rights or for which we have responsibilities? Or can we treat with the administration on two levels, seeking intellectual and logistic support at a high administrative level while at the same time endeavouring not to become identified with the administration at the local level? Do these problems arise in all field research or only when some aspect of administrative activity is one of the principal topics under investigation?

Spillius (1957:123-125) has discussed many of these issues at length and I would merely reiterate his plea for a dispassionate view of colonial government as a social system. Yet an intellectual appreciation of the aims and methods of a colonial government does not entail approval of its methods, and the problem of how much and in what ways the ethnographer should seek its support still remains.

This dilemma is easier to solve in practice when fieldwork is undertaken in territory controlled by an administration that is entirely foreign to the investigator. Under these circumstances he is likely to have very little influence and is entirely dependent on the co-operation of the foreign administration. The ethnographer will then often try to make his research work appear harmless rather than useful. But when research is planned in some territory with which the ethnographer, or the institution supporting him, has some connection, a choice is open. The whole-hearted co-operation of the administration can either be consciously sought or carefully avoided, or some intermediate position adopted. Clearly the main consideration will be the attitude of the group being studied towards its administrators.

Relationships to the administration do not impinge merely at the point of getting or not getting an entry permit. We all hope that we shall win the confidence of our informants, but when this confidence extends to confidential administrative documents, we have to walk warily. When we are told in confidence that A is not really the father of B we decide how to make use of this information principally by reference to our own professional ethics, illdefined though these are. But when we are told 'official' secrets other considerations enter, for the administration has effective sanctions to protect its interests. The ethnographer has to be clear from the start that co-operation with the administration may entail obligations as well as advantages.

It may be hazardous for the ethnographer to become identified with the administration, or with any one segment of the society he is studying. Yet without sponsorship at all he may be in difficulties. Informants in subordinate or insecure positions may be unwilling to co-operate unless responsibility for the ethnographer's presence has been taken by someone in authority. If there is no one to indicate to the community that the ethnographer has his approval, the research worker may have to explain his presence, describe his objectives and methods, and allay suspicion in each fresh context and with each new informant. In some field situations, particularly in towns, the ethnographer may well go out of his way to look for some publically recognized organization enjoying wide-spread support that can act as his local sponsor. Yet such bodies do not always exist and the field worker may have to resign himself to explaining over and over again what he wants to do.

Moral judgments in the field. Under the microscope there could be no moral judgments. They had their code and we had ours, and the two never met (cf. Evans-Pritchard 1946:92; Shils 1959:116). There was a double standard of morality, one for informants in their world and the other for the ethnographer, the society he belonged to, his colleagues and his readers. Furthermore, in the colonial era before the advent of 'development', even the administration's ideas of right and wrong impinged on the lives of its dependent peoples only in a limited number of contexts. But if tribesmen, administration and ethnographer are now all part of one social system, this inter-cultural ethical indifference disappears. More and more of the daily lives of tribesmen becomes subject to legal and moral evaluation by the administration, even though their respective codes differ widely. More and more the ethnographer finds himself in situations in which he cannot avoid evaluating the actions of his informants in terms of his own moral code. If he refrains from acting on these evaluations, it is because of the way he has defined his role as a scientific investigator and not because of the cultural gulf between him and his informants. But sometimes he cannot refrain. For example, we often find that many of the social actions taken in a tribal community are regarded as illegal by the administration (cf. Whyte 1955:312-317). These practices may have their origin in pre-contact conditions, or they may have evolved during colonial times or they may be directly linked with attempts to change or subvert the existing regime. The ethnographer is in a quandary. He may feel he has a duty to the administration to report illegalities. Even if he does not think he has this duty, the administration may think he has. The ethnographer may equally well feel that he has a duty to his informants to conceal his knowledge from the administration. He may feel a duty to the ideals of scientific inquiry not to intervene in the field situation, and yet the same sense of duty may require him to publish the facts of this illegal activity if this forms part of the basis of his analysis of social life, even if he disguises his evidence. Participation in community activities may involve the ethnographer himself in illegal acts. In extreme situations the ethnographer may well consider that, quite apart from any duty he may feel towards administration, informants, or science, his own personal values override other considerations: surely all of us would try to intervene to save a life. Spillius (1957: 18ff.) has described clearly his own intervention on Tikopia during a famine and the consequences this had for his role as a research worker. But there are many situations that are not so clear cut, and the ethnographer is often under continual pressure from his informants, and sometimes from the administration, to intervene on their behalf (cf. Gallin 1959). If he supplies information in confidence to the administration or some other body, he must be aware that though he may be on his guard against betraying his informants, when he himself becomes an informant, his confidence may be betrayed, either by accident or design (cf. Goodenough in Keesing 1959: 5, f.n.l.).

No simple formula will apply to all circumstances. The ethnographer has to define his role, or try to do so, so that he can retain the good will of his informants and of the administration, continue to gain the flow of information essential to his research task, and yet remain true to his own basic values. This ideal may not always be possible, and the ethnographer has to decide which if any of these desiderata he should forego. If he cannot reach an acceptable solution, he should not waste everyone's time but should switch to some other research topic. We have no reason to assume that all possible social situations can, in principle, be studied objectively by an ethnographer on the spot. Atomic explosions can be studied only from a safe distance, and similarly some social situations cannot be studied dispassionately by any ethnographer, however competently trained and whatever his personal code of values, except from a safe distance in time and space. Nor should we assume that if a given social situation can be studied successfully by one adequately trained ethnographer, it can equally well be studied by any other. Trained ethnographers are not interchangeable units, differentiated only by age and sex. Each has his own temperament and his own set of values and convictions as a citizen. These impose limits on what he can study as a scientist, limits which differ from one ethnographer to the next.

Role definition. Difficulties in role definition arise continually because of the multiplicity of contexts in which most ethnographers hope to make their observations. Some ethnographers may still hire informants by the hour and even follow an office routine beginning with the first informant at nine o'clock in the morning and pausing for a coffee break when informants may smoke (cf. Hilger 1954: 26-33; Holleman 1958:34-37). Many of the problems discussed here do not arise when research inquiries are made in this way. Another method of working, springing from quite different premisses, also limits contact between the investigator and the object of his inquiries. In the Glacier project, an investigation into certain aspects fo the social life of a London factory, correct roles for the research team were carefully worked out, but it was emphasized that outside the research situation members of the team had no relevant role at all. Jaques writes:

... the Research Team has limited its relationship with members of the factory to strictly formal contacts which have to do with project work publicly sanctioned by the Works Council ... this has meant refusing invitations to people's homes, to play tennis on the factory's courts, to discuss with individual members of a group occurrences which took place earlier at a meeting, and many other activities which could be construed as outside the terms of reference. (Jaques 1951:14-15).

Here the model of the natural science laboratory has been discarded in favour of the psychiatric clinic with group therapy in progress.

Both these methods where extra-professional contacts are shunned seem incompatible with the conventional ethnographic method of inquiry epitomized in Evans-Pritchard's classic phrase: 'to get to know well the persons involved and to see and hear what they do and say' (Pitt-Rivers 1954: x). By the first method, the ethnographer collects his information only in the artificial context of formal interviews and neglects opportunities for direct observation. The second method method may be appropriate when the boundaries of the research field are agreed and distinct, but in many field inquiries there are no terms of reference agreed to by all parties and there is no representative body like a Works Council able to give formal approval to research activities. Furthermore, the ethnographer usually limits himself to observing and understanding and does not primarily aim to assist the group he is studying to see its own difficulties more clearly and to take action to overcome them; he does cast himself in the role of therapist. Only through informal association with his informants can he gain the rich flood of complex and conflicting information he needs; yet unequivocal identification with one faction may dry up the flow of information from all others. Sometimes it may be unwise to play tennis with the District Officer, to drink beer with one lineage and not with another, to attend a sacrifice to the ancestors but to stay away from Mass: sometimes it may be even harder to do both. A neutral role can often be defined so that the ethnographer can observe conflict situations from more than one standpoint and his neutrality may still entail twenty-four hours work a day.

In some field situations the ethnographer may have little latitude in defining his role for it will be done for him. Most commentators on fieldwork methods caution the ethnographer against becoming too closely identified with one faction within the community he is studying, although I think that this danger is often exaggerated. Yet if there is a major cleavage between the administration and the local community, it may be difficult for the ethnographer to find a neutral position where he can retain the confidence of both sides. In some recent situations (particularly in Africa) government approval has implied for the people that the ethnographer was a spy, while positive approval by the people has implied for the government that he was subversive. Similar difficulties have been encountered in the study of factories, where management approval has implied trade union suspicion, and vice versa (Gullahorn and Strauss 1954). In their study of Deep South, Davis and Gardner, one a Negro and the other a White, worked each on his own side of the colour line (Warner and Davis 1939: 234), but this division of labour would be impossible in many field studies and the ethnographer has to try to straddle the cleavage. Even in situations of severe social conflict some community of interest remains and it may still be possible to do effective fieldwork even in situations where, to give a recent example, informants are fined in court for speaking to the ethnographer. But in some situations of conflict there are no neutral roles and impartial social inquiry is impossible.

Two ways have been suggested for avoiding these difficulties in role definition. One is to do research covertly. Many of us might say simply that this is dishonest and inexcusable. Yet it is not uncommon for an ethnographer, when trying to explain the purpose of his work to tribesmen and to administrators, to stress those aspects that seem innocuous such as, say, the collection of legends and of information on technology, rather than topics such as land tenure and social control, which are more likely to be controversial. This is in fact an attempt to disguise our main interests (cf. Colson 1953: vi-viii; Holleman 1958; Mead 1932:16; Shils 1959:123). I well remember the surprise with which a District Officer greeted my naive remark that I was studying him too, and I think I was more circumspect thereafter. Clearly there are limits of comprehension that make necessary some kind of modified statement of one's research aims when talking to different audiences. But completely misleading statements of intentions will come home to roost with publication, and even if the ethnographer is by then well removed from his scene of study, the reputation of the profession suffers.

In completely covert research the ethnographer seeks his information while ostensibly filling some quite different role. The absence of any suitable alternative role for a visiting scientist in many tribal situations is probably the reason why covert research has not received more discussion among anthropologists. Covert research can sometimes yield results that are significant and which could perhaps not be obtained in any other way: *When prophesy fails*, by Festinger and others, a study of a small sect in the Middle West of the United States awaiting the destruction of the earth, is an outstanding example. Yet in my view this method is simply dishonest and we should not use it. Furthermore, I think we should say that we will not undertake covert research. If we wish to enjoy public support as a responsible profession we must not only avoid acting as spies even in the best causes; we must make it clear in advance that we will not act in this way.

The other method is to come completely out into the open, state one's neutral position in advance, and endeavour to get both sides to accept one as an intercalary figure. This procedure has been followed with success in several studies of industrial situations. However, an essential feature of these investigations seems to be a long period of preliminary negotiation during which the investigator gains acceptance from both the management and the trade unions. Only after this does fieldwork start in earnest. A procedure of this kind is obviously impracticable where the fieldwork is to be carried on among illiterate or unsophisticated people living thousands of miles away who may not be organized in an hierarchical structure. Yet the ethnographer may well endeavour to move into a neutral role as his fieldwork progresses. In particular he may prefer to facilitate the exchange of ideas between administration and people rather than give direct advice to one side about how to deal with the other.

Publication. Research work that does not lead to published reports is usually a waste of time and money. Yet, when we publish, our eye is more often on our colleagues than on our informants. Articles may sometimes lie unnoticed in the decent obscurity of learned journals, but books find their way far into the bush and if they are not always well understood they are easily misunderstood. Some may say that no harm is likely to be done if people see themselves described in print. Indeed, the fieldworker is sometimes recommended to win the support of his tribal informants by saying that he is trying to write a book about them. Other tribes are already in the books; don't they want to be honoured in the same way (cf. Keesing 1959:28)? Yet in research in Western society the usual procedure is to disguise the identity of individuals, locations and times, and this is done at the request of informants. Why this difference? There are two questions to answer. Why and when should we try to minimize the effects that publication may have on the field situation? If we want to minimize effects, how can it best be done?

Ethnographic and other sociographic publications find their way back into the field. The Trobriand Islanders now know of Malinowski's books and one of them has reported that Malinowski did not understand their system of clans and chiefs (Groves 1956). At one extreme, Rattray's books on Ashanti have become authorities accepted by Ashanti courts. At the other, in the community in the United States described by Vidich and Bensman under the pseudonym of Springdale, it is said that no further research will be possible for 'many, many years' (Risley 1958-59). The first effect may be good, the second is obviously bad. In general every field situation should be kept open for possible future research. Even if everyone in the community knows of A's misdeeds, he and they may not relish seeing them recorded for posterity. As Whyte points out with reference to the Springdale affair, there is a significant difference between public knowledge circulating orally in a community and stories appearing in print (Whyte 1958:1). Furthermore, if actions are illegal according to a set of regulations imposed from outside or are regarded by outsiders as particularly reprehensible, this may be a strong additional reason for protecting the actors (cf. Evans-Pritchard 1937:511). When publishing in the hope that action may be taken the ethnographer needs to be sure that the expected action is wanted by those who provided him with information; but in not publishing lest action might be taken the ethnographer has to consider his obligations to those who have supported his research and to the profession to which he belongs.

One way of controlling the effect of publication is to make sure that those affected agree to what is being said about them. The number of people who may possibly be affected by the publication of the results of a social inquiry is immense, and if the ethnographer tried to get unanimity he would certainly publish nothing. In practical terms all that can be done is to clear the manuscript with those most closely concerned. Two groups of people are typically involved: the administration, to whom the ethnographer is probably beholden for much confidential information as well as innumerable services such as hospitality, transport, advice and companionship; and certain key informants. With some justification, we tend to regard censorship by government as sinister and regrettable; at the same time we may regard discussion of draft manuscripts with informants as scientific and enlightened. Yet administrations are much harder to disguise than individuals, and are particularly sensitive to criticism in those territories where articulate opposition is not yet accepted as normal and legitimate. On the other hand administrators are capable of defending their own interests much more effectively than are private citizens and hence the effects of anthropological publication rarely constitute a serious threat to them. I hope that I am not alone in maintaining the old-fashioned view that governments should exist only to serve their peoples and I would argue that it would be regrettable if ethnographers were able to publish only manuscripts approved by the administration. Individuals are, for the most part, relatively defenceless and our duty towards them is consequently greater. There are two situations in which informants may be asked to comment on a manuscript before publication. They may be asked merely to check the accuracy of the statements. This is an admirable though not always feasible procedure and need not concern us further. In addition, informants may be asked if they will agree to statements about themselves appearing in print. Their privacy is being invaded, their confidences revealed and they are asked to agree to this, either because they are indifferent or because what is described they now regard as past history (cf. Jaques 1951: xvi). Bott worked through her manuscript with two of her London couples and found that this procedure resulted, among other things, in more confidential material becoming available for publication (Bott 1957:47). This lengthy procedure entails further contact between ethnographer and informants after the main research has been concluded, and is impossible in many field situations. It requires a level of sophistication for the informants not too far removed from that of the investigator and an awareness of the consequences of appearing in print. Nevertheless, it may well sharpen the understanding of the investigator as well as reassure the informant.

On the other hand, it may not be easy to find the appropriate body with whom to discuss a manuscript. A factory is a corporate body with a hierarchical structure and hence it was possible for Jaques and his colleagues to find groups in the factory able to take responsibility for approving his manuscript. Bott's couples took responsibility for the sections of her book which concerned themselves. But in a study of a stateless society, or of a village community, there may be no representative bodies who can act for the whole, and the whole may be too large for each individual to be approached. If there are several factions in a community, approval by one faction may well imply rejection by the others. The faction fight would be continued over the manuscript while the poor ethnographer waits in vain to get something into print.

One way of protecting informants from the effects of publication is to give them pseudonyms. Sometimes the names of individuals are disguised, sometimes places and times. Even the tribal name may be concealed (Colson 1949:1, f.n.1; Mead 1932: xi, 16), and in at least one instance (West 1945) the identification of time and place has been further impeded by using a pseudonym for the author. Case material is sometimes distorted in presentation, and there is then a particularly onerous responsibility on the writer both to ensure that none of the details altered is likely to be significant, and to indicate that distortion has been introduced. Often these disguises are only partly successful; informants can usually recognize themselves. But perhaps that does not matter much if strangers cannot recognize them. For what are the undesirable effects of publication? Bott's couples did not want their neighbours to know they were in her book (Bott 1957:11). Festinger and his colleagues say that they disguised their informants to protect them from the curiosity of unsympathetic readers (Festinger et al. 1956: vi). Both these studies were made in industrial societies enjoying self-government, and unwelcome publicity may well there be the most serious danger. But under tribal conditions there may be others, including the possibility of criminal prosecution or of being put at a political disadvantage. Mead and others have mentioned the dangers of publishing undisguised accounts of tribal practices which may later become illegal (Mead et al. 1949), but some socially significant actions are already illegal. Publication of such material obviously calls for great care by the ethnographer, and it may be necessary to delay publication for some years if the interests of informants are to be adequately protected.

With publication we run the risk of making public that which our informants would prefer to keep secret. The limits of privacy vary with time and place. Informants may object to a great variety of disclosures; photographs of sacred objects reserved for men now published for women to see; initiation procedures revealed to the uninitiated; details of tabooed characteristics such as income, sexual behaviour, medical histories; reprehensible actions as well as good deeds done by stealth. Where laboratory conditions prevail, a promise can sometimes be made to ensure that publication of secret material will not affect secrecy within the society studied. For instance, permission has sometimes been given by Aboriginal groups in Australia for the filming of secret ceremonies on condition that the films will not be shown to mixed audiences in Australia, where Aboriginal women might be present. Where publication takes place within the group studied, the investigator has to be guided by the tolerance of his informants. In Britain we often assume that individuals do not wish others to know details of their income and expenditure. Income tax returns, where these details are set out, are well guarded and after a number of years are burnt, never becoming part of the public records. On the other hand if a man appears in court, or is involved in an accident, we expect his name to appear in the newspaper. Yet in Norway details of income and tax assessed for each individual are published annually, while in rural areas the policy is to report court cases and accidents anonymously. There are cultural fashions in secrecy and publicity, and they change through time. It is easier than it was a hundred years ago to publish medical and sexual information about individuals. The procedure followed by Bott and her colleagues enabled her informants to accept in print statements about their own personalities which previously they had not accepted consciously at all. But although the area of tolerance may be growing, the ethnographer may always be left with a problem. Some of the actions he has to describe and analyse are bound to be despicable, immoral, illegal or reprehensible, and most of the people concerned will prefer to keep them unheralded and unsung. In the semi-therapeutic relationships established by both Bott and Jaques, individuals and groups may be enabled to realize the truth about themselves and acquiesce in its publication; but the ethnographer has also to work with unregenerate social systems whose on-going activity contains significant amounts of deception, self-deception and secrecy. Even while the research is going on, the field inquiries may stimulate or force members of the community studied to look closely at aspects of their common life they normally repress or ignore. The authors of *Crestwood Heights*, while their research was in progress, made partial reportings to the community of tentative findings, which, they say, were in many cases 'deeply disturbing, not to say shocking', to their informants (Seeley et al. 1956:24). Publication, with its potentially wider audience, may be even more disturbing. Francis Williams (1962:15) argues that the press has a social function 'to cut public figures down to size' and to show 'that even great men often have feet of clay'. Would we argue that the ethnographer has the function of showing that the bullroarer is only a slab of wood, that the masked figure is not an ancestor but a neighbour in disguise, and that the chief who can do no wrong is as venial as his subjects? In other words, if we protect our informants, is it right to expose the myths of their institutions?

Some writers have maintained that social scientists have a duty to do research and to publish the results even if some informants find this unpleasant (cf. Holleman 1958:253). Vidich and Bensman (1958-59:5) argue that

if social science is to have some kind of independent problems and identity and, if a disinterested effort is to be made to solve these problems, a certain number of social scientists, presumably residing at universities, must be willing to resist the claims for planned, popular, practical research.

Vidich clearly regards the research he did at Springdale as part of this dis-interested effort. The pseudonyms he gave to the individuals he mentions in his book were not effective in Springdale itself, for, after the book had been published, the individuals concerned drove in procession in a Fourth of July pageant wearing masks and bearing the names given to them by Vidich (Whyte 1958:1). The disturbance caused in Springdale seems to be justified for Vidich and Bensman (1958-59:4) by the research done and they assert that 'Negative reaction to community and organizational research is only heard when results describe articulate, powerful and respected individuals and organizations'.

This observation may well be empirically correct, and perhaps explains why Festinger and his colleagues do not find it necessary in their book to discuss the ethics of covert research, although they give a detailed account of their methods of inquiry. Their investigation was conducted without the consent or knowledge of the group studied. The authors told their informants that they were 'businessmen', and two of their assistants said falsely that they had had supernatural experiences. Notes were made in secret, and magnetic tapes made by the group were copied by the investigators. The authors write: '. . . we faced as much a job of detective work as of observation' (Festinger et al. 1956:25).

This attitude towards research contrasts sharply with that adopted, for example, by Evans-Pritchard when he found it difficult to gain information on the training of witch-doctors by direct enquiry. His personal servant became a pupil and from him Evans-Pritchard got his information. He writes (1937: 151, 153): 'We acted straightforwardly in telling him [the witchdoctor] that his pupil would pass on all information to me' and he notes that the witch-doctors well understood that the pupil 'was a sponge out of which I squeezed all the moisture of information which they put into it'. Yet even the limited and reluctant co-operation Evans-Pritchard got from his informants may not have many analogues in situations where the written word is better known. Despite the deception practised by the Festinger team, were their informants harmed by this? How many of us have not written down afterwards information that we dare not record openly? Even if some harm was done to Festinger's informants, is this justified by the scientific value of the book that reports the research?

Shils (1959:130-138) draws a careful distinction between private and public life, and argues that it is right to make inquiries in the public domain, as he defines it, even if illegalities are thereby exposed and popular myths refuted. Outside the public domain, on the other hand, the investigator should be most careful not to abuse the individual's right to privacy. This distinction between public and private is however often difficult to apply in tribal societies and in face-to-face communities in the modern world.

Vidich and Bensman say that negative reactions are heard only from powerful groups of informants, and argue that this should not prevent us from carrying on research among such people. I argue differently. Negative reactions, by which I take it they mean annoyance, disillusionment with the investigators and opposition to further inquiries, may be heard only when the group studied is powerful and articulate, but there seems every reason for assuming that similar sentiments develop among weak and inarticulate groups of informants if they are treated in the same way. Their protests may be unheard and ineffective, but this does not permit us to ignore them. The groups we study are often far from articulate, powerful or respected and we should therefore be particularly on our guard to ensure that we do not betray the trust our informants have placed in us.

In fact we know almost nothing about the effects of publication, negative or positive. Most monographs tell us a good deal about preparations for the field research and the way in which it was carried on, perhaps even how the manuscript was checked, but there the story stops. Only in a second edition is it possible to report on the effects, if any, of publication. We hear more of the scandals, when unapproved publication of tribal secrets, private misdeeds or government blunders has led to overt hostility towards further visits from investigators, and less of those instances where publications have been well received by those persons described in them. Whyte's account, in the second edition of *Street corner society* (1955:342-358) of the local effects of his book indicates that publication does not necessarily ensure publicity. It also suggests that the ethnographer should reconcile himself to becoming inevitably somewhat of a disappointment to his informants.

As professional sociologists and anthropologists we have an abiding interest in seeing that we are regarded as responsible professionals by all those we work with, and the interests of the profession outlast those of the specific investigation or investigator. A professional code of ethics would not make any easier the solution of the many problems discussed here, but it might at least remind ethnographers that these problems do have to be solved and cannot be ignored. The 'wide uncontaminated open stretch of nature', postulated by Malinowski, no longer separates our informants from the wide world or from us, and we have to allow for this.

references

E. J. BOTT (1957) Family and social network: roles, norms and external relationships in ordinary urban families, London.

CAMBRIDGE ANTHROPOLOGICAL EXPEDITION TO TORRES STRAITS (1901-1935) Reports, Cambridge, 6 vol.

E. D. CHAPPLE (1952) The applied anthropologist – informal or professional *HO* 11 (♯ 2): 3-4.

E. COLSON (1949) Assimilation of an American Indian group, *Rhodes-Livingstone Journal* 8:1-13.

E. COLSON (1953) The Makah Indians: a study of an Indian tribe in modern American society, Manchester.

E. E. EVANS-PRITCHARD (1937) Witchraft, oracles and magic among the Azande, Oxford.

E. E. EVANS-PRITCHARD (1946) Applied anthropology, *Africa* 16:92-98.

L. FESTINGER, H. W. RIECKEN and S. SCHACHTER (1956) When prophesy fails, Minneapolis.

B. GALLIN (1959) A case for intervention in the field, *HO* 18:140-144.

M. GROVES (1956) Trobriand Island clans and chiefs, *Man* 56:164, art. 190.

J. GULLAHORN and G. STRAUSS (1954) The fieldworker in union research, *HO* 13 (♯ 3): 28-33.

M. I. HILGER (1954) An ethnographic field method, in: R. F. Spencer ed., Method and perspective in anthropology, Minneapolis.

J. F. HOLLEMAN (1958) African interlude, Capetown.

E. JAQUES (1951) The changing culture of a factory, London.

F. M. KEESING (1959) Field guide to Oceania, Washington D.C., National academy of sciences – National research council, Publication no. 701, Field guide series 1.

C. LÉVI-STRAUSS (1950) Introduction à l'œuvre de Marcel Mauss, in: M. Mauss, Sociologie et anthropologie, Paris: IX-LII.

L. P. MAIR (1957) Studies in applied anthropology, London.

B. MALINOWSKI (1930) The rationalization of anthropology and administration, *Africa* 3: 405-430.

M. MEAD (1932) The changing culture of an Indian tribe, New York.

M. MEAD et al. (1949) Report of the committee on ethics, *HO* 8 (♯ 2): 20-21.

J. A. PITT-RIVERS (1954) People of the sierra, London.

R. RISLEY (1958-1959) 'Freedom and responsibility in research': comments, *HO* 17 (♯ 4): 5.

J. R. SEELEY, R. A. SIM and E. W. LOOSLEY (1956) Crestwood heights, New York.

E. A. SHILLS (1959) Social inquiry and the autonomy of the individual, in: D. Lerner ed., The human meaning of the social sciences, New York: 114-157.

J. SPILLIUS (1957) Natural disaster and political crisis in a Polynesian society: an exploration of operational research, *Human Relations* 10: 3-27; 113-125.

A. VIDICH and J. BENSMAN (1958-1959) 'Freedom and responsibility in research': comments, *HO* 17 (# 4): 2-5.

W. L. WARNER and A. DAVIS (1939) A comparative study of American caste, in: E. T. Thompson ed., Race relations and the race problem, Durham, N.C.: 219-245.

J. WEST (*pseud.*) (1945) Plainville, U.S.A., New York.

W. F. WHYTE (1955) Street corner society: the social structure of an Italian slum, Enlarged ed., Chicago.

W. F. WHYTE (1958) Freedom and responsibility in research: the 'Springdale' case, *HO* 17 (# 2): 1-2.

F. WILLIAMS (1962) The right to know, *Twentieth century* 170: 6-17.

I I

*annotated bibliography on
anthropological field work methods*

P. C. W. GUTKIND AND G. SANKOFF

Introduction. Those who insist that anthropology belongs more properly to
the humanities might well find justification should they ask 'How do anthropologists do their work and what methods, if any, do they employ'? In this
regard, one of the outstanding features is that, although there is a great deal
of material available on field work methodology, this material is scattered, and
little attempt at systematization of method has been made. Many anthropologists would probably feel that this is in some respects a good thing – a set
of rules, of ordered steps or sequences of method is often felt to be too re-
strictive, to be detrimental to the heuristic character of anthropological studies.
Nevertheless, the authors of this selected and annotated bibliography feel that
there is a definite need, if not for a systematization, at least for a collection of
statements on method. We know of no such work existing at present.

Much information on methodology exists. Availability of this material,
relating both to general and to highly specific and varied problems would be
invaluable to others who will encounter, or are now facing, such problems.
These reasons alone are, we feel, illustrative of a need for a bibliography such
as the one we have prepared.

In essence, only methods and techniques directly pertaining to social and
cultural anthropologists have been covered. Within this wide area, the bibliography is not complete in the sense of including all available statements on
methodology and field work. It is intended rather to be a representative sample
of the writings on major methodological problems encountered. Items were

selected for inclusion according to diverse criteria. 'Classical' or seminal works were included as well as reviews containing a complete exposition of a problem and its history. Also selected were recent papers containing modern methods and viewpoints. Increasingly, anthropologists are working in new and different capacities. This opens up many new methodological areas, in which techniques are often borrowed from other fields, such as psychology and sociology. We have, however, retained a fairly traditional viewpoint of anthropology, feeling that many treatments of methodological problems in other areas are readily available to anthropologists who are interested in them. Particular relevance to anthropology was required. Though it was often difficult to draw the line between sociological and anthropological topics, particularly as far as contemporary studies are concerned, problems such as those of survey research and of interviewing *per se* (except where applied to non-Western societies), of urban and community studies (except where specifically 'anthropological' techniques were used), and of industrial studies have generally been omitted. Also, in fields such as psychological testing, which is marked by a copious and redundant literature, only a small portion could be included.

We have generally omitted statements of broad general outlook, setting out an orientation to both theory and methodology, except for early classic papers by noted anthropologists such as Boas and Radcliffe-Brown. We also omitted many short statements (anywhere from a paragraph to several pages) on methodology in monographs. Many personal and anecdotal materials had to be excluded, as being of limited general applicability. Lastly, where an author, over a period of time, had written several articles on the same topic, we tried to include only the latest and/or most complete. Thus, for example, Rivers' 1900 paper on genealogical method was discarded in favour of his 1906 work on the same topic.

Although our definition of the subject matter implied generally omitting work mainly defined as belonging to another discipline, it did not mean that we left out statements on the methodology of topics being pioneered specifically by anthropologists. Thus, we have included sections on applied anthropology, and on formal analytical techniques.

The data for the bibliography have been collected partly by P. C. W. Gutkind and G. Sankoff, whose entries are initialled Gu-Sa, and partly by D. G. Jongmans, C. Jonker, A. J. F. Köbben and L. M. Serpenti, whose entries are initialled Jgm, Jk, K and Se respectively.

We are grateful to all those who have drawn our attention to relevant items, especially to Dr. Margaret Mead who sent us a copy of a non published bibliography on Ethnographic Research (Theory, Methods, Technique) by H. C. Conklin.

annotated bibliography

contents

I   *general*

1   R. N. Adams and J. J. Preiss eds. (1960) Human organization research, field relations and techniques, Homewood, Ill.
A collection of thirty-two papers, mainly on field research and the utilization of case material. Approximately half appeared originally in *Human Organization*. General topics dealt with include researcher and informant behaviour, relationships of researcher with clients and other researchers, field techniques and analysis. (Many of the component papers have been indexed separately). Gu-Sa.

2   M. Mead and R. Metraux eds. (1953) The Study of culture at a distance, Chicago.
A collection of essays describing and giving examples of various methods of studying cultures not accessible to direct contact. See particularly Part IV – working with informants, Part V – written and oral literature, Part VI – film analysis. Gu-Sa.

3   G. P. Murdock, C. S. Ford, A. C. Hudson, R. Kennedy, L. W. Simmons and J. W. M. Whiting (1950) Outline of cultural materials, 3rd rev. ed., New Haven.
Originally designed to aid in classifying materials for cross-cultural studies, the Outline is of use to the field worker in delimiting a wide range of phenomena and as a system for classifying field notes. Gu-Sa.

4   A committee of the Royal Anthropological Institute of Great Britain and Ireland (1951) Notes and queries on anthropology, 6th ed., London.
The fieldworker's Bible – a highly practical guide of 'what to do's', including lists of topics on which information should be collected and how to go about it, solutions to difficulties of collecting and assembling many kinds of materials. Main sections on physical anthropology, social anthropology, material culture and field antiquities. Also included are appendices on photography, cinematography, collecting and packing, preservation of bones, and paper squeezes. Gu-Sa.

4a   H. C. Conklin (1961) Bibliography on Ethnographic Research (Theory, Method, Techniques), New York: Columbia University, Department of Anthropology. (Mimeographed).

5   Selected papers in method and technique (1963) *AA* 65 (# 5): 1001-1230.
Six papers on current methodological issues and problems. (Separately indexed). Gu-Sa.

6   R. F. Spencer ed. (1954) Method and perspective in anthropology, St. Paul, Minn.
Many of the component chapters deal with general issues in methodology and theory, often in the form of a historical review. Linguistics and archeology are discussed as well as social and cultural anthropology. (Papers of particular relevance have been indexed separately). Gu-Sa.

7   S. Tax et al. eds. (1953) Problems of process: methods, Ch. VI of An appraisal of anthropology today, Chicago: 85-103.
A symposium in which a number of anthropologists discuss the six methodological papers in Antropology today (see 29). Gu-Sa.

B   METHODOLOGICAL SURVEYS

8   J. W. Bennett (1948) The study of cultures: a survey of technique and methodology in field work, *ASR* 13: 672-89.
Discusses many techniques in cultural anthropology, including participant observation, use of local language, interviewing, personal documents, direct observation, statistics, and psychological tests. Emphasizes participant observation and the holistic viewpoint, and discusses the relationship between method and technique. Presents three methodological issues, involving type of problem and when to formulate it, and kind of concepts and theories to be used. Gu-Sa.

9   M. Griaule (1957) Méthode de l'ethnographie, Paris.
Exposition of the method followed by Griaule in his research into religion. Important on the subject of observation of ritual events and institutions, with particular emphasis on the use of questionnaire and interview. Jgm.

10   A. I. Richards (1939) The development of field work methods in social anthropology, in: F. C. Bartlett et al. eds., The study of society, London: 272-316.
A historical survey of social anthropological field techniques, as related to types of investigation, methods of observation, and presentation of material. Contains many examples and references. Gu-Sa.

11   B. J. Sarevskaja (1963) La méthode de l'ethnographie de Marcel Griaule et les questions de méthodologie dans l'ethnographie française contemporaine, *Cahiers d'Études Africaines* 4:590-603.
A review of Griaule's Méthode de l'ethnographie. (See *9).

12   M. G. Smith and G. J. Kruyer (1957) A sociological manual for extension workers in the Caribbean, *Caribbean Affairs Series*, Un. College of the West Indies.
A practical general guide to fact-finding and interpretation. Discusses field techniques, survey design and execution, individual area studies, survey analysis, and samples and errors. Especially meant for welfare workers in the Caribbean but also has ? wider application. Jk.

C   GENERAL ORIENTATIONS TO METHODOLOGY

13   G. Bateson (1941) Experiments in thinking about observed ethnological materials, *Phil. Sci.* 8: 53-68.
Personal account of ordering and reworking of ethnological materials, which includes use of analogy

and borrowing from other sciences; use of loose concepts, later sharpened and reworked; heuristic process of problem formulation. Gu-Sa.

14 J. Beattie (1964) Other cultures. Aims, methods and achievements in social anthropology, London: 78-90.
Justification of the cultural anthropologist's moving in fields in which he is not specialized. Warning against onesided stressing of the past. Process to which the ethnographer is subjected, first frustration, followed by a slowly increasing knowledge of and living in the new culture. Observation based on hypotheses which are adapted and renewed. Functional approach essential for modern field work. Statistical evidence should be aimed at, but not without profound qualitative research. Se.

15 J. H. Bell (1954) Field-techniques in anthropology, *Mankind* 5 (# 1): 3-8.

16 F. Boas (1920) The methods of anthropology, *AA* 22: 311-321.
Gives a justification for and a general treatment of the detailed historical method in anthropology, as opposed to evolution, some types of diffusion, and psychology. Gu-Sa.

17 H. C. Bredemeier (1955) The methodology of functionalism, *ASR* 20: 173-180.
Different meanings of the term 'functional' (e.g. the consequences of a particular pattern vs. the causes of the pattern, individual needs vs. requirements for the maintenance of the system) are discussed, showing what constitutes a satisfactory analysis as related to each meaning. Examples of the incest taboo, the Hopi rain dance, and social stratification are cited. Gu-Sa.

18 D. T. Campbell (1961) The mutual methodological relevance of anthropology and psychology, in: F. Hsu ed., Psychological Anthropology, Homewood, Ill.: 333-352.
Shows how psychology bears on the problem of interpretation and of methodological choices in anthropology. Conversely, anthropological data is important for psychological theorizing. Problems of verifiability, and of statistical cross-cultural studies in culture and personality are discussed briefly. Gu-Sa.

19 F. Eggan (1961) Ethnographic data in social anthropology in the United States, *The Sociological Review* 9: 19-26.
Discusses some complications in connection with the use of case materials as brought forward by Gluckman (see * 23), namely the sampling problem and problems concerning the scope of the case that is used. Jk.

20 E. E. Evans-Pritchard (1954) Fieldwork and the empirical tradition, Ch. 4 of his Social anthropology, London: 64-85.
Outlines history of field work in social anthropology, and discusses standard methods of field work at the time of writing. Includes a brief discussion of the anthropologist's personality and temperament. Gu-Sa.

21 R. Firth (1951) Elements of social organization, London: 17-28.
Distinctive characteristics of social anthropology are (1) 'the intensive detailed character of the systematic observation of people in group relations', (2) its holistic implication, and (3) the emphasis on comparison. Problems to be considered in examining the validity of anthropological methods are observation, assignment of meaning, and the problem of expression. Many examples from various localities. Gu-Sa.

22 M. Freilich (1963) The natural experiment, ecology and culture, *SWJA* 19: 21-39.
The natural experiment is one in which a researcher capitalizes on naturally occurring situations of 'clear and dramatic change', as providing a natural laboratory in which 'variables are in a state of control, so that the effects of an independent variable (the change) can be studied'. Culture system models within the framework of cultural ecology, are constructed and compared. East Indians and Negroes in Trinidad. Gu-Sa.

23 M. Gluckman (1961) Ethnographic data in British social anthropology, *Soc. Rev.* 9: 5-17.
Treats the extensive influence of Malinowski on the collection of ethnographic data, and traces a change in the use of 'cases' since Malinowski's time. Two main uses were (1) as apt illustration, in which incidents were not shown to be connected and (2) to extract a general rule (of social morphology) from a case. Now it is necessary to demonstrate process through a series of connected cases. This extended-case method is evaluated, and examples are given. Gu-Sa.

24 Guía de campo del investigador social (1956), Primera parte: Antropología social, Washington, Unión panamericana, Manueles téchnicos III.

25 M. J. Herskovits (1954) Some problems of method in ethnography, in *6: 3-24.
Relationship of theory and method discussed, as well as the influence of the conceptual scheme on formulation of the problem, research design and execution. Problems of duration of fieldwork, communication and rapport, historic depth, presentation of data, and reliability and validity also mentioned. Gu-Sa.

26 P. E. de Josselin de Jong (1956) De visie der participanten op hun cultuur, *Bijdragen Taal-, Land- en Volkenkunde* 112: 149-168; revised version (1967) under the title of The participants' view of their culture, in D. G. Jongmans and P. C. W. Gutkind eds., Anthropologists in the field, Assen.

27 P. Kaberry (1957) Malinowski's contribution to fieldwork methods and the writing of ethnography, in: R. Firth ed., Man and culture, London: 71-91.
Malinowski's approach to fieldwork placed in historical perspective, showing his stress on empiricism and documentation. Theoretical orientation and ethnographic works summarized, noting problems of presentation of such rich data, and his influence on ethnographic writing. Gu-Sa.

28   A. Lesser (1939) Problem vs. subject matter as directives of research, *AA* 41: 574-582.
A good discussion of the advantages of a problem orientation. Discusses the formulation of the problem, the nature and use of hypotheses, and the uses of history. Gu-Sa.

29   O. Lewis (1953) Controls and experiments in field work, in: A. L. Kroeber ed., Anthropology Today, Chicago: 452-475.
Discusses the scientific status of anthropology. Controls involve the 'personal equation' (i.e. relationship of ethnologist to the culture being studied), and the use of teams of field workers. Also treated are sampling, quantification, the comparative method, psychological testing, historical methods, and restudies, all in relation to controls. Contains many examples and a large bibliography. Gu-Sa.

30   R. H. Lowie, Ethnologist. A personal record (1959) L. C. Lowie ed., Berkeley, Calif. etc.
A record of the author's professional life. Methods of field work receive special attention, illustrative material being derived from the author's own experiences. Jk.

31   B. Malinowski (1922) Argonauts of the western Pacific, London: 4-25.
Malinowski's philosophy of field work and his general approach to it are presented, as well as an outline of the types of material to be collected. Participant observation by an isolated observer is stressed. Trobriands. Gu-Sa.

32   B. Malinowski (1948) Magic, science and religion and other essays, Glencoe, Ill.: 237-254.
Discusses some general rules that have to be framed in the field in order to allow the investigation of religion to reduce variations and discrepancies in information to a scientifically useful form. Jk.

33   B. Malinowski (1953) Coral gardens and their magic, London, vol. 1: 317-340.
Describes the method of field work used when studying land tenure among the Trobianders. Initial errors and the process of organizing data are presented in detail. Jk.

34   M. Mauss (1947) Manuel d'ethnographie, Paris.
Text of a series of lectures given by Mauss in Paris from 1926 to 1939. A short chapter on observation methods is followed by chapters on social morphology, technology, economy, religion, etc., aimed at providing some practical directives for the observation and classification of phenomena. Jk.

35   M. Mead (1933) More comprehensive field methods, *AA* 35: 1-15.
Discusses necessity of studying all parts of a culture, especially the problem of studying 'unformalized, inexplicit aspects of culture'. Specific methods of studying child behavior are outlined. Gu-Sa.

36   R. Piddington (1957) An introduction to social anthropology, London, vol II: ch. xiv and xv.
Two chapters dealing with field work. Method applies to the general approach and the theoretical

conceptions on the basis of which the anthropologist works, technique to the practical problems the anthropologist meets in the field. The technique varies form one situation to another. Method does not, it is connected with the conceptual framework. The anthropologist must recognize the inter-relationship between the facts observed. From these facts he must reconstruct the system. Partici-pants do not know the abstract system. Questions must be significant for the culture concerned. Need to distinguish between ideal and real, between majority and minority opinions. The anthro-pologist should also pay attention to non-explicit values. Limitations of the participant observation technique. Checking of the interview. Need for and risks of contact with other Europeans. Lan-guage as an instrument in field work. Value of life-histories, teamwork and follow-up studies. In publications a statement of the anthropologist's situation is necessary. Publication of certain data may be undesirable in the case of literate peoples on account of possible repercussions. Se.

37 J. Pouwer (1961) Practische wenken voor ethnologisch onderzoek in Nederlands-Nieuw-Guinea, *Nieuw Guinea Studiën* 5 (# 1): 10-36.
Concise manual for students at the Administration Institute, Hollandia. In the course of his enquiry, the investigator will come into contact with missionaries and teachers. It is necessary to realize the backgrounds and motives of their activities. Some practical advice for getting into contact with the population, choosing one's place of residence, the genealogical method and the collecting of general data. For an intensive village investigation observation may be very useful in addition to interviewing. Se.

37a H. Powdermaker (1967) Stranger and Friend; the way of an anthropologist, London.
The author's experiences as a fieldworker in Lesu, Mississippi, Hollywood and Northern Rhodesia (Zambia). Among the topics discussed are: The selection of area and/or problem. Problems of getting started, of establishing a routine of living and a pattern of systematic work, and of functioning within the indigenous power structure. Development and changes in problems. Techniques of interviewing in the larger context of the anthropologist's role and his relations with informants. Mistakes (such as over-projection and hidden involvements) and successes. Discouragements and becoming fed-up, due to continuous concentration on unending notetaking, to awareness of one's limitations and those of anthropology, to tensions and anxieties; ways of meeting these problems and of 'escape'. Pleasures in getting the 'feel' of the society, in close friendships with a few native peoples, of collecting some particularly good data, and of seeing it in perspective. The use of insight in determining the field worker's behavior and in understanding his informants, when knowledge is insufficient and theories and techniques inadequate. The ever-present role of involvement and detachment, a major theme throughout the book; the ethics of fieldwork. K.

38 A. R. Radcliffe-Brown (1958) Method in social anthropology, M. N. Srinivas ed., Chicago: Part I: 3-129.
A collection of five of Radcliffe-Brown's methodological essays. They deal mainly with his general orientation to social anthropology, and stress inductive, natural science methods. Papers of particular note have been indexed separately. Gn-Sa.

39   P. Radin (1933) The method and theory of ethnology, New York.
Examines the presuppositions of the ethnological method in the United States – the methods of
Boas and his school, as well as ethnological method in England and on the continent. Contains a
discussion of the quantitative method and the reaction against it. Treats 'factors in the determination
of the ethnological record' as well as reconstruction from internal evidence and the role of the individual. Gu-Sa.

40   R. Redfield (1948) The art of social science, *AJS* 54: 181-190.
Through an examination of De Tocqueville's Democracy in America, Sumner's Folkways, and
Veblen's The theory of the leisure class, Redfield concludes that at least three other-than-scientific
skills are required of great social scientists: humane insight, the ability to see the general in the
particular, and a freshness of vision. Advocates humanistic education and understanding as an
adjunct to scientific method. Gu-Sa.

41   S. A. Rice ed. (1931) Methods in social science; a case book, Chicago.
Comprises a series of analyses of the methods employed by the authors of significant contributions
to social science. Includes articles by R. E. Park on W. I. Thomas and F. Znaniecki, A. L. Kroeber
on Wissler, I. H. Allport and D. A. Hartmann on Stuart Chapin and A. L. Kroeber, and H. D.
Lasswell on B. Malinowski. Jk.

42   M. W. Smith (1959) Boas' 'Natural History' approach to field method, in: W. Goldschmidt ed.,
The anthropology of Franz Boas, Memoir 89 of the Amer. Anth. Assoc.: 46-60.
Boas' 'natural history' approach to field method is contrasted with the 'social philosophy' approach
of British social anthropologists. Indicates some implications of these different ways of approach
for the selection of field data, the use of sociological techniques, the investigator's attitude towards
informants, and the conducting of interviews. Jk.

43   B. K. Stavrianos (1950) Research methods in cultural anthropology in relation to scientific
criteria, *Psych. Rev.* 57: 334-344.
Outlines the development of method in cultural anthropology, reviews some current anthropological
literature with respect to the scientific presentation of research studies, and discusses techniques
related to objectivity, to isolation and control of variables (pertinency), and to reliability. Numerous
examples. Gu-Sa.

44   S. Tax (1963) Penny capitalism. A Guatemalan Indian economy, Chicago: 186-207.
The course of the enquiry is followed step by step and the method used is indicated. Starts by defining, both socially and territorially, the area to be investigated. Followed by house to house census,
genealogical research, etc. Determining and localizing differences in wealth. Se.

45   M. Titiev (1955) The science of man. An introduction to anthropology, New York: 329-337.
Advantages of participant observation. Knowledge of the language makes for less dependence on

interpreters. Use more than one informant on a particular subject. Internal consistency of material a check on its reliability. Field worker should stay at least one whole year. Preferably visit the area more than once. Se.

46   J. H. Weakland (1951) Method in cultural anthropology, *Phil. Sci.* 18: 55-69.
Emphasizes a general pattern-seeking approach, and the establishment of a comparative basis of observation. Discusses types of observations made, use of informants, possible checks which can be used, as well as the validity and applicability of conclusions reached. Deals mainly with culture and personality and national character studies. Gu-Sa.

47   K. W. Wolff (1945) A methodological note on the empirical establishment of culture patterns, *ASR* 10: 176-84.
The 'objective' (where one concentrates on scientific method, and approaches culture by way of preconceived contentual divisions) and the 'cultural' (where one concentrates on the 'cultural equation', i.e. the way in which one's own cultural background affects his view of the new culture, and where he looks for patterns, not content) approaches to anthropological study are outlined, with respect to how to establish patterns empirically, and how to prove that these patterns are an adequate interpretation of the culture. Includes a brief discussion of prediction. New Mexico. Gu-Sa.

2   *field relations*

A   GENERAL

48   D. F. Aberle (1966) The Peyote religion among the Navaho, *Viking Fund publications in Anthropology* 42: 227-243.
Detailed description of the course of research; discusses in what way an initial misconception of the fieldworker influenced his research and his results. K.

49   C. Baks, J. C. Breman, E. W. Hommes, I. Ronner and K. W. v. d. Veen (1965) De betrouwbearheid van informatie in een kastesamenleving in Gujerat, India, *Sociologische Gids* 12: 167-174.
Discusses how the reliability of data collected in a caste society was affected by the dependence of each caste on the dominant one, by caste cohesion and by the identification of the researcher with the dominant caste. Jk.

50   J. Beattie (1965) Understanding an African Kingdom: Bunyoro, New York etc.
A description of the investigation carried out by the author in Bunyoro (Uganda), following the enquiry step by step from the preparations for the field work to the writing down of the results. Attention is paid both to participant observation and to more formal techniques of data collection. Jk.

51   G. D. Berreman (1962) Behind many masks: ethnography and impression management in a Himalayan village, *Society for Applied Anthropology Monograph* # 4, Ithaca, N.Y.
Description and analysis of field relations in a hostile North Indian village in terms of impressions the participants (himself, his interpreters, various caste groups of villagers) wanted to convey to the others. Includes a description of some rapport-inducing devices, and an explanation of how use of different interpreters gave access to different information. Gu-Sa.

52   J. Dollard (1949) Caste and class in a southern town, New York: 1-41.
Participation in social life in two roles, as a Yankee studying the Negroes and, more intensively, noting down life-histories. Two kinds of observation 1. of what the people say 2. of what they do and appear to feel. No fixed questionnaires were used. Special attention given to the investigator's own emotional reactions and to those of the people in concrete social situations. In the collecting of life-histories many precautions had to be taken with respect to place and manner of interviewing to avoid suspicion on the part of either the white or the negro population (important since negro-women were also interviewed). Notes were taken on the spot since many subtleties might otherwise be lost. Necessity of anonymity of informants and place of enquiry. Se.

53   E. E. Evans-Pritchard (1940) The Nuer, Oxford: 7-15 and 82-84.
An unusually frank description of fieldwork under difficult conditions. Problems of entree of a fieldworker with an 'enemy' role into a largely hostile population, with no assistance available in language learning. Gu-Sa.

54   W. J. Hanna (1965) Image-making in field research: some tactical and ethical problems of research in tropical Africa, *Am. Behavioral Scientist* 8: 15-20.
The image of a study presented to host officials and informants is created by controlling characteristics and behavior of the researcher. In the ideal study the satisfactions of the host and informants are maximized, study is legitimate and presents a minimum threat. The ideal may be approached by describing the investigation as 1. nonpolitical, 2. one of several, 3. informal and 4. helpful, and the investigator as professor, peer, friendly participant, sympathetic neutral, stranger, and American. Gu-Sa.

55   D. G. Haring (1945) Comment on field techniques in ethnography; illustrated by a survey in the Rijūkijū Islands, *Southwestern Journal of Anthropology* 10 (# 3): 255-267.
Informants very helpful and interested in the investigation. Reason: science is held in high esteem on this island. The people are proud of their educational system, many institutions collaborate in the investigation. Value of photographs, films, and tape recordings. Importance, in studying a literate people, of explaining reasons and results. Movies should always be shown and tape-recordings played back. Questionnaires were drawn up or revised by the people themselves. Results, too, were shown to and criticized by them. Se.

56   F. Henry (1965) Some comments on the role of the fieldworker in an explosive political situation, paper read at the Annual Meeting of the American Anthropological Association, Denver.
Revised version in: *CA* (1966) 7: 552-559, with comments by J. A. Barnes, H. Befu, P. C. W. Gutkind, A. Weingrod and N. E. Whitten jr.
Discusses the problem of maintaining impartiality, role changes necessary in public political situations and the role of the female fieldworker. Also deals with the problems of verifying data, size of the political community and accessibility of data. Gu-Sa.

57   M. J. Herskovits and F. S. Herskovits (1934) Rebel destiny: among the Bush Negroes of Dutch Guiana, New York and London.
The field work methods used in this investigation are described in the course of the book, interspersed among the ethnographic description. Data were obtained exclusively through casual observation, chance happenings, and conversations arising out of these. Fragments of conversations are reproduced throughout the book. Jk.

58   M. J. Herskovits (1948) Man and his works, New York: 79-93.
Discusses techniques used in the field, involving relationships with informants and how to get at and understand materials. Also treats the 'Notes and Queries' approach, the genealogical approach, village mapping, use of the native language and use of biographies. Many examples, including Surinam Bush Negroes, Nuer. Gu-Sa.

59   Sister I. Hilger (1954) An ethnographic field method, in *6: 25-42.
Based on personal field experiences in studying children. Discusses preparation (take notebooks, camera, presents), interviewing and observation, use of a field assistant, selecting and motivating informants, and problems of validity (cross-checking with other informants, with documents, by observation). Indians of the southwestern U.S.A. Gu-Sa.

60   J. F. Holleman (1958) African interlude, Cape Town.
Describes the anthropologist in the field. It is the personal story of the six years of research that lie behind the compilation of the author's Shona Customary Law. Jgm.

61   Junker, B. H. (1960) Field work: an introduction to the social sciences, Chicago.
This useful book includes material on observing, recording and reporting; the field work situation; roles and adaptations of the field worker; a valuable section on learning to do field work, and an extensive classified bibliography. Many examples are given throughout. Gu-Sa.

62   H. Kuper (1947) An African aristocracy, London: 1-10.
Difficulty of overcoming distrust with respect to investigator. For female investigator participation in certain aspects of the culture is limited. Reactions to the anthropologist not the same for the various classes (upper, middle, lower). Not only observable facts important, but also attitudes and ideas regarding these facts. Se.

63 S. F. Nadel (1953) The foundations of social anthropology, Glencoe, Ill.: 35-55.
Discusses use of informants and of native language, the personal equation (coming to grips with one's subjectivity, making explicit one's evaluations), application of anthropological knowledge. Gu-Sa.

64 D. Nash (1963) The ethnologist as a stranger: an essay in the sociology of knowledge, *SWJA* 19: 149-167.
The ethnologist's role influences his viewpoint. Adaptive difficulties can significantly affect perception. Two polar responses of strangers to host culture are approach (empathy) and avoidance (authoritarian ethnocentrism). Discussion of 'modal personality' of the anthropological community. Gu-Sa.

65 P. L. Newman (1965) Knowing the Gururumba, New York: 5-16.
Account of the difficulty of explaining the aims of one's visit to the population. No equivalent for role of researcher in the culture studied. Expectations of material wealth through the arrival of a white man. Se.

66 F. C. Mann (1951) Human relations skills in social research, *Human Relations* 4: 341-345.
Considers role of social researcher in regard to 1. informing his subjects about his work, 2. maintaining balanced relationships, 3. involving leaders and members of the research situation in active participation, 4. accustoming people to research activity. Mentions possibilities of developing these skills through field experience, case-book materials and role-playing in simulated situations. Gu-Sa.

67 D. Maybury-Lewis (1965) The Savage and the innocent, London and New York.
An account of the way field-work was carried out among the Sherente and Shavante Indians of Brazil. Describes the making of first contacts, relations with informants, problems and successes during the investigation, and the field-worker's personal experiences and adventures. Contains many conversations reproduced verbatim. (from a book review by Ch. Wagley, *AA* 68: 536-537).

68 H. Papanek (1964) The woman field worker in a purdah society, *HO* 23: 160-163.
A Western woman field-worker has two advantages in a purdah society, where women are secluded: (1) she can have contact with women, which would be impossible for a male field worker, and (2) she has a flexible role within the whole society, an impossibility for 'fullfledged participants in the local culture'. Greater flexibility is possible because of the many opportunities for the individual to contribute to her own role definition. Pakistan. Gu-Sa.

69 B. D. Paul (1953) Interview techniques and field relationships, in: A. L. Kroeber ed., Anthropology today: 430-451.
Entering the community and choosing a role. The question of ethics in role playing. Community participation, interviewing techniques and the use of informants. The interpretation of language and note-taking. Contains a good bibliography. Gu-Sa.

70   G. Plimpton (1966) The story behind a nonfiction novel, *The New York Times Book Review* 71
(# 3): 2-3; 38-43.
Interview with Truman Capote on how his nonfiction novel In cold blood (New York 1965) came
into being. The author tells of his interviews, his relations with the principal figures, and how, by
selecting his data in a certain way, he incorporated his own views in the book. Jk.

71   H. Powdermaker (1962) Copper Town: changing Africa, New York: xiii-xxi.
Shortness of time available makes it difficult to learn the language. Impossible to live in African
quarter. First problem solved by employing African students. Second by making assistant write
down all conversations of his own home. Se.

72   S. A. Richardson (1953) A framework for reporting field relations experiences, *HO* 12 (# 3): 31-37.
Also in *1: 124-139.
Besides the framework list of topics, the article treats the problems of preparation for entry and
structuring of role, timing of activities and importance of initial activities, dealing with rumours, and
sources and types of information. Gu-Sa.

73   J. W. Schoorl (1967) The anthropologist in government service, in: D. G. Jongmans and P. C. W.
Gutkind eds., Anthropologists in the field, Assen.

74   A. J. Shelton (1964) The 'Miss Ophelia' syndrome as a problem in African field research,
Practical Anth. XI: 259-265.
Presents three cases where young anthropologists' lack of adaptability to situations involving physical
contact (refusing food and drink, refusal to shake hands appropriately, unwillingness to enter house)
has disastrous effects on research attempted and on relationships with Africans. Urges greater self-
examination by potential fieldworkers before entry into field. Gu-Sa.

75   E. Smith-Bowen (1956) Return to laughter, London.
A fictional account (based on experience) of an anthropologist's field work. Problems of rapport, of
communication, of getting at difficult information, of factionalism, of gaining the confidence of
one's informants, etc., are discussed through examples of various incidents. A description of troubles
involving ethical judgement in dealing with people, culture shock and adaptation problems of the
anthropologist. Africa. Gu-Sa.

76   R. H. Wax (1957) Twelve years later: an analysis of field experience, *AJS* 63: 133-142. Also in *1:
166-178.
Describes three stages of fieldworker's definition of his role: insecurity, gradual role definition, and
validation, during which time he must teach informants the role behaviour which will enable him
to learn from them. Wartime study of an American Japanese relocation centre. Gu-Sa.

77 W. F. Whyte (1955) Appendix to Street corner society, 2nd ed., Chicago: 279-358.
A perceptive account of personal experiences which influenced a 3½-year slum community study before, during and after field research. Includes comment on the after effects of the study on informants and others. Also discusses problems of entree, of establishing relationships, of interviewing selected informants, participant observation and recording. Gu-Sa.

78 M. Zelditch, Jr. (1962) Some methodological problems of field studies, *AJS* 67: 566-576.
Three broad classes of desired information are matched with three methods: participant observation, informant interviewing, and enumeration and sampling, each of which is discussed in detail. Criteria to evaluate methods are suggested, 1) informal adequacy and 2) efficiency. Gu-Sa.

B PARTICIPANT OBSERVATION

79 N. Babchuck (1962) The role of the researcher as participant observer and participant – as – observer in the field situation, *HO* 21 (# 3): 225-228.
The author distinguishes between the role of participant observer (the researcher being a full member of the group) and participating -as-observer (the researcher being accepted as such by the group). The latter role, according to the author, offers better possibilities of research: the researcher's task is situated outside the group studied, which affords him freedom of movement while he loses no time in non-research activities. The researcher's status is not determined by a formal position within the group, enabling him to come into contact with all members of the system in the same way. Jk.

80 H. S. Becker and B. Geer (1957) Participant observation and interviewing: a comparison, *HO* 16: 28-32.
Participant observation favoured over unstructured interviewing because of greater completeness and accuracy, through increased access to people under study and greater sensitivity produced in the researcher. Participant observation provides more context for interpretive purposes. Gu-Sa.

81 H. S. Becker (1958) Problems of inference and proof in participant observation, *ASR* 23: 653-660.
The three stages of field analysis are 1) selection and definition of problems, concepts, indices. 2) checking on frequency and distribution of phenomena. 3) incorporation of individual findings into a model of the organization under study (construction of social system model). Final analysis and presentation of results should include a description of the characteristic forms that data took at each stage of research. Gu-Sa.

82 R. M. Berndt (1962) Excess and restraint – social control among a New Guinea Mountain People, Chicago: VI-XIV.

83 R. M. Berndt and C. H. Berndt (1941) A preliminary report of fieldwork in the Ooldea region, Western South Australia, *Oceania* 12: 305-315.

84   D. Brokensha (1963) A study of Larteh, Ghana, *CA* 4 (# 5): 533-534.

85   S. Bruyn (1963) The methodology of participant observation, *HO* 22 (# 3): 224-235.
Inquiry concerning the place of participant observation in the methodology of the social sciences, discussion of the epistemological background of participant observation. Mentions eight points that constitute a guide for adequate research. Jgm.

86. K. Burridge (1960) Mambu, London: 1-14.
Description of experiences during an ethnographic enquiry into a cargo-cult (N. Guinea). Jk.

87   L. Festinger, H. W. Riecken and S. Schachter (1956) When prophesy fails, Minneapolis: 237-252.
This investigation was exclusively carried out by participant observers posing as ordinary members of the group they were studying. The difficulties that arose in this are discussed in detail in the Methodological Appendix. Jk.

88   R. Firth (1936) We, the Tikopia: a sociological study of kinship in primitive Polynesia, London: 1-12.

89   R. L. Gold (1958) Roles in sociological field observations, *Soc. Forces* 36: 217-223.
Analyzes, with respect to their effects on field work, four possible field-worker roles, as seen in the work of Junker (See *61): complete participant; participant-as-observer; observer-as-participant; and complete observer.
These are 'master roles', in which numerous lesser role relationships can be developed, and they are analyzed in terms of the self-demands and role-demands on the researcher. Role selection depends partly on what aspects of society are being studied. Gu-Sa.

90   H. Geertz (1961) The Javanese Family, Glencoe: 161-171.
Discusses the difficulties of participant observation in a larger town K.

91   R. I. Goldstein (1964) The participant as observer, *Phylon* 25 (# 3): 270-279.
This paper discusses some positive advantages to the sociologist as scientist accruing from community participation. These include: 1. An increased awareness of the need for a broad social science framework. 2. An inside view of the day-by-day dynamics of a social movement. 3. Perception of functional relationships between civil rights activities at various levels. 4. An increased sensitivity to the limitations of public documents. 5. An understanding of the community through the opportunity to observe its life from many status vantage points. Gu-Sa.

92   R. W. Janes (1961) A note on phases of the community role of the participant-observer, *ASR* 26: 446-450.
On the basis of his field work in a small town the author discerns five phases in the investigator's community role, and shows how this affects the content of the information acquired in each phase. (United States). Jk.

93 F. R. Kluckhohn (1940) The participant-observer technique in small communities, *AJS* 46: 331-343.
Nature and purpose of participant observation outlined. Key to participant observer techniques is understanding by ethnographer of his general and specific roles in the community. Although participant observation entails some disadvantages (for example, ethnographer's role may limit his access to material), its advantages include increasing of range, relevance, and reliability of data through 1) increased opportunities for observation and 2) balance between behavioristic type investigation and that which seeks meaning. Small village in southwestern U.S.A. Gu-Sa.

94 A. J. F. Köbben (1967) Participation and quantification; field work among the Djuka (Bush-Negroes of Surinam), in: D. G. Jongmans and P. C. W. Gutkind eds., Anthropologists in the field, Assen.

95 J. Kolaja (1956) Contribution to the theory of participant observation, *Social Forces* 35 (# 2): 159-163.
Kolaja develops two analytical categories in terms of performance and concept of performance, cross-tabulated with the categories of correspondence and non-correspondence between the self and the role. This is applied to the processes of participant observation and interview. In the interview the correspondence between the self and the role changes in the same circumstances as in participant observation. In participant observation the investigator switches from performance to concept of performance when he finds that the other person's motives differ from his own. In the interview he does so for instance when the interviewee is not sufficiently communicative. The interviewer then plays up to the other person, as it were, to bring him round. Se.

96 C. J. Lammers (1960) De participerende waarneming, *Sociologische Gids* 7: 193-218.
Briefly compares participant observation with other methods of empirical investigation, after which the relations between participant observation and sociological theory, and the relations between participant observation and statistics, are discussed. Distinguishes four variables which determine the participant observer's position in the group he studies, and various types of role conflict between or within his roles as a participant (group member) and as an observer (professional scientist) Jk.

97 P. Mayer (1962) Townsmen or tribesmen, Cape Town: 295-297.
Differences in methods of rural and urban field work are indicated. Jk.

98 S. M. Miller (1952) The participant observer and 'over rapport', *ASR* 17: 97-99.
In a case study of a local labor union, Miller found that, while a high degree of rapport with union leaders supplied him with valuable information, this rapport closed certain antagonistic areas to examination and reduced his objectivity towards lower members of the organization. Gu-Sa.

99 L. Pospisil (1963) Kapauku papuan economy, New Haven: 17-26.

100   K. E. Read (1965) The high valley, New York.
An account of two years of anthropological field work in New Guinea. Describes particular aspects of the culture on the basis of particular individuals known to and situations experienced by the author. Highly autobiographical. Jk.

101   H. W. Riecken (1956) The unidentified interviewer, *AJS* 62 (# 2): 210-212.
Describes the role of the investigator who cannot or does not wish himself to be known as such. Draws on the Methodological Appendix of *87. Jk.

102   A. J. Rube (1966) The method of participant observation: Fieldwork in Mexiquito, New York etc.

103   M. S. Schwartz and C. G. Schwartz (1955) Problems in participant observation, *AJS* 50: 343-353.
The process of participant observation involves registering, interpreting, and recording. Interaction between observer (who may have either a passive or an active role) and observed influences the data. Kinds and causes of distortion are discussed. Handling of anxiety and bias is particularly important. Gu-Sa.

104   Th. Schwartz (1962) The Paliau movement in the Admirality Islands, 1946-1954, *Anthropological Papers of the Am. Museum of Natural History* 49 part 2, New York: 292-301.
Investigation of a cargo-cult.

105   M. G. Silverman (1962) The resettled Banaban (Ocean Island) community in Fiji: A preliminary report, *CA* 3 (# 4): 429-431.

106   M. Trow (1957) Comment on 'Participant observation and interviewing: a comparison', *HO* 16: 33-35.
Condemns exclusive preoccupation with one method and suggests that different techniques should be used to get at different kinds of data. Gu-Sa.

107   A. J. Vidich (1955) Participant observation and the collection and interpretation of data, *AJS* 50: 354-360.
The participant observer's role and the respondents' image of him affect data greatly. Two problems of data collection are (1) tactical maneuvers in the field (involving problems of conformity and identification) and (2) evaluation of data. Participant observation is of particular importance for the study of change. Problems of category-formation and validity are also discussed. Small town in New York State. Gu-Sa.

108   J. West (1945) Plainville, U.S.A., New York: VII-XV.

109 W. F. Whyte (1951) Observational field work methods, in: M. Jahoda, M. Deutsch and S. W. Cook eds., Research methods in social relations, New York: 493-513.
Guiding principles in the use of participant observation. Problems that arise in setting up an appropriate position for observation. Discusses the content of observation, its recording, the reliability of data and the training of the observer. Jgm.

C INFORMANTS AND INTERVIEWING

110 *American Journal of Sociology* (1956) 62 (♯ 2).
Issue devoted to the interview. (Papers of particular relevance have been indexed seperately). Jk.

111 K. W. Back (1956) The well-informed informant, *HO* 14 (♯ 4): 30-33.
Informants may be either well-informed (the usual anthropological informant on factual matters) or interpretive. Traits and tasks of the well-informed informant outlined (must have knowledge, motivation, ability to transmit information). Short section on selection of informants. Gu-Sa.

112 M. Benney, D. Riesman and S. A. Star (1956) Age and sex in the interview, *AJS* 62 (♯ 2): 143-152.
Statistical analysis of the influence of various combinations of age and sex of interviewer and interviewee on the informant's answers, on the interviewee's honesty as judged by the interviewer and on the degree in which both of them appreciated the interview. Jk.

113 H. Blanc (1956) Multilingual Interviewing in Israel, *AJS* 62 (♯ 2): 205-209.
An illustration of the problems that arise in translating questions into the languages of different cultures. Jk.

114 J. B. Casagrande ed. (1960) In the company of man, New York.
This collection of 'twenty portraits by anthropologists' contains essays about particularly interesting or noteworthy people (often informants) with whom they came in contact during field trips. Through the perceptive recounting of many incidents, we are given an idea of the character of the anthropologist's relationships with people in the field. Gu-Sa.

115 J. P. Dean and W. F. Whyte (1958) How do you know if the informant is telling the truth? *HO* 17 (♯ 2): 34-39.
The authors distinguish between information on subjective and on objective data. They name the factors which in their opinion influence the reliability of such information and indicate some ways of detecting distortion. Jk.

116 L. A. Dexter (1956) Role relationships and conceptions of neutrality in interviewing, *AJS* 62 (♯ 2): 153-157.

Cooperation in the interview is best attained if the interviewer adopts the terminology and style of speech of the informant, which makes the informant feel that the interviewer shares his point of view. According to the author this makes the interviewer neutral in the eyes of most informants. Jk.

117   B. S. Dohrenwend (1956) Some effects of open and closed questions on respondents' answers, *HO* 24 (# 2): 175-184.
The conclusion reached by the author is that closed questions may be less efficient though no confirmation is to be found for the assumption that open questions produce more depth and more reliable answers. Jk.

118   B. S. Dohrenwend and S. A. Richardson (1964) A use for leading questions in research interviewing, *HO* 23 (# 1): 76-77.
Shows how leading questions may be a useful tool for eliciting volunteered information. Jk.

119   E. E. Evans-Pritchard (1932) Withchraft among the Azande, *JRAI* 62: 291-336; also in: (1933) The Zande corporation of witchdoctors, *JRAI* 63: 63-100.
Statement of the way in which information was secured on the esoteric life of the Zande corporation of witch doctors and on the training of a novice by using a substitute to be initiated and by creating rivalry between practitioners. Jk.

120   R. L. Gorden (1956) Dimensions of the depth interview, *AJS* 62 (# 2): 158-164.
The author discusses the barriers to communication on the interviewee's part in so far as these are connected with the depth of the interview. Eight 'dimensions of depth' are distinguished; degree of ego-threat; degree of forgetting; degree of generalization and of subjectivity; consciousness of original experience; trauma; etiquette; chronology. Jk.

121   M. J. Herskovits (1950) The hypothetical situation: a technique of field research, *SWJA* 6: 32-40.
Devising hypothetical situations to provoke comment, speculation on the outcome, etc., may be useful in probing areas about which informants are reluctant to speak (esoteric, mysterious, or undesirable activities), or about things taken for granted by informant. Examples given of use in many areas. Gu-Sa.

122   Cl. Kluckhohn (1940) Navaho witchcraft, Cambridge; (1962) Boston: 13-20.
On the difficulties of obtaining information on witchcraft and on the manner in which the material was collected (interview methods). Jk.

123   K. L. Little (1951) The Mende of Sierra Leone, London: 11-16.
Difficulties in obtaining information on secret societies. Educated members of the society are found to be the best informants. Reasons for not reporting part of the material. Jk.

124   J. A. Loewen (1965) Self exposure: bridge to fellowship, *Practical Anthropology* 12 (♯ 2): 49-62.
Friendliness and communicativeness on problems that are preferably not talked about may be brought about by telling the informant something of the problems one is wrestling with oneself. Show that for us, too, there is a discrepancy between ideal and reality. Se.

125   E. E. Maccoby and N. Maccoby (1954) The interview: a tool of social science, Ch. 12 in: G. Lindzey, Handbook of social psychology, vol. 1: 449-487.
Historical review of the use of the interview, standardized and unstandardized, in social research; phrasing of questions; interviewing techniques; role relationships and cooperation; problems involving children, other societies; validity and sources of error; comparison of interviewing and other research techniques. Includes a good bibliography. Gu-Sa.

126   D. Metzger (1963) Asking questions and questioning answers in ethnography, paper presented at meeting of the Southwestern Anthr. Assoc., Riverside, Cal., *in*: Symposium on Ethnographic Procedures and Descriptive Format.

127   S. F. Nadel (1939) The interview technique in social anthropology, in: Bartlett (see *10): 317-327.
Use of informant to provide information on social reality, check with observation and/or other interviews, dealing with inaccurate or distorted information, use of abstractions and concrete material, stimulation of informant intellectually and emotionally, use of leading questions, problems of note-taking, interviewer's social role. Gu-Sa.

128   H. Passin (1942) Tarahumara prevarication: a problem in field method, *AA* 44: 235-247.
Five alternately possible reasons for lying suggested: fear of sorcery, fear of displeasure of outsiders, prestige-lying for self-aggrandizement, personal factors, ethnologists affiliation with one faction of community. Lies can be interpreted to point out stresses and patterns in the culture. Gu-Sa.

129   M. A. Tremblay (1957) They key informant technique: a nonethnographic application, *AA* 59: 688-701.
Focused use of key informants for specialized information on particular topics as a preliminary stage in a study involving mainly survey technique. Good discussion of research design, objectives of the focused key informant technique, criteria and methods of selection of informants (more were used than is general in ethnographic work). Rural eastern Canada. Gu-Sa.

130   R. H. Wax (1952) Reciprocity as a field technique, *HO* 11 (♯ 3): 34-37. Also in (♯ 4): 90-98.
In order to better interpret and evaluate the data received, the fieldworker should be aware of what the (possibly atypical) informant derives from their relationship, for example, release of aggression, satisfaction of curiosity or of need to give advice, relief of loneliness or boredom. Gu-Sa.

131   W. F. Whyte (1960) Interviewing in field research, in *1: 352-374.
Research interview (involving neither questionnaires nor schedules) discussed in terms of stages in interviewing, verification of both evaluative and descriptive data, use of projective aids and recording, indexing and classifying unstructured material. Notes importance of making informant specify names, places, etc., since otherwise misinterpretation is easy. Gu-Sa.

132   F. W. Young and R. C. Young (1961) Key informant reliability in rural Mexican villages, *HO* 20: 141-148.
Reliability defined as agreement between persons and/or individual informant's internal consistency and stability. Key informants were found most reliable in 'reporting on the community as a whole rather than on the typical behavior of the residents, when the information concerns directly observable phenomena such as physical properties or stable institutions in the community, and in matters requiring little evaluation or inference'. Guttman scales may be helpful in determining intra-informant reliability. Mexican villages. Gu-Sa.

3   *observation and recording*

133   J. H. Bell (1955) Observation in anthropology, *Mankind* 5 (# 2): 55-60.

134   R. L. Birdwhistell (1952) Body motion research and interviewing, *HO* 11 (# 1): 137-138.
Interaction in interviews goes farther than communication by speech. Interviewers can be taught to interpret body motions. Examples given of eye behavior and hand behavior in the U.S. Gu-Sa.

135   S. Ceccato (1965) Suggestions for anthropology: the machine which observes and describes, in: D. Hymes ed., The use of computers in anthropology, The Hague: 465-500.
Describes a project for building a machine capable of observing and verbally recording what takes place in its environment, (antecedents, results and operation of the machine). Indicates four ways in which this research can contribute to anthropological inquiries. Jk.

136   E. D. Chapple (1940) Measuring human relations: an introduction to the study of the interaction of individuals, *Genetic Psychology Monographs* 22: 3-147.
An attempt to apply 'the methods of the exact sciences' to human behavior, the inferences made being limited to those derived from observation. Discusses units of observation and of measurement, and applications of mathematics to analysis. Many examples include several drawn from the areas of family, kinship, industry. Gu-Sa.

137   E. D. Chapple (1949) The interaction chronograph: its evolution and present application, *Personnel* 25: 295-307.
The Interaction Chronograph is 'a computing machine which continuously records and integrates

measurements of the time aspects of the way one person adjusts to another'. The article illustrates its use in evaluating interviews non-subjectively. Psychiatric patients, personnel work, job performance in industry. Gu-Sa.

138   J. L. Fischer (1958) The classification of residence in censuses, *AA* 60: 508-517.
Proposes a general typology of individual residence which classifies everyone, not only simple families, for use in taking censuses in any society. Discusses relationship of this system to that currently in use. Truk. Gu-Sa.

139   E. T. Hall (1963) A system for the notation of proxemic behavior, *AA* 65: 1003-1026.
Cross-cultural differences exist in the interpretation of different physical interpersonal features. This system permits recording of such proxemic behavior on the dimensions of (1) postural-sex identifiers (2) sociofugal-sociopetal orientation (3) kinesthetic factors (4) touch code (5) retinal combinations (6) thermal code (7) olfaction code (8) voice loudness scale. Analysis involves proxemic systems as communication. Gu-Sa.

140   R. W. Heyns and R. Lippitt (1954) Systematic observational techniques, in: Lindzey (see *125): 370-404.
Historical review of observer techniques in social psychology. Observer's main tasks (categorizing and rating behavior) outlined. Properties of observer systems discussed and illustrated for face-to-face groups, two-person groups, for field- and therapy settings, and for social behavior of children. Extensive bibliography. Gu-Sa.

141   G. P. Kurath (1950) A new method of choreographic notation, *AA* 52: 120-22.
Three aspects of dance must be recorded: ground plan, steps and gestures, rhythmic beat and structure. Plan to integrate all three applied to Iroquois choreographies, and illustrated by one simple dance. Comparative choreology requires study of psycho-religious functions and cultural significance of dance, but adequate recording is a precondition of these. Gu-Sa.

142   D. N. Larson (1964) Making use of anthropological fieldnotes, *Practical Anthropology* 11 (# 3): 142-144.
The taking of notes as an important means of gauging one's own reactions to the alien world. They show the extent of one's own adaptation to the other culture at the time of taking the notes. Se.

143   M. Mead (1940) The mountain Arapesh, *Anthropological Papers, Amer. Museum of Natural Hist.* 37: 325-338.
Deals with methods of recording, types of material collected, relationship of theory to data in field situations. In reporting one's material, there is a need to specify theoretical bias, methods, and language used in the field, as well as the sequence of formulating and checking hypotheses.

40: 173-178.
On the necessity of detailed records of events, because of the discrepancy between articulate forms and actual practices.

41: 293-302.
Some methodological points regarding the collection of autobiographical statements: verbatim versus dictated materials; recording in native or in communication language; various purposes for the collection of life histories and the advantages of employing informants who are of the same disposition and cast of mind as the anthropologist himself. Gu-Sa-Jk.

144   M. Mead (1956) New lives for old, London: 481-501.
The methods used in this restudy are compared with those used in 1929 (Growing up in New Guinea, New York 1930). 'Fine-grain note-taking' on small behavior sequences, as used in the restudy, is preferred to dictation by a trained informant. Omissions in the material gathered in 1929 are indicated. Illustrated with examples of note-taking. Jk.

145   M. Melbin (1954) An interaction recording device for participant observers, *HO* 13 (♯ 2): 29-33.
Illustrates the use of a card system for recording interaction by an unknown participant observer in a department store. Gu-Sa.

146   M. Melbin (1960) Mapping uses and methods, in *1: 255-266.
Reviews many mapping techniques in social science (diagrams, floor plans, aerial photos, etc.). Methods of mapping discussed with respect to purposes, procedure (including problems of scale, symbols, materials), sampling observations, and reliability and validity. Gu-Sa.

147   M. F. A. Montagu (1945) Sociometric methods in anthropology, *Sociometry* 8: 62-63.
Advocates use of sociometric methods in mapping 'interactive relationships' among all members of the (usually small) group being studied by the anthropologist. Gu-Sa.

148   P. Pollenz (1949) Methods for the comparative study of the dance, *AA* 51: 428-435.
History of notation systems (including letter notation, track drawings, and stick figures) for recording dance steps discussed. The Von Laban system of stenochoreography is described, and suggested as useful for recording motions used in agriculture, the hunt, carrying children, etc., as well as dances and ceremonials. Illustrated with some of own work. Gu-Sa.

149   F. L. W. Richardson, Jr. (1950) Field methods and techniques, *HO* 9 (♯ 2): 31-32.
Deals with data gathering and presentation in four types of 'internal mapping': (1) spatial arrangements in general, (2) spatial arrangements of objects important in regularizing people's activities, (3) seating arrangements and groupings of people during periodic gatherings, (4) traffic-flow maps. Gu-Sa.

150   R. F. Salisbury (1962) From stone to steel: economic consequences of a technological change in New Guinea, Melbourne: 162-183.
A carefully detailed account of an economic experiment in a field work situation. Shows the technique used for collecting data and discusses the theoretical importance of complete records. Gu-Sa.

151   G. Saslow and E. D. Chapple (1945) A new life-history form, with instructions for its use, *HO* (*Applied Anth.*) 4 (♯1): 1-18.
Presentation of a life-history form which can 'furnish an objective account, permitting independent verification' and satisfying certain criteria of a good case-history. Instructions for interviewing and filling in the form are given. Gu-Sa.

152   W. A. Smalley (1960) Making and keeping anthropological fieldnotes, *Practical Anthropology* 7 (♯ 4): 145-152.
Practical hints for non-professional anthropologists. How to collect and how to preserve data. Chronological or topic recording. General, or bearing on a particular topic. Photography, participation, selection of informants. Se.

153   W. C. Sturtevant (1959) A technique for ethnographic notetaking, *AA* 61: 677-678.
Note-taking by means of small paper squares, a piece of cardboard, and a short pencil concealed in one's pocket for unobtrusive note-taking during all-day ceremonies where note-taking is 'inadvisable'. Explicit instructions are given. Gu-Sa.

154   J. Wilson (1962) Interaction analysis: a supplementary fieldwork technique used in the study of leadership in a 'new style' Australian aboriginal community, *HO* 21 (♯ 4): 290-294.
Discusses a technique for determining in a systematic way the broad outlines of the social organization of a group, through observation of the frequency of mutual contact between persons. Suggests some ways of using this technique, for instance in studying social change. Jk.

155   K. H. Wolff (1960) The collection and organization of field materials: a research report, in *1: 240-254.
Describes collection and classification of field notes by topic in the field (this included cross-referencing), and reclassification at home by categories. Includes use of supplementary materials, reorganization and writing-up of data, many tables. Examples from own research in a village in the southwestern U.S.A. Gu-Sa.

4   *technical aids: photography, films, recordings*

156   J. Collier (1957) Photography in anthropology: a report on two experiments, *AA* 59: 843-859.
Exposition of two direct uses of photography in social science research 1) an application of photographic surveying to establish a typology for evaluating housing conditions, and 2) experimentation with the use of photography as a semi-projective technique in interviewing. Both a control and an experimental group were used here, and generally better interview material was obtained from the experimental group. Gu-Sa.

157   N. G. Dyhrenfurth (1952) Film making for scientific field workers, *AA* 54: 147-152.
Useful article containing practical information on types of equipment, and its care and handling in different climates and situations, as well as techniques of shooting (varying angles and distances, how to record long sequences, problems of transition) which help to make the film more interesting. Gu-Sa.

158   J. T. Hitchcock and P. J. Hitchcock (1960) Some considerations for the prospective ethnographic cinematographer, *AA* 62: 656-674.
On the making of short descriptive films for recording purposes by relatively inexperienced ethnologists. Discusses types, costs, and care of film, other equipment, editing, sound, and distribution. Contains a glossary of cinematographic terms and lists other sources of information and a sample script as an example. Gu-Sa.

159   M. Mead (1956) Some uses of still photography in culture and personality studies, in: D. G. Haring ed., Personal character and cultural milieu, 3rd revised ed., Syracuse: 78-105.
Discusses development of still photography as a major research tool 'rather than a helpful little supplement', with considerable attention to the technology of photography. Treats uses of photography as both a recording and a communication device. Many examples, including photographs and discussion, from Bali, Manus, America. Gu-Sa.

160   I. Polunin (1965) Stereophonic magnetic tape recorders and the collection of ethnographic field data, *CA* 6 (♯ 2): 227-230.
A stereo tape recorder makes it possible to make a sound recording of an event and of information on that event independently but exactly synchronized. The equipment suitable for these operations is briefly described. Jk.

161   J. H. Rowe (1953) Technical aids in anthropology: a historical survey, in: Anthropology today (see *29): 895-940.
As well as discussing techniques useful mainly to physical anthropology and archaeology, the following, for social anthropology and ethnology, are mentioned: photography, motion pictures, X-rays (archaeology and phonetics), microfilm and reflex copying, aerial reconnaissance and photography surveying, sound recording, experimental phonetics, index and calculating machines, bacteriology and dietetics. Many examples and a lengthy bibliography are included. Gu-Sa.

162   B. M. Schwartz (1963) Induced competition: a technique to increase field data and rapport, *AA* 65: 1112-1113.
Tape recorder used to encourage people to tell stories (competing in doing so) and other information. Useful both in gaining rapport and in collection of texts. Gu-Sa.

163   A. G. Smith (1957) Gaining rapport quickly, *AA* 59: 875.
Use of tape recorder to convey messages from one island to another (thereby gaining rapport of both sender and receiver) during brief visits to numerous islands in Micronesia. Gu-Sa.

164   S. Tax et al. eds. (1953) Technological aids in anthropology, Ch. 12 of An appraisal of anthropology today, Chicago: 191-217.
A symposium in which participants discuss Rowe's paper, *161. Gu-Sa.

5   *language learning and applications of linguistic techniques*

165   P. Brown et al. (1955-1959) Review: Bohannan, Tiv farm and settlement; and subsequent
correspondence, *AA* 57: 1321-22; 58: 557; 59:716-17; 60:161-63, 940-42; 61:681-82.
On the anthropologist's use of linguistics.

166   A. P. Elkin (1941) Native languages and the field worker in Australia, *AA* 43: 89-94.
Language is an integral part of culture to be understood and interpreted.   Virtuosity an ideal, useful
in problems of relating kinship to rest of culture, in work with texts, in analysis of rituals. Gu-Sa.

167   J. Henry (1940) A method for learning to talk primitive languages, *AA* 42: 635-641.
Stresses common need to learn a language in a short time. This can be done through a combination
of preparation, use of linguistic techniques, use of informants, and concentrated hard work. Includes
section on special problems where no native talks any language but his own. Based on experience
with Kaingang and Pilaga. Gu.-Sa.

168   D. H. Hymes (1959) Field work in linguistics and anthropology, *Studies in linguistics* 14 (# 3-4):
82-91.
Annotated bibliography containing 119 titles.

169   D. H. Hymes ed. (1964) Language in culture and society, New York.
A comprehensive reader on the various ways anthropology is concerned with language, both theoretical and practical. Several topical bibliographies are offered, including a bibliography on fieldwork
and linguistics (25-26). Jk.

170   C. Kluckhohn and D. Leighton (1947) The Navaho, Cambridge: 182-215.
On the importance of knowing the language, since differences in language structure go hand in hand
with differences in perception and thinking. With concrete and detailed examples. Jk.

171   W. P. Lehmann (1962) Methods employed in the gathering and analysis of material, Section II
of Historical linguistics: an introduction, New York: 63-146.
Method in historical linguistics, including the use of written records, the comparative method, the
method of internal reconstruction, lexicostatistics (an interesting critical discussion, including a
pertinent, annotated bibliography), dialect geography and model construction. Gu-Sa.

172 F. G. Lounsbury (1953) Field methods and techniques in linguistics, in: Anthropology today (see *29): 401-416.
A historical review of methods and techniques in gathering linguistic field data. Outlines problem areas to which data at each level, simple to complex, are relevant. Contains a good bibliography. Gu-Sa.

173 R. H. Lowie (1935) The Crow Indians, New York: xvii-xx.
An introduction, a plea for the using of an interpreter in addition to learning the language. Se.

174 R. Lowie (1940) Native languages as ethnographic tools, *AA* 42: 81-89.
Takes the position, contrary to Mead (see *175), that language virtuosity is a decided asset. Thorough language knowledge is always valuable, and interpreters are used only because there is no other choice (considering the length of time required for fluency in any language). Gu-Sa.

175 M. Mead (1939) Native languages as field work tools, *AA* 41: 189-205.
General discussion of contact languages versus native languages. Learn language as a tool, not to demonstrate virtuosity. Includes types of problems not requiring knowledge of language. Language needed for asking questions, establishing rapport, and giving instructions. Importance of learning names and general terms. Interpreter useful even after one knows language, for example, to give time for note-taking. Gu-Sa.

176 D. L. Oliver (1949) Human relations and language in a Papuan speaking tribe of Southern Bougainville, an essay on methodology, *Peabody Museum Papers* 29 (‡ 2).
By tracing his efforts to define a single Papuan word for 'chief', the author shows the levels of meaning a central concept may have and discusses the manner in which he uncovered several meanings of the word as he traced it for several months. Gu-Sa.

177 H. P. Phillips (1960) Problems of translation and meaning in field work, in *1: 290-307.
Stresses the importance of accurate translation, especially in areas such as culture and personality. Discusses the effects of interpreters on the informant, on the communication process, on translation. Illustrates methods, listing instructions used for translating a sentence-completion test into Thai, and discussing many problems involved in this work. Gu-Sa.

178 C. F. Voegelin and Z. S. Harris (1945) Linguistics in ethnology, *SWIA* 1: 455-465.
The authors point out the relations between linguistic details and the associated culture and indicate various ways in which these may help the anthropologist in detecting cultural details. Jk.

179 I. C. Ward (1937) Practical suggestions for the learning of an African language in the field, Supplement to *Africa* 10 (‡ 2).
Discusses the practical problems facing the worker in Africa who is not primarily a linguistic student and gives suggestions on how they may be met. Jgm.

6   *problems of validity and objectivity*

180   J. Bennett (1946) The interpretation of Pueblo culture: a question of values, *SWJA* 2: 361-374.
Discusses the divergent interpretations of the same (Pueblo) cultural facts by different field workers.
Jk.

181   F. Cancian (1963) Informant error and native prestige ranking in Zinacantan, *AA* 65: 1068-
1075.
Presents a technique for possible resolution of Wallace & Atkins' problem (see *196) of distinguishing
'psychological reality' from 'structural reality'. Contains an example of how the psychological reality
of a prestige ranking scale was demonstrated through informant error. Statistical (correlational)
analysis used. Gu-Sa.

182   K. J. Cooper (1959) The modified Q-technique in rural-urban field research, *HO* 18 (# 3):
135-139. (also in *1: 338-351).
Treats comparability of data obtained by the same research method from rural and urban populations.
Contains discussion of development of research tools, data collection, and an evaluation of the
method. Examples taken from a study of attitudes toward leadership roles in Mexico. Gu-Sa.

183   F. DeLaguna (1957) Some problems of objectivity in anthropology, *Man* 57: 179-182.
To be more objective and valid in his interpretation, the ethnographer should have a holistic conception of culture and a sense of the past (an arbitrary present lacks objectivity), avoid preoccupation
with one problem, and use 'creative intuition' (not basing work exclusively on scientific techniques).
Gu-Sa.

184   A. N. J. den Hollander (1965) Soziale Beschreibung als Problem, *Kölner Zeitschrift für Soziologie*
17: 201-233; reprinted (1967) under the title of Social description; the problem of reliability and
validity, in: D. G. Jongmans and P. C. W. Gutkind eds., Anthropologists in the field, Assen.

185   Li-An-Che (1937) Zuñi: Some observations, *AA* 39: 62-76.
An illustration of the fact that the cultural background of the ethnographer may influence his outlook
on the society he studies. Jk.

186   J. J. Maquet, (1964) Objectivity in anthropology, *CA* 5: 47-55.
Reviews African studies in anthropology and discusses their relationship with colonialism. Discusses
whether or not anthropological knowledge is scientific, and concludes that although the anthropologist's knowledge is not 'impersonal', his results are 'valid and perspectivistic'. The social perspective of anthropology is considered, as well as its inductive and deductive aspects. Gu-Sa.

187   W. J. McEwen (1963) Forms and problems of validation in social anthropology, *CA* 4: 155-183.
Presents three general forms of data-handling for 'determining the empirical validity of propositions':

1) illustration, or case analysis, 2) comparison, or type analysis, and 3) testing or statistical analysis. Discusses all three with respect to working procedures of the researcher. Advocates improved validation possibilities through changing data collection methods and research strategies, and increased use of mathematical methods. Includes comment by numerous anthropologists and a large bibliography. Gu-Sa.

188   M. P. Redfield ed. (1962) Human nature and the study of society. The papers of Robert Redfield, Chicago: 70-84.
Discussion of the way in which the investigator's values and those of his own community affect his scientific work (for instance in his choice of a subject and in his conclusions) and of how the results of social science affect the values of the community studied. Jk.

189   A. Vidich and J. Bensman (1954) The validity of field data, *HO* 13 (♯ 1): 20-27. (Also in *1: 188-204).
Deals with sources of error related to various types of interviewing techniques 'in the context of enduring and intimate contact'. Refers mainly to community studies. Bibliography included. Gu-Sa.

7   *genealogical method and kinship analysis*

190   M. P. Banton (1956) A technique for tabulating the kinship structure of households, *Man* 16: 60-62.
For mathematical processing of quantitative data a simple coding system is needed. A numeral is used to show for each person his relationship to the head of the family. The first digit indicates the generation, the second one the canonical degree of kinship in the collateral line. Se.

191   J. A. Barnes (1947) The collection of genealogies, R-LJ ♯ 5: 48-55.
Advocates including other material about the individual (e.g. migration history, economic status) along with the genealogy. Discusses methods of asking questions, collecting and checking material, and presentation, illustrating a possible format. Problems of chronology and 'structural amnesia' mentioned. States minimum amount of information required to estimate population trends scientifically. Discusses briefly advantages and limitations. Gu-Sa.

192   I. R. Buchler (1964) Measuring the development of kinship terminologies: scalogram and transformational accounts of Crow-type systems, *AA* 66: 765-788.
Illustrates the use of Guttman scaling in analyzing Crow kinship terminologies, combined with Lounsbury's method (see Lounsbury article in Goodenough, see *193) of using transformational analytic rewrite rules. Shows how to create a typology of Crow systems from the scalogram model. Gu-Sa.

193   H. C. Conklin (1964) Ethnogenealogical method, in: W. Goodenough ed., Explorations in Cultural Anthropology, New York: 25-55.
Gives criteria for evaluating the adequacy of ethnographic statements. Reviews standard literature on genealogical method, starting with Rivers and the 'classical genealogical method'. Compares this with requirements for an adequate ethnography. States minimum requirements for adequate genealogical method, illustrates use of this method and expansion of it in one segment of an ethnographic analysis. Discusses social significance of genealogical connections. Very extensive bibliography. Hanunóo, Philippines. Gu-Sa.

194   W. H. R. Rivers (1910) The genealogical method of anthropological enquiry, *Soc. Rev.* 3: 1-12.
Deals with collection and recording of genealogical materials, outlining possible difficulties and ways of solving them. Mentions some uses to which material may be put: (establishing kinship terminologies and 'systems of relationship', studying marriage regulation, descent, property inheritance, and migration). Among the method's advantages are its concreteness and the greater accuracy it makes possible. Gu-Sa.

195   D. L. Schusky (1965) Manual for kinship analysis, New York.
Practical guide, with exercises, for the studying of kinship relations and their reproduction in diagrams. Jk.

196   A. F. C. Wallace and J. Atkins (1960) The meaning of kinship terms, *AA* 62: 58-80.
The paper examines 'traditional techniques of kin-type analysis and . . . more recent procedures of componential analysis'. Presents, in a straightforward way, steps in the method of componential analysis as applied to kinship (recording terms, defining them in the traditional manner, identifying principles of grouping, defining terms by means of symbolic notation, stating semantic relationship among terms), and gives examples. Discusses at length several analytical problems in componential analysis. Gu-Sa.

197   C. H. Wedgwood (1952) Anthropology in the field: a 'plan' for tackling kinship, *South Pacific* 6: 291-293, 299, 320-324, 396-406, 433-438.
Notes, queries and directives for analysing different forms of social organization in the sphere of kinship. Jgm.

8   *formal analytical methods and model building*

198   M. B. Black (1963) On formal ethnographic procedures, *AA* 65 (# 6): 1347-51.
Discusses some of the assets and limitations of the technique set forth by D. Metzger and G. E. Williams (see *202). Jk.

199   P. Kay (1963) Tahitian fosterage and the form of ethnographic models, *AA* 65: 1027-1044.
General discussion of the characteristics of formal models and their relationship to field observation, illustrated by a formal model of 'practices relating to the fostering of children in various Tahitian communities'. Gu-Sa.

200   J. L. Kennedy (1955) A 'transition-model' laboratory for research on cultural change, *HO* 14 (# 3): 16-18.
(A slightly modified version appears in *1: 316-323). Demonstrates the laboratory simulation of 'complex manmachine organizations called information-processing centers' as a transition stage between laboratory and field procedures. Studies the development of culture and stages of organizational growth over a six-week period in four model organizations. Gu-Sa.

201   E. R. Leach (1961) Rethinking Anthropology, London (London School of Economics, Monographs on Social Anthropology, No. 22).
Seven essays (all previously published) illustrating various logical and formal methods of treating specific ethnographic data. Gu-Sa.

202   D. Metzger and G. Williams (1963) A formal ethnographic analysis of Tenejapa Ladino weddings, *AA* 65: 1076-1101.
Presents a method for ethnographic description in terms of categories which parallel those of the people under study, intended to be free of investigator's pre-definition of the problem, of 'any particular theoretical stance' and of 'investigator's own implicit perception or assumption of descriptive units'. Procedures for identification of units described, illustrated with an example of the analysis of weddings. Gu-Sa.

203   D. L. Oliver (1958) An ethnographer's model for formulating descriptions of social structure, *AA* 60: 801-826.
Dimensional terms for describing group interaction suggested and described. These terms then subcategorized, with further illustration. Three alternate methods given for describing the structure of any society. Gu-Sa.

9   *large-scale society and cultural anthropology*

204   J. W. Bennett and M. Nagai (1953) The Japanese critique of the methodology of Benedict's, Chrysanthemum and the Sword, *AA* 55: 404-411.
Summarizes the principal observations made by Japanese scholars on organization of empirical data, conceptual approach and approach to historical change. Jk.

205   R. Bierstedt (1948) The limitations of anthropological methods in sociology, *AJS* 54 (# 1): 22-30.

Discusses the differences between primitive and civilized societies which restrict the efficacy of anthropological methods when applied to the latter. Jk.

206   S. N. Eisenstadt (1961) Anthropological studies of complex societies, *CA* 2 (# 3): 201-222. On the basis of a survey of the concepts and methods of approach of social anthropology the author points out the contributions made by social anthropologists to the study of complex societies and indicates for which aspects of social organization in these societies their analysis fell short. Jk.

207   J. Gillin (1949) Methodological problems in the anthropological study of modern cultures, *AA* 51: 392-399.
Several important propositions taken from general cultural theory (e.g. holism, existence of themes in culture, culture as learned, functioning of culture) and considered as to their applicability to modern cultures. Two main methodological approaches outlined: deductive (as in the work of Benedict and Gorer) and inductive (e.g. community studies). Problems of studying modern culture include its complexity, diversity, existence of subcultures, urban-rural differences, large size, high rate of borrowing, etc., but there are advantages in the availability of written records, political support, and material aids. Adequate study requires money, many well-trained anthropologists, and cooperation with other specialists. Gu-Sa.

208   S. T. Kimball (1955) Problems of studying American culture, *AA* 57: 1131-1142.
Reviews work on American culture, stressing methodology and emphasizing the specifically anthropological contribution. Examines such questions as the adequacy of methodology and research techniques, the quality of findings, influences from and relations with other disciplines, and the effects of incorporation and modification of new techniques upon outlook and theory. Gu-Sa.

209   D. G. Mandelbaum (1953) On the study of national character, *AA* 55: 174-187.
Partially a comment on Mead's paper in *Yearbook of Anthropology*, the paper discusses approaches to and methods of national character study in general. Mentions three points on which there is much disagreement in national character study: relationship to applied anthropology, relationship to psychological theory, and problems of sampling. Gu-Sa.

210   D. G. Mandelbaum (1955) The study of complex civilisations, *Yearbook of Anthropology* 1: 203-226.
Review of some of the anthropological literature dealing with complex civilizations published 1952-1954, with special reference to general methodological problems. Jk.

211   J. H. Steward (1956) Introduction to J. H. Steward, R. A. Manners et al., The people of Puerto Rico, Urbana, Ill.: 5-27.
In connection with the demands made on the investigator's methods and concepts by the study of a complex society such as Puerto Rico the concept of 'culture' is subjected to a critical analysis and the

concept of 'levels of sociocultural organization' is introduced. The procedures and methods used in this investigation (community study method, study of the national culture and field studies) are briefly treated. A detailed discussion is devoted to the manner of selection and delimitation of the different groups that were studied and to the theoretical and practical considerations that played a part in this. Jk.

212   E. R. Wolf (1956) Aspects of group relations in a complex society; Mexico, *AA* 58: 1065-78. Description of Mexican society from the point of view that in studying complex societies one must proceed from a study of communities or national institutions to a study of the ties between social groups on all levels of the society. Jk.

10   *urban and community studies*

213   C. M. Arensberg (1954) The community study method, *AJS* 60: 109-124.
Community seen as a locus of the 'basic cultural and structural whole'. The special characteristics of the method are its holism, the relationship between method and technique, its treatment of extant data, and its structural, qualitative, topographic outlook. Stages of the study process are outlined, with emphasis on the naturalistic, non-quantitative approach. Gu-Sa.

214   C. M. Arensberg (1961) The community as object and as sample, *AA* 63: 241-265.
Solutions are offered for four problems often mentioned in connection with the community study method, namely: is the community representative, how is it to be bounded, in how far should the community contain the institutions of the whole society and to what degree should it be an integrated whole. Jk.

215   R. K. Beardsley (1954) Community studies in Japan, *The Far Eastern Quarterly* 45 (# 1): 37-53. Critical analysis of community studies by Japanese and foreign scholars. Jgm.

216   J. B. Casagrande (1959) Some observations on the study of intermediate societies, in : V. F. Ray ed., Intermediate societies, social mobility, and communication, *Am. Ethnol. Society*, Seattle: 1-10. Intermediate societies: introduction and content of the concept, connection with and distinction from related concepts such as peasant society and composite society. Productive lines of enquiry in connection with research strategy are indicated. Jk.

217   I. Chiva (1958) Rural communities. Problems, methods and types of research, *Reports and Papers in the Social Sciences* no. 10.
A methodological guide for world-wide research in rural communities based on a study of existing literature. Bibliography. Jgm.

218   M. H. Fried (1954) Community studies in China, *The Far Eastern Quarterly* 45 (♯ 1): 11-36.
Critical analysis of eight community studies. Jgm.

219   D. P. Gamble (1963) Sociological research in an urban community (Lunsar) in Sierra Leone, *Sierra Leone Studies* ♯ 17: 254-268.
Outlines problems created by large size and diversity of population. The research included use of a sample census, a town plan based on aerial photographs, an infant mortality survey, occupational and opinion surveys, materials written by literate Africans, and other documentary material. Includes categories of data collected. Gu-Sa.

220   P. C. W. Gutkind (1967) Orientation and research methods in African urban studies, in: D. G. Jongmans and P. C. W. Gutkind eds., Anthropologists in the field, Assen.

221   E. Hellman (1935) Methods of urban field work, *Bantu Studies* 9: 185-202.
To adequately study the life (including numerous adaptation problems) of urban Africans, a heterogeneous population, it is necessary to take into account three environments: the tribal environment, and the home and work environments in the town. Summarizes 5 urban studies. Discusses informants, sampling and statistical method, the collection and use of budget information. Gu-Sa.

222   J.-P. Lebeuf (1960) An outline of survey methods for the study of urbanisation in Africa South of the Sahara in housing and urbanisation, Publication No. 47, C.C.T.A., London: 106-113.
Proposes that studies of African urbanization be carried out on the assumption that traditional tribal tendencies are always present in towns. In order to understand these tendencies he suggests 1. determination of ethnic groups in the town being studied. 2. study of these groups in their traditional rural settings, and 3. study of same groups in urban areas. Gu-Sa.

223   Mc. Kim Marriott (1955) Little communities in an indigenous civilization, in: Mc. Kim Marriott ed., Village India. Studies in the little community, *Am. Anthr. Assoc. Memoir no.* 83: 171-222.
In the light of a concrete example the author discusses the question to what extent an Indian village may be regarded as a whole in itself, and how much our knowledge about one village contributes to our knowledge of the greater culture and society in which the village is embedded. Jk.

224   R. Redfield (1960) The little community and peasant society and culture, Chicago.
Gives a short survey of methods in community studies of recent years and offers suggestions concerning ways of modifying traditional anthropological research to make it useful for the study of complex cultures. Jk.

225   W. B. Schwab (1954) An experiment in methodology in a West African urban community, *HO* 13 (♯ 1): 13-19.
Discusses methods used in surveying a heterogeneous and changing Yoruba community. Includes

problems involved in securing entree and gaining rapport, taking of censuses, a thorough investigation of a sub-sample of families during a period of a year, use of African assistants. Gu-Sa.

226 W. B. Schwab (1965) Comparative field techniques in two African towns, *HO* 24 (# 4): 373-380. Compares problems of entree, of administering a sample census, and of assuring the representativeness of data in two African towns. Treats the influence of hostility, stability of social structures, capabilities of field assistants. Nigeria and Rhodesia. Gu-Sa.

227 A. W. Southall (1956) Some problems of statistical analysis in community studies, illustrated from Kampala, Uganda, in: Social implications of industrialization and urbanization in Africa south of the Sahara, Paris: 578-590.
Concerned with 'uses and limitations of the quantitative approach in urban social research'. Mentions 3 types of data (ideal, activity remembered by informant, and activity observed by ethnographer), saying that since these vary greatly in a heterogeneous, rapidly changing urban community, a statistical definition of behavioral frequency is important. Discusses complicating features, problems of classification, combination of survey work with participant observation. Illustrates with questionnaire and categories of classification for coding responses used in Kampala survey. Gu-Sa.

228 J. H. Steward (1950) Area research: theory and practice, *Bulletin of the Social Science Research Council* no. 63, New York.
Discussion of the theoretical background of community selection for research in Puerto Rico. Representativeness with respect to the principal crops, coffee or sugar, the system of land tenure, individual or communal, degree of urbanization, etc. The questionnaire was not used until the end of the enquiry at a stage where it was known what questions would be most productive. Se.

229 A. J. Vidich, J. Bensman and M. R. Stein eds. (1964) Reflections on community studies, New York.
A series of articles by different authors on their experiences in community studies. Part One: 'The Community Sociologist Discovers the World' contains articles concerning the investigator's emerging consciousness of problems not anticipated in the original plans of the study and the changes to which research methods are subjected in the course of an enquiry. Part Two: 'Community Sociology as Self-Discovery' is particularly focused on the relations between the author's life history and psychological background, and his enquiry. Part Three: 'Public Responses to the Community Study' discusses problems with respect to publication, reaction of informants to the enquiry and the ethical problems of the relations between the investigator and the community he studies.
Although most of these articles refer to the western world this book is important for the social and cultural anthropolgist. Jk.

230 W. L. Warner (1941) Social anthropology and the modern community, *AJS* 46: 785-796.
Briefly outlines the social anthropological method of community study, stressing the problem of

social status classification in modern communities. Presents a quantifiable system of study, in which the units are relationships, not individuals. Gu-Sa.

231   W. L. Warner and P. S. Lunt (1941) Chapter 3, The field techniques used and the materials gathered, in: The social life of a modern community, New Haven, Conn: 38-75.
Treats many problems of community research, including criteria for the selection of the community, testing the criteria, and gaining an entrance into the community. Techniques *per se* include interviewing, observation, use of schedules and questionnaires, case histories, life histories, biographics, genealogies, documents and other written materials, and newspapers; and the types of survey methods used. Gu-Sa.

I I   *surveys*

232   E. Ardener (1962) Divorce and fertility, Oxford: 5-20.
Some current points of view in anthropology and demography on the choice of units of study are stated, followed by a description of the way in which villages were selected for the purpose of this study and of the procedure of the interviews. Jk.

233   K. W. Back and J. M. Stycos (1959) The survey under unusual conditions; methodological facets of the Jamaica human fertility investigation, *Society for applied anthropology monograph* no. 1.
This enlightening description pertains mainly to general field relations, especially the problems of entree and of conducting the interview in private. Selection, training, supervision and evaluation of interviewers discussed at lenght. Gu-Sa.

234   P. Deane (1949) Problems of surveying village economies, *R-LJ* # 8: 42-49.
The only really satisfactory way of getting accurate economic data on production, consumption, and allocation of resources is by intensive observation. Surveying and sampling are, however, necessary, because of the amount of data needed quickly. Discusses sampling (involving the definition of a household), the kinds of questions which should be asked, advantages of the joint interview, problems posed by migrant laborers and their effects on the village. Gu-Sa.

235   R. Fink (1963) Interviewer training and supervision in a survey of Laos, in *242: 21-34.
Discusses setting and population, questionnaire design, interviewer selection and training, interviewer supervision (including the problem of finding sufficiently trained supervisory personnel), and sampling in rural villages. Makes some suggestions for the training of interviewers and supervisors in situations where no survey research has previously been done and there are no trained personnel available. Gu-Sa.

236   H. Flegg and W. Lutz (1959) Report on an African demographic survey, *Journal for Social Research*, Pretoria, 10: 1-24.
Discusses use of a preliminary investigation of the area, the sampling scheme, and the training of African native field personnel for interviewing, and demonstrates the estimation of the age and sex structure of the population under consideration. Gu-Sa.

237   M. Fortes, R. W. Steel and P. Ady (1947) Ashanti survey, 1945-46: an experiment in social research, *The Geographical Journal* 110: 149-179.
The study was experimental in its use of African field personnel, and in involving teamwork among specialists in three fields: anthropology, geography, and economics. Discusses sampling, census, questionnaires, all in the context of social change. Each of the three major disciplinary aspects is discussed separately, but their interdependence and articulation is stressed. Gu-Sa.

238   R. Galetti, K. D. S. Baldwin, and I. O. Dina (1956) Nigerian cacao farmers, Oxford: XXIII-XXXIX.
Discusses the manner in which a sample of localities and farming families was composed for a survey of the economics of cacao-farming when random sampling was impossible. How the material for the survey was obtained while the methods of questionnaires and interviews could not be used. Discusses the method used for testing the reliability of data as well as some causes of erroneous information. Jk.

239   P. Hill (1956) The Gold Coast cacao farmer; a preliminary survey, Oxford.
Study of budgets of cacao farmers. Inextensive study using mainly the cooperative as sample. With the help of the cooperative's secretary a questionnaire was drawn up, taking into account the interests of the members. With the secretary's help most farmers were interviewed by the investigator. Se.

240   R. Hill, J. M. Stycos and K. W. Back (1959) The family and population control; a Puerto Rican experiment in social change, New Haven.
Contains a detailed account of the evolution of the research problem and the development of the research design. The various stages of the investigation, ranging from a pilot study to large-scale surveys, and research strategies are described. Chapters 10 and 11 discuss a field experiment to test the conclusions of the survey. Jk.

241   J. Holleman ed. (1964) Experiment in Swaziland, London and New York.
Report of the Swaziland Sample Survey 1960 which consisted of a random sample population survey of the rural area, urban surveys, a labor survey and livestock and land use surveys. Part I (1-98) outlines the methods employed and the aims of the survey treating in detail sampling methods, content, coding, etc. of the questionnaire, and the training of enumerators. Jk.

242   *International Soc. Sci. Journal* (1963) 15 (♯ 1).
Opinion surveys in developing countries. Includes some papers of a methodological nature. Two

such have been indexed separately. See also Introduction by Alain Girard on sampling, use of interviews and questionnaires, and interviewer selection and training, all with respect to the content of the included papers. Gu-Sa.

243 E. L. Jones (1963) The courtesy bias in South-East Asian surveys, in *242: 70-76.
To eliminate possible effects of the respondent's courtesy, include in the questionnaire only those questions which have no obviously pleasing answer, make the respondent more comfortable in expressing critical, negative, or 'impolite' answers (several devices are suggested), utilize the positive elements of courtesy. The interviewer's image should be defined as that of an impartial observer. Gu-Sa.

244 G. O. Lang and P. Kunstadter (1957) Survey research on the Uintah and Ouray Ute reservation, *AA* 59: 527-531.
Describes the selection, training, and use of native interviewers for a survey of Ute acculturation. Interviewer efficiency discussed, as well as the effects of using native interviewers on the information received. Gu-Sa.

245 E. R. Leach (1958) An anthropologist's reflections on a social survey, *The Ceylon Journal of Historical and Social Studies* 1 (# 1): 9-20; reprinted (1967) in: D. G. Jongmans and P. C. W. Gutkind eds., Anthropologists in the field, Assen.

246 D. Lerner (1956) Interviewing Frenchmen, *AJS* 62 (# 2): 187-194.
Describes in what way, for a large-scale survey by means of interviews, the questions of the interview, the manner of interviewing, the role of the interviewer and the sponsoring of the project were altered and adapted in connection with national character traits, codes of social behavior and political circumstances. Jk.

247 *Public Opinion Quarterly* (1958) 22 (# 3).
Special issue: attitude research in modernizing areas, Part I. Research experiences, problems, methods. Particularly relevant papers have been separately classified. Gu-Sa.

248 L. Rudolph and S. H. Rudolph (1958) Surveys in India: field experience in Madras state, in *247: 235 -244.
There are several assumptions implicit in survey research in the U.S., for example, that most people hold 'articulatable' opinions, the individual is the unit of opinion, all opinions are equal. This paper examines whether or not these assumptions hold in underdeveloped countries, and mentions modifications which might be made, taking such factors into account. India. Gu-Sa.

249 I. Silberman (1954) The urban social survey in the colonies, *The Colonial Review* 8: 170-171.
Discusses various types of survey, particularly (a) the census, (b) the sample social survey, and (c) a

subsample of houses studied more intensively. Treats problems of sampling, and various ways of collecting information by questionnaire techniques. Evaluates utility of surveys in the collection and interpretation of data. Gu-Sa.

250   J. D. Speckmann (1967) Social surveys in non-Western societies, in: D. G. Jongmans and P. C. W. Gutkind eds., Anthropologists in the field, Assen.

251   H. Stanton, K. W. Back, E. Litwak (1956) Role-playing in survey research, *AJS* 62 (# 2): 172-176.
On the basis of three investigations the authors show how role-playing by informants may be used to gather data for a survey. Especially useful for studying the informant's behavior in situations of emotional tension, his attitude towards other persons and for personality tests. Jk.

252   G. F. Streib (1952) The use of survey methods among the Navaho, *AA* 54: 30-40.
Contrasts the use of survey techniques in two Navaho communities. In the first, there was a two-month orientation period, and in the second, a more direct approach was used. The second approach was judged more effective because it gave a clearer role definition to the researcher on entry into the community. Questionnaire construction discussed (techniques, topics, wording, and areas of discussion must be fitted to known facts about Navaho culture). Mentions sampling problems with respect to a highly mobile population. Gu-Sa.

253   J. M. Stycos (1954) Unusual applications of research: studies of fertility in underdeveloped areas, *HO* 13 (# 1): 9-13.
Outlines some of the ways problems of sampling and casefinding, rapport, questionnaire-construction and interviewer-training were dealt with in two projects concerning family planning in Jamaica and Puerto Rico. Jk.

254   J. M. Stycos (1960) Sample surveys for social science in under-developed countries, in *1: 375-388.
Surveys are feasible, and may have a very low refusal rate (An example of this is cited from the West Indies).
Reliability and validity of survey data can be improved by good interviewer selection and training methods, by making unstructured exploratory investigations. Unreliability is caused by non-intentional errors of respondents, or by instrument error. Gu-Sa.

255   R. B. Textor (1962) A statistical method for the study of Shamanism. A case study from field work in Thailand, *HO* 21 (# 1): 56-60.
Use of survey techniques in an investigation into shamanism to supplement unstructured enquiry. Certain problems were cleared up in this way and new correlations discovered. Se.

256 E. C. Wilson (1958) Problems of survey research in modernizing areas, in *247: 230-234.
Discusses sampling, interviewer selection and training, establishing rapport, reliability and validity.
Gu-Sa.

12   *culture change, culture contact, acculturation*

257 G. K. Garbett (1960) The replication study, in: Growth and change in a Shona ward, Occasional
paper no. 1, University College of Rhodesia and Nyasaland: 27-34.
Discusses the field problems involved in 1) 'deciding whether discrepancies between my work and
(the previous field worker's) were due to changes actually having occurred or to mistakes in recording',
and 2) difficulties arising from the practice of changing personal names. Also discusses general
considerations in the method of replication with respect to social change. Gu-Sa.

258 G. K. Garbett (1967) The restudy as a technique for the examination of social change, in: D. G.
Jongmans and P. C. W. Gutkind eds., Anthropologists in the field, Assen.

259 International African Institute (1938) Memorandum 15, Methods of study of culture contact in
Africa, London.
A collection of papers, previously published in *Africa*, on methodology of studying culture contacts.
Contents include an introductory essay by Malinowski, as well as papers by Mair, 'The place of
history in the study of culture contact; Hunter, and Schapera, 2 papers on 'Contact between European
and Native in South Africa'; A. T. and G. M. Culwick, 'Culture contact on the fringe of civilization'; Richards, 'The village census in the study of culture contact'; Fortes, 'Culture contact as a
dynamic process'; and Wagner, 'The study of culture contact in its practical applications'. Gu-Sa.

260 F. M. Keesing (1953) Methodology, in: Culture change: an analysis and bibliography of anthropological sources to 1952, Stanford, California: 92-94.
A brief review of methodological treatments and problems in the culture change literature. Gu-Sa.

261 O. Lewis (1951) Life in a Mexican Village: Tepoztlan restudied, Urbana, Ill: xi-xxvii.
Outlines general methodological considerations in carrying out the replication study. Two aspects
of special note are the techniques used for the intensive case-study of seven families, and the 'program
of services (organized) as a corollary to the research project'. Gu-Sa.

262 E. Schlesier (1964) Der Völkerkundler als Kontaktpartner. Erfahrungen in Neu Guinea
1961-1962, *Sociologus* 14 (# 2): 128-136.
The anthropologist is a factor in acculturation. He may be traversing the acculturation purposes of
administration and mission. He may contribute to the disintegration of the society and give rise to
tensions, for instance by causing a shortage of food in certain families through his use of interpreters.
Dangers of buying ethnographic objects. Se.

263   G. Spindler and W. Goldschmidt, (1952) Experimental design in the study of culture change, *SWJA* 8: 68-83.
Paper stresses importance of rigorous methods in acculturation studies, sharpening of conceptual apparatus through use of careful research design, importance of the latter for interdisciplinary work and for hypothesis testing. Presents a design for interdisciplinary research in acculturation, used among Menomini. Criteria for determining the degree of social acculturation (the 'independent' variable) suggested; use of Rorschach to get at psychological variable. Problems of sampling and selection of a control group also discussed. Gu-Sa.

264   W. P. Zenner (1957) Methodological considerations in the study of intergroup relations, *AA* 59: 1081-1082.
Possible ways of studying cultural processes include semantic analysis of terms used in referring to outgroups, the observation of contact situations between two groups (e.g. social contacts, inter-marriage, trading), and the examination of early folklore stereotypes to derive inferences about culture history. Gu-Sa.

13   *statistical methods*

265   M. Ascher and R. Ascher (1963) Chronological ordering by computer, *AA* 65: 1045-1052.
The paper sets forth a procedure for operationalizing a method proposed by Robinson in 1951, for chronological ordering, applicable to many kinds of anthropological data. Also demonstrates the implementation of the procedure on a digital computer. Gu-Sa.

266   J. A. Barnes (1949) Measures of divorce frequency in simple societies, *JRAI* 79: 37-62.
Much vagueness exists in this area, and the need for adequate measures is stressed. Four kinds of calculation of the numerical frequency of divorce are given: 1) present marital state of the population, 2) measures of cumulative marital experience, 3) proportion of marriages ending in divorce, and 4) rates (number of divorces granted within a given time). Gu-Sa.

267   H. M. Blalock, Jr. (1960) Correlational analysis and causal inferences, *AA* 62: 624-631.
Treats the question of 'whether or not it is possible to make causal inferences, given only a knowl-edge of the intercorrelations among items at a relatively fixed point in time', with special reference to evolutionary theory. Uses a mathematical solution as proposed by Simon, illustrating with some of Driver and Massey's North American Indian data. Gu-Sa.

268   R. L. Carneiro (1962) Scale analysis as an instrument for the study of cultural evolution, *SWJA* 10: 149-169.
Presents a description of the Guttman scaling technique, in which formal properties of scales, in-cluding concepts of scalability, are discussed. Treats applicability of scaling to theories of cultural

evolution, and possible implications for the study of cultural process. Gives an example in which 8 culture traits are scaled for 9 South American societies. Sampling, trait selection, and interpretation of errors are also handled. Gu-Sa.

269   F. E. Clements (1954) Use of cluster analysis with anthropological data, *AA* 56: 180-199.
Principles fundamental to proper use of statistical analysis in treating anthropological data specified. Cluster analysis claimed to be analogous to factor analysis, and the latter's complexity to be unnecessary for many purposes. An example, including step by step description, is given of cluster analysis of some of Kroeber's northwest California data. The results are highly similar to those obtained by Kroeber, using another method. Gu-Sa.

270   H. E. Driver (1939) The measurement of geographical distribution form, *AA* 41: 583-588.
Investigates the conformity of (the range of) a geographical distribution of a trait to certain theoretical forms. Elliptical and circular distributions are considered, with examples from Sun Dance and Peyote. Gu-Sa.

271   H. E. Driver (1953) Statistics in anthropology, *AA* 55: 42-59.
A good review of the use of statistics as a tool for accomplishing the ordering of 'adequate samples of worldwide data' in physical anthropology, archaeology, linguistics, ethnology and social anthropology. Advocates greater awareness of methodological problems in designing and carrying out field studies. Gu-Sa.

272   H. E. Driver and K. F. Schuessler (1957) Factor analysis of ethnographic data, *AA* 59: 655-663.
Factor analysis deemed to have many advantages over cluster analysis of cultural traits for purposes of cultural classification and typology construction. Gu-Sa.

273   W. H. Goodenough (1963) Some applications of Guttman scale analysis to ethnography and culture theory, *SWJA* 19: 135-150.
Outlines basic assumptions and methods of constructing a Guttman scale (for both dichotomous and trichotomous items). Discusses two applications: 1) to the 'formal organization of interpersonal relations' (here, duties and rights are dealt with) and 2) to problems of evolution (including 'quasi-scales', use of scales for sorting vs. hypothesis-testing, problems of straight-line vs. cyclical views of time). Gu-Sa.

274   J. Honigmann and I. Honigmann (1955) Sampling reliability in ethnological field work, *SWJA* 11: 282-287.
The familiar anthropological 'opportunistic' sample (selection, by chance, of available, willing informants) is compared with a random sample, stratified where possible, in a study of the effects of American films on Pakistanis. No real differences are found in the variable being investigated, but the two samples differ in some respects (e.g. education, class). Although it is difficult to generalize

from one experiment on one topic, they conclude that an opportunistic sample will probably not approximate a random sample in all respects. Gu-Sa.

275   W. Milke (1949) The quantitative distribution of cultural similarities and their cartographic representation, *AA* 51: 237-252.
Relates geographical distance and cultural similarity of ethnic units. Reviews earlier work by Keiter, and says differences might arise from the particular coefficient chosen as a measure of similarity. Selects cultural areas, and considers particular cultural elements for the case of southeastern Melanesia and California. Gu-Sa.

276   J. C. Mitchell (1963) Quantitative methods and statistical reasoning in social anthropology, *Sudan Society* ♯ 2: 1-23.
Discusses the use of statistics in cross-cultural studies analyzing secondary data, and of quantitative methods in field work. Also considers types of quantitative data, as well as their use in analysis. Sampling and generalization are treated. Anthropologists are urged to familiarize themselves with statistical techniques. Gu-Sa.

14   *psychological techniques in anthropology*

277   C. J. Adcock and J. E. Ritchie (1958) Intercultural use of Rorschach, *AA* 60: 881-892.
Five possible ways to use Rorschach interculturally are suggested. Data on Maoris and Europeans in New Zealand are examined for relevance to the problem of Rorschach validation. Caution is advised. Gu-Sa.

278   S. Biesheuvel (1958) Objectives and methods of African psychological research, *Journal of Social Psychology* 47: 161-168.
Three objectives of African psychological research are discussed 1) To gain an understanding of the behavior of African peoples. 2) To provide a means of testing the general validity of psychological hypotheses concerning human behavior (which have developed from the study of western individuals). 3) To measure the limits of modifiability of human behavior and to define the environmental factors that determine these limits. The problems involved in longitudinal studies designed to implement these objectives are discussed. Gu-Sa.

279   C. DuBois (1937) Some psychological objectives and techniques in ethnography, in: M. H. Fried ed., Readings in Anthropology II: 45-58. Also in: *Journal of Social Psychology* (1937) 8: 285-300.
Discussion of some aspects of field work, including personality factors of the field worker and difficulties peculiar to the ethnographic interview, especially in connection with the increasing attention at that time for psychology in anthropology. Jk.

280   J. Fried (1954) Picture testing: an aid to ethnological field work, *AA* 56: 95-97.
Pictures pertaining to unspecific conflict situations designed to provoke from informants descriptions of possible content of various conflicts, and information on the ideal norms held by informants. Includes cautions regarding the scope and use of this type of test. Tarahumara. Gu-Sa.

281   T. Gladwin and S. B. Sarason (1953) Truk: man in paradise, New York: 433-456.
On the use of Rorschach-tests in culture-and-personality studies. Special attention is devoted to sources of error emanating from the psychologist, the informant and the anthropologist. Discusses congruence as a criterion of test validity. Jk.

282   W. Goldschmidt and R. B. Edgerton (1961) A picture technique for the study of values, *AA* 63: 26-47.
Pictures depicting 'choice' situations can be used to study values. This article contains an outline of the purposes of the test, a description of the test situation, some results and conclusions and a large bibliography. Menomini examples cited and nine pictures are included. Gu-Sa.

283   A. I. Hallowell (1945) The Rorschach technique in the study of personality and culture, *AA* 47: 195-210.
General introduction to the role of anthropology in personality theory. Appraisal of Rorschach (first projective technique used in a non-European environment) includes an outline of the Rorschach technique, a treatment of problems in securing responses from non-literate people, some principles of interpretation, a discussion of the psychological significance of group results and of problems of intra-group variability in personality. Concludes that Rorschach should be used as a supplement to other approaches. Gu-Sa.

284   A. I. Hallowell (1951) The use of projective techniques in the study of the socio-psychological aspects of acculturation, *J. Proj. Tech.* 15: 27-44.
Illustrates the use of projective techniques in the study of 'the socio-psychological aspects of acculturation among the Ojibwa'. Gu-Sa.

285   J. Henry and M. E. Spiro (1953) Psychological techniques: projective tests in field work, in: Anth. Today (see *29): 417-429.
Outlines development of psychological interest in anthropology. Explores Rorschach, TAT, free drawings, doll play, and the Bender Gestalt test, mentioning problems of test selection and interpretation. Provides a useful table with information on 24 anthropological studies using projective tests. Bibliography. Gu-Sa.

286   J. Henry et al. (1955) Symposium: projective testing in ethnography, *AA* 57: 245-270.
Communication by Henry on the usefulness of projective testing in ethnography (largely negative in appraisal of Rorschach utility), and comments by Nadel, Caudill, Honigmann, Spiro, Fiske, Spindler, Hallowell. Gu-Sa.

287   W. E. Henry (1961) Projective tests in cross-cultural research, in: Kaplan (see *288): 587-596. Discusses many aspects of the use and application of projective techniques, for example, their use as a check on field observations vs. reliance on projective test data alone. Also treats problems of team-work and of analysis. Gu-Sa.

288   B. Kaplan (1961) Cross-cultural use of projective techniques, in: F. L. K. Hsu ed., Psychological anthropology, Homeswood, Ill: 235-254.
Sets forth purposes of culture and personality study. Utility of tests should be judged in relation to these. States own position regarding data required in the culture and personality field and prospects of obtaining them with projective techniques. Comments upon problems of sampling, scoring and interpreting in descriptive studies. Points out, to researchers, existing problems in the cross-cultural use of projective tests and the development of research on how to study personality, using tools with depth and validity. Gu-Sa.

289   B. Kaplan ed. (1961) Studying personality cross-culturally, New York.
A well-planned collection of thoughtful, methodologically oriented papers, generally focusing on methodological and theoretical issues, their interrelationships and implications, rather than on specific techniques and applications. Some of the topics include dream analysis, symbolic analysis, art, linguist-ics, and mental disorders. Several papers are separately indexed. Gu-Sa.

290   I. N. Mensh and J. Henry (1953) Direct observation and psychological tests in anthropology, *AA* 55: 461-480.
Psychological testing can be combined with observation, often as a check on it. (Cites example of mother-child behavior with food in two cultures). Practical problems of administration and inter-pretation of tests are discussed, as well as the issue of individual vs. group use of tests. Some benefits of multidimensional team research, with several cautions, are considered. Gu-Sa.

291   S. F. Nadel (1937, 1938) A field experiment in racial psychology, *British Journal of Psychology* 28 (# 2): 195-212.
Experiment with two groups in Northern Nigeria to determine correlation between culture and psychological differences. Tested were a number of 15-to 18-year-old schoolboys selected in such a way as to form a sample of their groups. Test consisted of a) repeated reproduction of a story and b) remembering a number of photographs. Se.

292   E. T. Sherwood (1957) On the designing of TAT pictures, with special reference to a set for an African people assimilating Western culture, *J. Soc. Psych.* 45: 161-190.
Presents 'criteria and procedures employed in designing a TAT series for . . . the Swazi, . . . (who are) . . . in the process of assimilating western cultures'. Chooses to study 'specific areas of personality' rather than to use techniques for eliciting 'spontaneous fantasy'. Contains a brief review of the litera-ture, as well as some of the pictures used. Gu-Sa.

293 R. Sommer and H. Osmond (1960) Association methods in anthropology, *AA* 62: 1051-1053.
Examines use of word association test in studying acculturation and special languages of subgroups.
Results involving core vocabulary appear to be stable over a fifty year period! Gu-Sa.

15   *historical materials,*
                          including documents and life histories

294   B. Berelson (1954) Content analysis, in: Lindzey (see *125): 488-522.
The history, uses, definitions, and categories of content analysis are examined. The characteristics
of content which should be taken into account are form, producers, audience, and effects. The
units of content analysis (a distinction is made between 'recording' and 'context' units) must always
be quantifiable. Technical problems of counting, reliability, sampling and inference are also dealt with.
Contains a large bibliography. Gu-Sa.

295   P. B. Foreman (1948) The theory of case studies, *Soc. Forces* 26: 408-419.
There are three broad categories of case materials: personal documents, participant observation
records, and third person reports. The utility of case techniques in general is examined, and five
major uses of case materials are considered: illustration, development of concepts and hypotheses,
hypothesis testing, prediction, and the testing and refinement of methods. Criteria for evaluating
the adequacy of case records as research tools are suggested. Problems of validity and of generalization from records are also discussed. Gu-Sa.

296   L. H. Gann (1956) Archives and the study of society, *Rhodes-Livingstone Journal* 20: 49-67.
Importance of studying archives for historical reconstruction, social change and processes. Risks
involved in interpretation. Se.

297   E. A. Hoebel (1961) The law of primitive man, Cambridge, Mass.: 29-45.
There are three main approaches in anthropological studies of law: (1) Ideological – having to do
with 'rules'; (2) Descriptive – dealing with practice, and; (3) Procedural rather than substantive –
the search for grievances, problems of motivation and result. A procedure for gathering legal data
and cases is outlined, stressing that different approaches are applicable in different cultures. Also
deals with problems of using more than one informant, problems of validity (i.e. how to treat the
historic case, the myth). Gu-Sa.

298   C. Kluckhohn (1945) The personal document in anthropological science, in: L. Gottschalk, C.
Kluckhohn, and R. Angell, The use of personal documents in history, anthropology, and sociology,
SSRC Bulletin 53, New York: 77-173.
Contains chapters on biographies; diaries, letters, and dreams; field techniques and methods; analysis
and interpretation of materials; and future research needs. A large bibliography is included. Gu-Sa.

299   L. L. Langness (1965) The life history in anthropological science, New York etc.

300   M. G. Smith (1961) Field histories among the Hausa, *J.Af. Hist.* 2: 87-101.
Illustrates field methods used to study a 150-year period of history in Zaria emirate, northern Nigeria.
The inquiry, which was based on the system of titled offices and dynastic genealogies, made use of
informants (a senior representative of each of four dynasties who, as dynastic historian, had memorized
the official inventory), as well as maps, cross-checking from knowledge of military history, and an
external check, involving the history known of a neighboring state with many connections. Gu-Sa.

301   B. Trigger (1966) Reconstructing the history of a non literate society, New York.

302   C. A. Valentine (1960) Uses of ethnohistory in an acculturation study, *Ethnohistory* 7 (♯ 1): 1-27.
When data on the past provided by native informants fail to produce coherence in a historical sense,
a detailed knowledge of local history from external sources may serve as an objective check on native
testimony as well as encouraging informants to attempt to conform to alien standards of historicity
in giving material. Illustrated by a study on the Lakalai (New Britain). Jk.

303   J. Vansina (1964) The oral tradition: a study in historical methodology, translated from the
French by H. M. Wright, Chicago.
A complete and detailed treatment of the collection and evaluation of 'the oral tradition', including
religious and ceremonials, genealogical and other data. Also deals with problems of historical
reconstruction and validation, and of working with informants. Gu-Sa.

304   J. Vansina (1967) History in the field, in: D. G. Jongmans and P. C. W. Gutkind eds., Anthropologists in the field, Assen.

305   J. Vansina, R. Mauny and L. V. Thomas (1964) The historian in tropical Africa, London.
Part I contains a general introduction in both French and English, describing historical techniques
(mainly archaeological, ethnographic, and linguistic), as well as particular aspects relevant to Africa.
Part II is a collection of studies. Gu-Sa.

16   *ethical problems in field work*

306   J. A. Barnes (1963) Some ethical problems in modern fieldwork, *British Journal of Sociology* 14:
118-134; reprinted in: D. G. Jongmans and P. C. W. Gutkind eds., Anthropologists in the field,
Assen.

307   R. L. Beals et al. (1967) Background information on problems of anthropological research and
ethics, *Fellow Newsletter of the American Anthropological Association* 8 (♯ 1).

This report by the Committee on research problems and ethics (appointed by the Association 1966) contains information on 1. the way governmental agencies make use of anthropological research and problems connected with employment by the government; 2. sponsorship (by government and private agencies) of anthropological research; 3. problems in connection with research in other countries. The data in this report are based on investigations and interviews among both anthropologists and individuals concerned with social science research in various U.S. government departments. Jk.

308   A. J. F. Köbben (1959) Ethisch toclaatbaar? *Sociologische Gids* 6: 183-184.
L. Festinger and S. Schachter (1960) Ethisch toelaatbaar? A reply to prof. Köbben, *Sociologische Gids* 7: 293-295.
Discussion on whether, and how far, the method of participant observation followed by Festinger, Riecken and Schachter (described by them in When prophesy fails) is ethically permissible (see 87*). Jk.

309   M. Mead, E. D. Chapple and G. Brown (1949) Report of the committee on ethics, *HO* 8 (♯ 2): 20-21.
Code of ethics for applied anthropologists stated. The applied anthropologist must take responsibility for both means and ends recommended or employed. His responsibilities to the groups he studies and assists are outlined. Gu-Sa.

310   A. Vidich, J. Bensman, R. Risley, R. Ries and H. S. Becker (1958) Comments on 'Freedom and responsibility in research', *HO* 17 (♯ 4): 2-7.
Commentators discuss issues arising from an Editorial (*HO* 17 (♯ 1): 1-2) pertaining to Vidich and Bensman's *Small town in mass society*. Among these issues are the ethical problems involved in deciding what may or may not be published, whether or not the people studied may be identified, who has publication rights in a large project involving many researchers. Gu-Sa.

17   *applied anthropology and participant intervention*

311   W. G. Bennis, K. W. Benne and R. Chin (1962) The planning of change, New York.
An interdisciplinary collection of 'readings in the applied behavioral sciences'. Discusses models of systems of change, dynamics of the influence process, and programs and technologies of planned change. Gu-Sa.

B. Gallin (1959) A case for intervention in the field, *HO* 18 (♯ 3): 140-144.
Discusses an instance of the ethnographer being more or less obliged to take sides actively in a conflict, which proved to offer certain advantages with respect to further research. Jk.

313   A. R. Holmberg (1955) Participant intervention in the field, *HO* 14 (♯ 1): 23-26.
Explores the potentialities of the intervention method, including its particular characteristics, the role of the investigator in its application, and possible contributions to the theory and method of culture change. Makes an experimental analogy, and discusses problems of control and context. Gu-Sa.

314   A. R. Homberg (1958) The research and development approach to change, *HO* 17 (♯ 1): 12-16.
Discusses the implications of the research and development approach, with examples from Vicos. This paper and *313 have been combined under the title 'The research-and-development approach to change: participant intervention in the field', in *1: 76-89.   Gu-Sa.

315   M. Jahoda and E. Barnitz (1955) The nature of evaluation, *Int. Soc. Sci. J.* 7: 353-364.
Steps in the evaluation of an action program are defining its aims, selecting the criteria by which accomplishment is judged and the methods of measuring them, deciding on the design, collecting and analyzing the data. Each of these is discussed separately, with examples. Gu-Sa.

316   L. R. Peattie (1958) Interventionism and applied science in anthropology, *HO* 17 (♯ 1): 4-8.
Examines the history of applied anthropology and discusses many of the important ethical issues involved. Deals with the joint issues of 'helping' and 'experimentation'. A short section on methodology is included. This paper is part of the 'values in action' symposium, *HO* 17 (♯ 1): 2-26. Gu-Sa.

317   J. F. Rychlak, P. H. Mussen and J. W. Bennett (1957) An example of the use of the incomplete sentence test in applied anthropological research, *HO* 16 (♯ 1): 25-29.
The persons tested are given a number of incomplete sentences to complete, from which their future adaptability may be predicted. This test measures the personality variable which will be positive or negative towards adaptation. Se.

318   J. Spillius (1957) Natural disorder and political crisis in a Polynesian society: an exploration of operational research, *Hum. Rel.* 10: 3-27; 113-125.
Part I describes a hurricane on Tikopia which caused a food shortage and a political crisis, and shows how R. Firth and Spillius assumed roles other than 'the traditional research role of the academic anthropologist'. Part II defines operational research as 'the attempt to produce an effect on the processes of social change while they are being studied' and also outlines some of its principles and aims, as well as the professional responsibilities of the anthropologist involved. Gu-Sa.

18   *interdisciplinary and team research*

319   J. Bennett (1954) Interdisciplinary research and the concept of culture, *AA* 56: 169-179.
A descriptive-holistic view of 'the cultural variable' is likely to be rejected by anthropologists doing

interdisciplinary work. The concept of culture must be broken down into a series of analytical variables; it is often taken to mean 'the pattern-construct aspect of any interactive process: in most cases, values and norms'. The development of interdisciplinary research has implications for a revision of anthropology's claim to being the only selfcontained, synthetic science of man. Gu-Sa.

320 W. Caudill and B. H. Roberts (1951) Pitfalls in the organization of interdisciplinary research, *HO* 10 (# 4): 12-15.
Discusses problem definition and temperament of researchers, the effects of the pressure of publicity that usually accompanies a large interdisciplinary project, and the establishing of a common denominator of knowledge. Instead of really collaborating, team members often act as experts, and increased conservatism (instead of creativity) can occur. Differences in academic orientation to field work may impede collection and working-up of data. Gu-Sa.

321 N. von Hoffman and S. W. Cassidy (1956) Interviewing Negro Pentecostals, *AJS* 62 (# 2): 195-197.
Dilemmas in role definition and division of tasks in a team studying a negro church-community. Jk.

322 E. E. LeClair, Jr. (1960) Problems of large-scale anthropological research, in *1: 28-40.
Discusses problems of a large team of workers in a village, illustrated by material from the Cornell India project. Major problem areas are rapport (both group and individual), staff administration (accomodation, food, and kitchen services, recreational facilities), data handling (classifying and identifying materials, and making them available to the whole staff), interpersonal relations, coordination of research efforts. Some benefits are the greater amount of work that can be accomplished, and the increased specialization of function possible. Gu-Sa.

323 M. B. Luszki (1957) Team research in social science: major consequences of a growing trend, *HO* 16 (# 1): 21-24.
The advantages and disadvantages of team research, its influence on the angle of the investigation, the formulation of the problem to be studied. Influence on the individual investigator, the problem of leadership. No teamwork for the sake of teamwork. Highly complex problems require tackling by a team. Se.

324 M. B. Luszki (1957) Some social problems of social research, *ASR* 22 (# 3): 333-335.
Advantages and problems of interdisciplinary team research, as manifested in ten very different projects (financing, reports, publicity, staff, leadership of the project). Jk.

325 M. B. Luszki (1958) Interdisciplinary team research: methods and problems, New York.
The book systematically reports the work of five committees investigating the problems of interdisciplinary research. The general area of mental health is chosen, and a case study of an interdisciplinary (sociology, psychology, anthropology) research project is presented. Major sections deal

with characteristics of the disciplines in the research setting, the planning and carrying out of an interdisciplinary project (formulation, conceptualization, design and methodology), administrative aspects (personnel recruitment, leadership, inter- and extra-team relations), and recommendations for more effective interdisciplinary research. Gu-Sa.

326   O. G. Simmons and J. A. Davis (1957) Interdisciplinary collaboration in mental illness research, *AJS* 63: 297-303.
Major barriers to team effort in an interdisciplinary project whose object was to develop a framework for research in community aspects of psychological rehabilitation were methodological, not conceptual (clinical vs. quantitative emphasis). Some solutions to such problems in difference of outlook are suggested. Team research demands individual role adjustments, and usually creates many strains. Gu-Sa.

19   *the study of special topics*

327   E. H. Ackerknecht (1945) On the collection of data concerning primitive medicine, *AA* 47: 427-431.
Indicates what important data on primitive medicine might be collected by anthropologists and points out the significance for both anthropology and modern medicine. Jk.

328   E. M. Albert (1956) The classification of values: a method and illustration, *AA* 58: 221-248.
Outlines a descriptive-analytic method for classifying values as elements of a value -system. Describes the theory and method of classification, including the system of categories. Illustrated with a description of the value system of the Ramah Navaho. Gu-Sa.

329   C. S. Belshaw (1959) The identification of values in anthropology *AJS* 64: 555-562.
Discusses various meanings and uses of the term 'value'. Presents an ideal scheme, 'showing the steps necessary to identify values and the difficulties of this as an empirical procedure'. Gu-Sa.

330   S. Biesheuvel (1958) Methodology in the study of attitudes of Africans, *J. Soc. Psych.* 47: 169-184.
Treats the combined interview and group discussion method, as well as the use of projective techniques, and an 'attitude inventory' technique in assessing attitudes of Africans during social change. Gu-Sa.

331   W. Bock (1965) Field techniques in delineating the structure of community leadership, *HO* 24 (# 4): 358-364.
Anthropological field methods to be used in ascertaining community leadership. Nine principles concerning community leadership are indicated which may be helpful in research. Jk.

332   V. L. Bohrer (1954) Punch cards applied to ethnobotanical research, *AA* 56: 99-103.
Presents and illustrates a system of indexing material on ethnobotany, with categories for the genus of the plant, the cultural group in which it is employed, the plant family, the use of the plant, and the author of the publication in which the information occurred. Gu-Sa.

333   N. Chance (1962) Conceptual and methodological problems in cross-cultural health research, *American Journal of Public Health* 52 (♯ 3): 410-417.
Describes adaptation of medical survey questionnaire (Cornell Medical Index) for use in Eskimo village in Kaktovic, Alaska. Conceptual framework, meaningful terminology, application and cultural bias are discussed with reference to examples from the Eskimo village. The author concludes that physical questions have validity but that Eskimo cultural attitudes influence psychiatric questions. Gu-Sa.

334   R. A. Ellis (1960) The prestige rating technique in community stratification research, in *1: 324-337.
Basic assumptions of stratification research are that it exists, that people are aware of it, that it is relevant to behavior patterning and interpersonal relations. Two methods of study are participant observation and assessments by selected community members. Research design involves selection of ratees (sampling unit) and of raters, use of a controlled rating procedure, and the choice of a method for combining ratings. Concludes with a general discussion of the utility of the prestige rating technique. Gu-Sa.

335   R. Firth (1946) Malay Fishermen: their peasant economy, London: 300-317.
Explains the difference between the method of the anthropologist and that of the historian, geographer, or agriculturalist, pointing out its advantages and disadvantages. Direct observation is valuable. Tentative assumptions can be 'tested' through provocative questions, or deliberately neglecting to follow a custom. The collection of quantitative data and the use of sampling methods are particularly important in economic investigations, but a census or questionnaire is best taken at the end of the research. Contains an enumeration of the types of record collected. Gu-Sa.

336   L. C. Freeman and A. P. Merriam (1956) Statistical classification in anthropology: an application to ethnomusicology, *AA* 58: 464-472.
Applies correlational techniques (Fisher's 'discriminant function' method) to problems of classification, using interval counts as a musical measure to differentiate between groups of songs. Illustrates the method with African-derived music in Brazil and Trinidad. Gu-Sa.

337   K. S. Goldstein (1964) A guide for fieldworkers in folklore, London.
A guide to collecting methods to be used in folklore field work (based on field experiences in the United States and Western Europe). Jk.

338   H. Haselberger (1961) Method of studying ethnological art, *CA* 2 (♯ 4): 341-384.
Presents in a systematic way some of the methods and objectives of the study of ethnological art:

collection and description of a work of art, criteria for classification of art objects, and psychological approaches to the personality of the artist. Jk.

339   Hilger, Sister I. (1960) Field guide to the ethnological study of child life, Behavior Science Field Guides, vol. 1, New Haven.
An outline of important topic areas (analogous to *3) in the study of children. Also contains an introduction on general field methods. Gu-Sa.

340   J. L. Kennedy and H. D. Lasswell (1958) A cross-cultural test of self-image, *HO* 17 (# 1): 41-43.
Description of an attempt to measure people's images of themselves (stature, weight) in relation to influential persons in their environment, in two cultures, in Peru and at a primary school in California. Result, undervaluation of own body. Difference between persons known at close quarters and abstract, distant persons. Se.

341   L. M. Killian (1956) An introduction to methodological problems of field studies in disasters, National Academy of Sciences – N. R. C. Publication 465 (Committee on Disaster Studies Report, # 8), Washington, D. C.
Treats many methodological problems of disaster studies. Main sections are on (1) research design, (2) selection of subjects, and (3) collection of data. Also discussed are problems of entree, of timing and retrospective interviews, and of analysis and reporting of findings. Gu-Sa.

342   G. P. Kurath (1956) Choreology and anthropology, *AA* 58: 177-179.
Traces the relationship between dance (and other types of movement patterns) and ethnology in general. Presents a list and brief description of interesting topics relating 'choreographic and social patterns'. Gu-Sa.

343   R. A. LeVine and B. B. Levine (1962) Studying child rearing and personality development in an East African community, *Annals of the New York Academy of Sciences* 96: 620-628.
Description and evaluation of some specialized techniques used in an intensive study of socialization
1   child rearing interviews for mothers.
2   systematic observation of child behavior.
3   a cross cultural child interview and verbal projective tests.
4   a pre initiation interview for boys and girls.
5   essay and story completion techniques for school children. Jgm.

344   E. J. Lindgren (1939) The collection and analysis of folklore, in: Bartlett (see *10): 328-378.
A comprehensive treatment of the history of folklore studies in Europe. Four methods are outlined and elaborated: the historical-geographical, the American anthropological, the functional, and the psychological. Gu-Sa.

345   W. B. Miller (1960) A system for describing and analyzing the regulation of coordinated activity, in: A. F. C. Wallace ed., Men and Cultures, Philadelphia: 175-182.
Offers an analytical system for anthropologists who wish to describe political organization in non-western societies. Western analytical categories cannot be applied to these societies. The starting point is the existence of coordinated group activity. This is subdivided into a number of segments called 'activity episodes'. These may again be distinguished according to the degree in which they follow a preconceived plan. The system of roles by which the activity takes place may be approached from two conceptions: the regulative function and the regulative agency. The regulative function, then, is an activity or a series of activities that are carried out in order to coordinate the collective activities. Se.

346   J. C. Mitchell (1949) The collection and treatment of family budgets in primitive communities as a field problem, *Rhodes Livingstone Journal* 8: 50-56.
When collecting family budgets in non-cashcrop areas it is best to ask where the money came from for each purchase during a particular period, since in such areas each sum of money is identified, that is, each purchase is made with a sum of money especially acquired for the purpose. Start with the purchases since on the whole expenditure is better remembered than income.
Discusses problems of representativeness of material and gives examples of how corrections may be applied. Se-Jgm.

347   B. Nettl (1954) Recording primitive and folk music in the field, *AA* 56: 1101-1102.
Some suggestions to the anthropological field worker on how to increase the value of his music recordings for subsequent research by ethnomusicologists. Jk.

348   J. W. M. Whiting (1953) Field manual for the cross-cultural study of child rearing, Social Science Research Council, New York.

abbreviations of journals

AA	American Anthropologist
AJS	American Journal of Sociology
ASR	American Sociological Review
CA	Current Anthropology
HO	Human Organization
HUM. REL.	Human Relations
INT. SOC. SCI. J.	International Social Science Journal
J. AF. HIST.	Journal of African History
JRAI	Journal of the Royal Anthropological Institute of Great Britain and Ireland
J. SOC. PSYCH.	Journal of Social Psychology
PRACT. ANTH.	Practical Anthropology
R-LJ	Rhodes-Livingstone Journal
SOC. FORCES	Social Forces
SOC. REV.	Sociological Review
SWJA	Southwestern Journal of Anthropology

author index

The numbers refer to items in the annotated bibliography